Palgrave Studies in Adaptation and Visual Culture

Series Editors
Julie Grossman
Le Moyne College
Syracuse, NY, USA

R. Barton Palmer
Atlanta, GA, USA

This series addresses how adaptation functions as a principal mode of text production in visual culture. What makes the series distinctive is its focus on visual culture as both targets and sources for adaptations, and a vision to include media forms beyond film and television such as videogames, mobile applications, interactive fiction and film, print and nonprint media, and the avant-garde. As such, the series will contribute to an expansive understanding of adaptation as a central, but only one, form of a larger phenomenon within visual culture. Adaptations are texts that are not singular but complexly multiple, connecting them to other pervasive plural forms: sequels, series, genres, trilogies, authorial oeuvres, appropriations, remakes, reboots, cycles and franchises. This series especially welcomes studies that, in some form, treat the connection between adaptation and these other forms of multiplicity. We also welcome proposals that focus on aspects of theory that are relevant to the importance of adaptation as connected to various forms of visual culture.

Advisory Board:
Sarah Cardwell, University of Kent, UK
Deborah Cartmell, De Montfort University, UK
Timothy Corrigan, University of Pennsylvania, US
Lars Ellestrom, Linnaeus University, Sweden
Kamilla Elliott, Lancaster University, UK
Christine Geraghty, University of Glasgow, UK
Helen Hanson, University of Exeter, UK
Linda Hutcheon, University of Toronto, Canada
Glenn Jellenik, University of Central Arkansas, US
Thomas Leitch, University of Delaware, US
Brian McFarlane, Monash University, Australia
Simone Murray, Monash University, Australia
James Naremore, Indiana University, US
Kate Newell, Savannah College of Art and Design, US
Robert Stam, New York University, US
Constantine Verevis, Monash University, Australia
Imelda Whelehan, University of Tasmania, Australia
Shannon Wells-Lassagne, Université de Bourgogne, France

More information about this series at
http://www.palgrave.com/gp/series/14654

Shannon Wells-Lassagne • Fiona McMahon
Editors

Adapting Margaret Atwood

The Handmaid's Tale and Beyond

Editors
Shannon Wells-Lassagne
University of Burgundy
Dijon, France

Fiona McMahon
University Paul Valéry Montpellier 3
Montpellier, France

ISSN 2634-629X   ISSN 2634-6303 (electronic)
Palgrave Studies in Adaptation and Visual Culture
ISBN 978-3-030-73685-9   ISBN 978-3-030-73686-6 (eBook)
https://doi.org/10.1007/978-3-030-73686-6

© The Editor(s) (if applicable) and The Author(s), under exclusive licence to Springer Nature Switzerland AG 2021
This work is subject to copyright. All rights are solely and exclusively licensed by the Publisher, whether the whole or part of the material is concerned, specifically the rights of translation, reprinting, reuse of illustrations, recitation, broadcasting, reproduction on microfilms or in any other physical way, and transmission or information storage and retrieval, electronic adaptation, computer software, or by similar or dissimilar methodology now known or hereafter developed.
The use of general descriptive names, registered names, trademarks, service marks, etc. in this publication does not imply, even in the absence of a specific statement, that such names are exempt from the relevant protective laws and regulations and therefore free for general use.
The publisher, the authors and the editors are safe to assume that the advice and information in this book are believed to be true and accurate at the date of publication. Neither the publisher nor the authors or the editors give a warranty, expressed or implied, with respect to the material contained herein or for any errors or omissions that may have been made. The publisher remains neutral with regard to jurisdictional claims in published maps and institutional affiliations.

Cover image: Hulu / George Kraychyk
Cover design: eStudioCalamar

This Palgrave Macmillan imprint is published by the registered company Springer Nature Switzerland AG.
The registered company address is: Gewerbestrasse 11, 6330 Cham, Switzerland

Contents

Introduction: Stories of Adaptation—Changing Objects with
Margaret Atwood   1
Fiona McMahon and Shannon Wells-Lassagne

Part I   Atwood Adapts   13

"Atwood's *Hag-Seed* and *The Heart Goes Last*, a Generic Romp"   15
Marta Dvořák

"Negotiating with the Dead": Authorial Ghosts and Other
Spectralities in Atwood's Adaptations   35
Ruby Niemann

Transforming the Human and the Novel: The Utopian
Potential of Resilience in Margaret Atwood's *MaddAddam*
Trilogy   49
Lena Crucitti

Atwood's Protean Poetics: Adaptation in the Service of Survival   63
Nicole Côté

v

Feminist Adaptations/Adaptations of Feminism: Margaret
Atwood's *The Penelopiad*   79
Penny Farfan

Part II   Atwood Adapted   93

The Unreliable Female (Narrator) in Mary Harron's
Miniseries *Alias Grace*   95
Anne-Marie Paquet-Deyris

The Figure of the Objectified Servant, from the Silent Biblical
Maid to the Twenty-First-Century Web TV Rebel   113
Ingrid Bertrand

Shallow Focus Composition and the Poetics of Blur in *The
Handmaid's Tale* (Hulu, 2017–)   127
David Roche

Feminism, Facts, and Fear: The Protean Reception of *The
Handmaid's Tale* (Atwood 1985, Miller 2017–)   143
Elizabeth Mullen

You Are Here: *The Handmaid's Tale* as Graphic Novel   157
Joyce Goggin

Offred at the Opera: Dimensions of Adaptation in Poul
Ruders and Paul Bentley's *The Handmaid's Tale*   177
Helmut Reichenbächer

Part III   Atwood in the World: Atwood Adaptation Practitioners   211

Staging *The Penelopiad*   213
Penny Farfan

Filming *Alias Grace*   229
Fiona McMahon

Filming *The Handmaid's Tale* 239
Shannon Wells-Lassagne

"Adapting (to) Atwood" 251
Linda Hutcheon

Index 263

Notes on Contributors

Ingrid Bertrand (PhD, 2011) is Assistant Professor of English Language and Literature at the Université Saint-Louis—Bruxelles and UCLouvain (Belgium). She has published several articles on biblical rewritings and Atwood's *The Handmaid's Tale*. Her research interests are dystopias and manifestations of silence in novels. She is the author of a book entitled *Biblical Women in Contemporary Novels in English: From Michèle Roberts to Jenny Diski* (2020).

Nicole Côté (Université de Sherbrooke) has published a number of articles and chapters about Canadian literatures. She co-directed an issue of *TTR*, "La traduction littéraire et les Amériques" and three anthologies: *Legacies of Jean-Luc Godard* (2014), *Expressions culturelles de la francophonie* (2008) and *Varieties of Exile. New Essays on Mavis Gallant* (2002). She has compiled and translated two anthologies of Canadian short stories: *Nouvelles du Canada Anglais*; *Vers le rivage: Nouvelles / Mavis Gallant*. She has also translated a number of Canadian authors, the last being Dionne Brand.

Lena Crucitti is Teaching Assistant (English Literature and Linguistics) at Université Saint-Louis—Bruxelles. She is working on a PhD under the supervision of Dr. Ingrid Bertrand on the forms and functions of the animal references in twenty-first-century dystopian literature (novels by Margaret Atwood, Kazuo Ishiguro, Naomi Alderman, etc.).

Marta Dvořák was born in Budapest and raised in Canada, going on to become Professor of Canadian and World Literatures at the Sorbonne

University, France. Arguing a dialogue among the arts within a global circulation of influence, she has most recently authored *Mavis Gallant: The Eye & the Ear* (2019). Marta Dvořák has contributed chapters to *Literary History of Canada* (2009) and *Companion* series, notably *The Cambridge Companion to Margaret Atwood* (2006/second edition in press) and *The Cambridge Companion to Canadian Literature* (2016, second edition). She has edited books on postmodern writers from Margaret Atwood and Nancy Huston to Carol Shields. Her other books include *Tropes and Territories* (with W. H. New, 2007), *Crosstalk* (with Diana Brydon, 2012), and *Translocated Modernisms* (with Dean Irvine, 2016).

Penny Farfan is Professor of Drama at the University of Calgary and the author of *Women, Modernism, and Performance* (2004) and *Performing Queer Modernism* (2017), as well as many articles and book chapters on modernism and performance and on contemporary women playwrights. She is also the editor with Lesley Ferris of *Critical Perspectives on Contemporary Plays by Women: The Early Twenty-First Century* (2021) and *Contemporary Women Playwrights: Into the Twenty-First Century* (Palgrave Macmillan, 2013), and a past editor of *Theatre Journal*. Her work has been recognized with the Association for Theatre in Higher Education's Outstanding Article Award, Excellence in Editing Award (for sustained career achievement), and Women and Theatre Program Achievement Award for Scholarship.

Joyce Goggin is Senior Lecturer in Literature at the University of Amsterdam, where she also conducts research in film, media studies, cultural studies, and art history. She has published widely on gambling and finance in literature, painting, film, TV, and computer games. Her most recent published work includes *Comedy and Crisis* (2020), a collection of essays and plays about the financial bubble of 1720, and "*Skyfall* and Global Casino Culture," in *The Cultural Life of James Bond: Spectres of 007* (2020). Her forthcoming work includes a translation of Umberto Eco's introduction to the Italian version of Huizinga's *Homo Ludens*, to be published in *Game Studies*.

Linda Hutcheon, University Professor Emeritus of English and Comparative Literature at the University of Toronto, is a specialist in modern and postmodern culture and critical theory (especially irony, parody, and adaptation), on which she has published nine books. She is guilty of having indulged in interdisciplinary work with Michael Hutcheon, MD, Professor of Medicine, U of T, on the intersection of medical and cultural history, studied through the vehicle of opera. They have published four books on topics such as disease, death, and the operatic body—and, most recently, *Four Last Songs: Aging and Creativity in Verdi, Strauss, Messiaen, and Britten* (2015).

Fiona McMahon is Professor of American Literature at the Université Paul Valéry Montpellier 3 (Montpellier, France), where she is editor of the series *Profils américains* at the Presses universitaires de de la Méditerranée (PULM). Her teaching and research address literary modernism, contemporary poetry and poetics (US/CAN), and intermediality in literature. She is the author of *Charles Reznikoff: une poétique du témoignage* (Éditions L'Harmattan, 2010) and *H.D. Trilogy* (2013). She has recently co-edited a book of essays: *Penser le genre en poésie contemporaine* (Éditions Classiques Garnier, 2019).

Elizabeth Mullen is Associate Professor of American Studies, Gender, Television and Film at the Université de Bretagne Occidentale in Brest, France. Her work focuses on questions of gender and aesthetics in American film (particularly masculinity and the grotesque) and she has recently written on *The Walking Dead* and *Westworld*.

Ruby Niemann is an early career researcher who recently completed her PhD in English at the University of Adelaide. Her research interests include theories of the Anthropocene, eco-criticism, nuclear and resource criticism, queer theory, and female novelists of the twentieth and twenty-first centuries. Her projects focus on the twenty-first-century novels of Margaret Atwood in the context of the Anthropocene, and how literature can help us understand a post-climate change planet, as well as how concepts such as the Anthropocene and the Great Acceleration figure into North American literature more broadly.

Anne-Marie Paquet-Deyris is Professor of Film and TV Series Studies and (African) American Literature at University Paris Nanterre. She is the co-editor of *Combining Aesthetic and Psychological Approaches to TV Series Addiction* with N. Camart, S. Lefait, and L. Romo (2018). Her latest volume is *Histoire, légende, imaginaire: Nouvelles études sur le Western* (Presses de l'ENS, 2018), which was co-edited with J.-L. Bourget and F. Zamour, about the history of the American West in the Western film genre. She recently participated in a special issue of *Post Script* on "Islands and Film" (2019).

Helmut Reichenbächer is an associate professor in the Faculty of Liberal Arts and Sciences, OCAD University, Toronto, where he teaches courses in cultural history, literature, and theater. In addition, he was appointed Senior Fellow at Massey College in the University of Toronto in 2018. He holds a PhD in English Literature from the University of Toronto and a joint master's degree equivalent (*Staatsexamen*) in English Philology and Music Education from the University of Cologne and the Cologne University of Music. He has published in the fields of Media Studies, Opera, and Canadian Literature. He is an avid fan of live performances.

David Roche is Professor of Film Studies at the Université Paul Valéry Montpellier 3, France, and President of SERCIA (www.sercia.net). He is the author of *Quentin Tarantino* (2018) and *Making and Remaking Horror in the 1970s and 2000s* (2014) and has recently co-edited *Women Who Kill: Gender and Sexuality in Film and Series of the Post-Feminist Era* (2020) and *Comics and Adaptation* (2018). His work has appeared in *Adaptation*, *CinémAction*, *Horror Studies*, *Miranda*, *Mise au Point*, *Positif*, *Post-Script*, *Transatlantica*, and *TV/Series*. He is writing a book on meta in film and series.

Shannon Wells-Lassagne is a professor at the University of Burgundy (Dijon, France), where she specializes in film and television adaptation. She is the author of *Adaptation and Serial Television* and co-editor of *Adapting Endings: Last Pages, Last Shots, Screening Text, De la page blanche aux salles obscures* (Presses Universitaires de Rennes), *Premières pages, premiers plans* (Mare et Martin), and *Filming the Past, Screening the Present: Neo-Victorian Adaptations*. Her work has appeared in journals like *Screen*, *The Journal of Adaptation in Film and Performance*, *Critical Studies in Television*, *The Journal of Screenwriting*, *TV/Series*, *Series*, and *The Journal of Popular Film and Television*, among others.

List of Figures

The Unreliable Female (Narrator) in Mary Harron's Miniseries *Alias Grace*

Figs. 1 and 2	E1: The mirror scene. Grace is "[a]ll these different things" at once	97
Fig. 3	Visual seepage: the obsessive image of Grace's desired body in virtually identical shots in E2 and E4	102
Fig. 4	Ending of E2: oblique-angle shots of Jordan as visual signs of dysfunction	103
Fig. 5	Ending of E6: Simon becoming in turn "as a blank space or page encoded by others" (Davies qtd. in Howells 61)	104
Fig. 6	Episode 6: Grace speaking in tongues during the session of neuro-hypnosis	106
Fig. 7	End shot of Episode 6, Grace looking straight at the camera: undecidable	108
Fig. 8	Episode 6: A narrative quilt of her own: the modified pattern, "all [of them] together" in the end	109
Fig. 9	Episode 6, end sequence: the gaps in the overall design/story/series	110

You Are Here: *The Handmaid's Tale* as Graphic Novel

Fig. 1	How real is fiction?	158
Fig. 2	A photo-shopped image of Melania Trump surveying her Christmas decorations in 2018	160
Fig. 3	One of two full-page panels from Renée Nault's graphic novel that pictorially communicate the claustrophobia of the text	171

Offred at the Opera: Dimensions of Adaptation in Poul Ruders and Paul Bentley's *The Handmaid's Tale*

Fig. 1	Based on Balea 445	183
Fig. 2	AUNT LYDIA	195
Fig. 3	OFFRED	195
Fig. 4	JOY	196
Fig. 5	Introspective, descending harp motif	198
Fig. 6	Full orchestral score	206

Staging *The Penelopiad*

Fig. 1	Megan Follows as Penelope in *The Penelopiad*, Nightwood Theatre, 2012; photo by Robert Popkin	220
Fig. 2	*The Penelopiad*, Alberta Theatre Projects, 2010. From left to right: Kathi Kerbes, Esther Purves-Smith, Vanessa Sabourin, Jamie Konchak, Elinor Holt, Meg Roe, Adrienne Smook, Janelle Cooper, Lindsay Mullan, Allison Lynch, Denise Clarke; photo by Trudie Lee	226

Filming *Alias Grace*

Fig. 1	Christmas figgy pudding party—augmenting candlelight with LEDs. (Photo courtesy of Brendan Steacy)	232
Fig. 2	The occult séance. (Photo courtesy of Brendan Steacy)	234
Fig. 3	The emigrant ship. (Photo courtesy of Brendan Steacy)	235
Fig. 4	Lighting the two openings in the ship's hold. (Photo courtesy of Brendan Steacy)	236
Fig. 5	Cancelling out the sun for the arrival in Toronto. (Photo courtesy of Brendan Steacy)	237
Fig. 6	Window. (Photo courtesy of Brendan Steacy)	237
Fig. 7	Window-arrival in Toronto. (Photo courtesy of Brendan Steacy)	238

Introduction: Stories of Adaptation— Changing Objects with Margaret Atwood

Fiona McMahon and Shannon Wells-Lassagne

> *When, at night, I look at the moon and stars, I seem stationary, and they to hurry. Our love of the real draws us to permanence, but health of body consists in circulation, and sanity of mind in variety or facility of association. We need change of objects.*
> Ralph Waldo Emerson, "Experience" in Essays. Second Series

> *All writers must go from now to once upon a time; all must go from here to there; all must descend to where the stories are kept; all must take care not to be captured and held immobile by the past. And all must commit acts of larceny, or else of reclamation, depending how you look at it. The dead may guard the treasure, but it's useless treasure unless it can be brought back into the land of the living and allowed to enter time once more—which means to enter the realm of the audience, the realm of the readers, the realm of change.*
> Margaret Atwood, "Descent: Negotiating with the Dead," in Negotiating with the Dead. A Writer on Writing

---

F. McMahon (✉)
University Paul Valéry Montpellier 3, Montpellier, France
e-mail: fiona.mcmahon@univ-montp3.fr

© The Author(s), under exclusive license to Springer Nature Switzerland AG 2021
S. Wells-Lassagne, F. McMahon (eds.), *Adapting Margaret Atwood*, Palgrave Studies in Adaptation and Visual Culture,
https://doi.org/10.1007/978-3-030-73686-6_1

In the Empson lectures that Margaret Atwood delivered at Cambridge University in 2000, Canada's premier literary figure offers up a rich meditation upon her beginnings as a writer and, more broadly, on the forms of duplicity attached to the art of writing. "I grew up in a world of doubles" (31)[1] begins one such lecture where the novelist, poet and essayist brings to the fore a lifetime of thinking about the identity of the writing self. Atwood draws upon her immense wealth of experience as a writer but also as a reader to explore the blueprint of a literary imagination invested in the doubleness of the writing "I." Its equivocal nature, Atwood explains, is learned from the stories we read, beginning with the mythical tale of Narcissus and its spectral variants in Shakespeare, Edgar Allan Poe and Lewis Carroll, to name only some of the principal canonical examples, through to the emblematic relationship that Atwood identifies, via Jorge Luis Borges, between the matter of authorship and "the Jekyll and Hyde theme" (44). Atwood takes a practitioner's view of Stevenson's novella, as a writer who is apt to allegorize the split of the psyche, choosing to sublimate it through forms of the grotesque. As George Woodcock, one of Atwood's earliest critics, has pointed out, her protagonists are forever straddling the dividing line between myth and reality, embracing hallucinatory contexts that distort an equally problematic world of actuality.[2] In Atwood's discussion of the formative library that has accompanied her throughout her career, she unearths the substratum exploration in novel-writing of the illusoriness attached to the authenticity of the self, as witnessed in the personae of literature and by association in that of the audience. Though Atwood is inclined in her critical corpus to highlight the practical concerns of the writer, focusing on the elemental "roots"[3] to novel-writing while amiably sharing with her readers answers to a host of

---

[1] "*Duplicity*: The jekyll hand, the hyde hand, and the slippery double. *Why there are always two*," in *Negotiating with the Dead: A Writer on Writing* (29–57).

[2] George Woodcock (26).

[3] "Spotty-Handed Villainesses. Problems of Female Bad Behaviour in the Creation of Literature," in *Moving Targets: Writing with Intent (1982–2004)* (161).

S. Wells-Lassagne
University of Burgundy, Dijon, France
e-mail: Shannon.Wells-Lassagne@u-bourgogne.fr

INTRODUCTION: STORIES OF ADAPTATION—CHANGING OBJECTS... 3

"how-to questions,"[4] her writing has demonstrated that it is no less interested in the postmodern charting of metaphysics that queries the designs of nature along with those of artistic processes. Long before the impermanence riddling and indeed defining the center of consciousness in Western literature was expertly mapped out in Atwood's critical corpus, the dialectical and shape-seeking route that travels between self-derealization and recreation was forming the basis of the poetics at play in her fiction and poetry.

The motif of metamorphosis envelops Atwood's corpus, bringing to life Ovid's instruction, according to which "Everything changes; nothing dies; the soul/Roams to and fro, now here, now there, and takes/What frame it will."[5] Atwood introduces us to the theme of changeability in her very first collection of poems, *The Circle Game* (1966), when, as though to appease readers grown weary of the trickery foisted upon them by illusion, the persona cautions: "([...] but if you look long enough,/eventually/you will be able to see me).[6] Ultimately however, the grip of a permanently transformative journey ("Journey to the Interior," as so named in *The Circle Game*) is envisioned in a redemptively restorative light, when it is sublimated by art:

> I may find
> an egg
> a sun
> an orange moon
> perhaps a skull; center
> of all energy
> resting in my hand
>
> can change it to
> whatever I desire
> it to be.
> ("Against Still Life," *The Circle Game*, 66)

The transformative drama performed by myth is an important apparatus of Atwood's literary imagination that has been widely commented upon by Atwoodian scholars interested in her predilection for mystical transformation and plots predicated upon either the recovery of primitive

---

[4] Ibid. (162).
[5] Ovid (357).
[6] "This is a Photograph of Me," (11).

worlds or the discovery of specular ones. A broad critical framework will entertain the idea that Atwood has acquired, in the words of Coral Ann Howells, one of Atwood's principal exegetes, the role of a "mythographer of the Canadian imagination,"[7] intent on exploring the mysteries of origins and prospective future worlds. Atwood's adherence to the revelatory premise of myth aptly underscores the reflexive frames that permeate her storytelling and her very identity as a novelist, poet, essayist, cartoonist, environmentalist and overall cultural figurehead. Myth provides an entry to explore not only the symbolic stage upon which imaginary landscapes unfold, bringing to the fore the vicissitudes of the psyche; it urges recognition of the lived experience of Atwood's career as a writer participating in innumerable media and genres (from poetry, novels, biography and criticism, to comic books and apps). With Atwood, the figure of the "Eventual Proteus" (31), appearing in *The Circle Game* (1966), is an early conceit of the imaginative life that connects with Atwood's long history of intertextuality and cultural recycling.[8] Though the prophetic feats expected of Proteus seem merely hypothetical in the postmodern age, as the visionary power of myth struggles to withstand the indefiniteness of experience, Atwood replicates its vital function through her involvement in adaptation. The alchemy of the writing self, a magical and intangible process, combines with that undergone by the medium of literature in the rapidly evolving landscapes of book publishing and more widely, of media production and distribution. Atwood's lively presence on digital and social platforms since the start of the 2000s has abundantly demonstrated her participation in the melding of print and digital media and the changes it has incurred with respect to the production and marketing of literature. The rise of a globalized market of print and digital media is refracted in some of her most recent novels, the weave of the *MaddAddam* trilogy for instance organized around shifts in technological frames that contrive to signal a future time for civilization and for storytelling.[9]

As a writer, Margaret Atwood has never fallen short of ways to parody novelistic conventions, beginning with the depiction of women's experience through the horrifying realities of the Gothic. The popularity of these novels (*The Edible Woman*, 1969; *Lady Oracle*, 1976; *Bodily Harm*, 1981) resonates with wider forms of entertainment appearing today across

---

[7] "Introducing Margaret Atwood," in *The Cambridge Companion to Margaret Atwood* (5).
[8] Lorna Irvine (202–213).
[9] Lorraine York.

different genre and media. Showtime's *Penny Dreadful* (2014–2016) is one example in television that draws upon the Gothic alignment of creativity and destruction, albeit more conspicuously, as a backdrop to the unfolding of a gendered narrative perspective. Atwood's career in adaptation is the story of a predilection for building upon narratives of wreckage that involves looking past the traditional boundaries of gender and of genre. It is also fundamentally a history of tampering with the lens through which the world is portrayed. Adaptation with Atwood takes its cue from Proteus, a mythic model across literature entangled in the volatility of life (Homer, Shakespeare, Wordsworth)—and the reanimated brainchild of Victor Frankenstein in *Penny Dreadful*, whose brief interlude and swift assassination acts as a reminder once again of how closely myth is intertwined with experimentation and reinvention in the realms of fiction. This is the same mythic intertext that helped lay the groundwork for the discussions underpinning the essays in this volume, all of which set out to explore Atwood's diverse corpus as a laboratory for the increasingly protean nature of adaptation.[10]

The popularity of Hulu's *The Handmaid's Tale* (2017–) was one of the inspirations for this volume (as witnessed by the numerous chapters referring to it), but its status as flagship series for a streaming platform highlights the changing nature of media in this new transmedial age, where past and present works can transcend the time and the culture in which they were made to an unprecedented extent:

> [w]e cannot isolate a text from its historical contexts of production and consumption—but also we cannot treat a text as a bounded, clearly defined, stable object of study. Especially (though not exclusively) in the digital era, a television program is suffused within and constituted by an intertextual web that pushes textual boundaries outward, blurring the experiential borders between watching a program and engaging with its paratexts.[11]

Like Proteus, Atwood's fictions and their adaptations link past, present and future and provide sometimes uncomfortable, if not cataclysmic,

---

[10] Atwood's work both as adaptor and as source for adaptation in media as varied as opera, theater, television, film or graphic novels was the focus of a symposium held in 2019 at the Université de Bourgogne (Dijon, France): "Adaptation and the Protean Poetics of Margaret Atwood." The event was organized by the Research Center, *Texte, Image, Langage* and the Center for Canadian Studies at the Université de Bourgogne.

[11] Jason Mittel (7).

truths. Foremost, however, they are all slippery creatures to take hold of, that erode the artifact and the structuring principles that separate the author from their audience.

The arrangement of this book, meanwhile, is largely inspired by one of the adaptation scholar Robert Stam's more famous (and popular) comments: "Film adaptations [...] are caught up in the ongoing whirl of intertextual reference and transformation, of texts generating other texts in an endless process of recycling, transformation, and transmutation, with no clear point of origin."[12] Though this book might be charged with according primacy of place to the author, ultimately what we see in all of these articles is the incessant exchange and interplay between different works, by Atwood, through Atwood, the whirl of intertextuality that Stam speaks of as being inherent to adaptation. Atwood therefore becomes our starting point for analysis, rather than a proposed "point of origin," since, as Julia Kristeva reminds us, "any text is constructed as a mosaic of quotations; any text is the absorption and transformation of another."[13]

As such, Part I seeks to highlight the way Margaret Atwood is herself an adaptor, and in so doing undercut any assumption of a hierarchical relationship between author and adaptation: "Atwood adapts". As we see very clearly in the work of our first five contributors, the author herself is always recreating, assimilating and subverting previous influences. Marta Dvořák, in the chapter entitled "Atwood's *Hag-Seed* and *The Heart Goes Last*, a Generic Romp", examines *Hag-Seed* and *The Heart Goes Last*, one an explicit adaptation of Shakespeare's *The Tempest* and the other, seemingly a new take on dystopia, but stresses the intertextual playfulness of both texts, foregrounding an aspect that goes unspoken all too often in adaptation studies—the pleasure of recognition, the "Where's Waldo?" approach to an adaptation, that allows the reader to be an active participant in their readings, and to acknowledge a shared background with character, narrator or author (or all of the above). Likewise, Dvořák's savvy choice of corpus also serves to highlight a recurrent trope of Atwood's fiction, the figure of the prison, which is contrasted with the hypotext of Milton's *Paradise Lost* and its meditation on the nature of free will, causing the reader to wonder if the single-text adaptation is itself a limitation that can only inspire rebellion: "Non serviam." Ruby Niemann, in her chapter, "'Negotiating with the Dead': Authorial Ghosts and Other

[12] Robert Stam (66).
[13] Julia Kristeva (37).

Spectralities in Atwood's Adaptations" explores the trope of the specter in several of Atwood's fictions (including *Hag-Seed*); spectrality becomes a tool to examine the haunted nature of previously occupied lands and narratives, thus emphasizing the postcolonial nature of her writings and, as Niemann says, "elud[ing] any chance of a totalising reading of either the original text or her adaptation—the spectre magnifies the fractured nature of the adaptation, and the totalising role of the author in the cultural imagination and in the colonial project." This fractured nature of the text also comes to the fore in Lena Crucitti's analysis of Atwood's *MaddAddam* trilogy, where she focuses on the author's choice of *Frankenstein* as an important hypotext (despite Shelley's postapocalyptic narrative, *The Last Man*, being perhaps a more obvious literary touchstone). In so doing, as Crucitti in her chapter, "Transforming the Human and the Novel: The Utopian Potential of Resilience in Margaret Atwood's *MaddAddam* Trilogy" posits, the monstrous nature of the human is foregrounded, and the reader's reluctance to identify with the posthuman characters, the Crakers, causes us to reassess the notion of human exceptionalism—and our own tendency to attribute a hierarchy to their discourses. Nicole Côté, in her chapter, "Atwood's Protean Poetics: Adaptation in the Service of Survival" continues the analysis of the *MaddAddam* trilogy in her examination of adaptation with respect to the thematics of survival developed by Atwood as a backdrop to Canadian literature in the 1970s. In Côté's discussion, the trope is linked with the aesthetic premise of adaptation as an economy of survival. Like Crucitti, Côté underscores the problematic nature of human exceptionalism and further defines the nature of the "human" as implicitly excluding both the female and the animal. Adaptation here is seen in its biological sense, as the ability to mutate in order to survive, to better face the challenges of a hostile world. Atwood dramatizes this struggle both in a society of savage capitalism and in a postapocalyptic Garden of Eden through the challenges faced by her characters to survive—but as Côté makes clear, this narrative effort at adaptation is intertwined with literary adaptation, in its novel use of well-known literary devices like narrative subjectivity and defamiliarization or literary genres like satire and speculative fiction. Finally, in her chapter, "Feminist Adaptations/Adaptations of Feminism: Margaret Atwood's *The Penelopiad*", Penny Farfan examines another "explicit" adaptation, Atwood's theatrical production of her novel *The Penelopiad*, to examine how Atwood has become an adaptor of her own work. Farfan's analysis draws upon the intricacies of intertextual circulation and the manner in which Atwood demonstrates the same reverent irreverence for her novel as for the iconic texts she has transformed elsewhere. In so doing, she seems to follow in the footsteps of Adrienne Rich:

> Re-vision—the act of looking back, of seeing with fresh eyes, of entering an old text from a new critical direction—is [...] an act of survival. Until we can understand the assumptions in which we are drenched we cannot know ourselves [...]. We need to know the writing of the past, and know it differently than we have ever known it; not to pass on a tradition but to break its hold over us.[14]

Each of the five contributors of this first section focuses on a variety of tropes for analysis that grow out of Atwood's experiments in forms of revisioning: all ultimately foreground not only Margaret Atwood's eager borrowings from various sources, but also her efforts to limit any form of totalizing discourse—including her own.

Farfan also makes an argument for the liberating nature of this theatrical adaptation as compared to the television adaptation of *The Handmaid's Tale*: "In addition [...] to exemplifying the usefulness of approaching adaptations as adaptations, *The Penelopiad* suggests the critical potential of feminist writing for the stage through its differences from an extended television series on related subject matter that aims to be feminist while at the same time functioning as popular entertainment for a mass audience." Her comparison of these two works brings us to Part II of this volume, "Atwood Adapted," which examines the ways in which Atwood's narratives are adapted to different media: television, graphic novel, opera, Halloween costume, internet meme and so on. *The Handmaid's Tale*, as Atwood's best known and most widely adapted text (particularly given the popular and critical success of Hulu's television adaptation), has pride of place in this section, but Anne-Marie Paquet-Deyris in her chapter, "The Unreliable Female (Narrator) in Mary Harron's Miniseries *Alias Grace*" offers an analysis of CBC/Netflix's *Alias Grace* as a case study in one of the principal stumbling blocks for adaptation of an Atwood text: the nebulous nature and status of the narrator's voice. She suggests that the very structure of the television adaptation may ultimately lend itself to a convincing equivalency of Grace Marks's unreliable narration: by dividing the

---

[14] Adrienne Rich (35). Our thanks to Armelle Parey for suggesting this quote.

narrative into episodes, and offering epigraphs and varying points of view, the adaptors resist the closure that remains elusive in the novel.

Ingrid Bertrand, in her chapter, "The Figure of the Objectified Servant, from the Silent Biblical Maid to the Twenty-First-Century Web TV Rebel" begins our case studies of Hulu's *The Handmaid's Tale*, examining how objects become signifiers for characterization of the Gilead universe and for the characters that inhabit it. By focusing on the appearance of the music box in Bruce Miller's series, Bertrand offers an exploration of the multiple intertexts of "The Red Shoes," as Hans Christian Anderson's tale or the 1948 film adaptation, appearing in the novel, in Atwood's biography, and on the small screen. In so doing, Bertrand posits, the series offers both a continuation and a proliferation of one of Atwood's own obsessions, bringing the impact of screen adaptations (*The Red Shoes* and *The Handmaid's Tale*) full circle.

David Roche's study of the television series centers on its purely filmic characteristics: in devoting his chapter "Shallow Focus Composition and the Poetics of Blur in *The Handmaid's Tale* (Hulu, 2017–)" to Reed Morano and Colin Watkinson's masterful use of shallow focus, he notes textual justifications in the novel, but above all seeks to establish a hallmark aesthetic unique to the screen fiction. If Roche's analysis implicitly foregrounds the series as an artwork in its own right, Elizabeth Mullen, in her chapter, "Feminism, Facts, and Fear: The Protean Reception of *The Handmaid's Tale* (Atwood 1985, Miller 2017–)" seeks to show the impact of the series on the larger world: her study of the reception of the Hulu series shows how *The Handmaid's Tale*, initially inspired by impossibly true facts, continues to intersect with contemporary politics and the ongoing gender wars in its audiovisual rendering. Joyce Goggin, in her chapter, "You Are Here: *The Handmaid's Tale* as Graphic Novel" confirms the hegemony of the *Handmaid* narrative in the zeitgeist, while highlighting the new avenues for exploration offered by the graphic novel adaptation by Renée Nault, which to date has been the object of sparse critical scrutiny. Finally, Helmut Reichenbächer in his chapter "Offred at the Opera: Dimensions of Adaptation in Poul Ruders and Paul Bentley's *The Handmaid's Tale*" offers an exhaustive analysis of how Gilead is deconstructed and reimagined within the context of opera. His detailed use of musical scores offers a semiotics of adaptation, where the decoding of signs both visual and auditory highlights how staging and composition produce an effect unique to this medium.

Our final part (Part III), "Atwood in the World," is a series of interviews with the adaptors themselves: Penny Farfan interviewed theater directors Kelly Thornton and Vanessa Porteous about their experience adapting *The Penelopiad* in her chapter, "Staging *The Penelopiad*"; Fiona McMahon interviewed *Alias Grace* cinematographer Brendan Steacy in her chapter, "Filming *Alias Grace*"; and Shannon Wells-Lassagne interviewed *The Handmaid's Tale* cinematographer and sometime-director Colin Watkinson in her chapter, "Filming *The Handmaid's Tale*". In so doing, we hope to pull back the curtain on some underexplored aspects of adaptation, both on stage and on screen, and attempt to pay respect to the practitioners of adaptation, bridging the gap between practice and theory recently examined by Kamilla Elliott in *Theorizing Adaptation*.

In *The Testaments*, Atwood's recent sequel to her 1985 novel *The Handmaid's Tale*, her decision to use polyphonic narrators and to frame these narratives once again within the context of an academic conference seems to emphasize the continuity between her two texts, not just diegetically, but also structurally—even while acknowledging the multiplicity of voices that are now telling their renditions of the tale, on the page, on the stage and on a variety of screens. In her afterword ("Adapting (to) Atwood"), Linda Hutcheon acknowledges the power of adaptation: "Offred will always be Elizabeth Moss for me now, and Aunt Lydia will always look and sound like Ann Dowd"—all while suggesting that new adaptations and new media will offer novel avenues for exploration. Modestly, we offer this volume as our own academic framing of a larger, richer narrative—of Atwood's creative imaginings and of adaptation itself.

Works Cited

Atwood, Margaret. *Negotiating with the Dead: A Writer on Writing*. Cambridge University Press, 2002.

———. *Moving Targets: Writing with Intent (1982–2004)*. Toronto: House of Anansi Press, 2004.

———. *The Circle Game*. Toronto: House of Anansi Press, 1966.

Elliott, Kamilla. *Theorizing Adaptation*. New York, NY: Oxford University Press, 2020. E-book.

Emerson, Ralph Waldo. "Experience," in *Essays. First and Second Series*. Boston: Houghton, Mifflin Co., 1883.

Howells, Carol Ann, ed. *The Cambridge Companion to Margaret Atwood*. Cambridge: Cambridge University Press, 2006.

Irvine, Lorna. "Recycling Culture: Kitsch, Camp, and Trash in Margaret Atwood's Fiction," in *Margaret Atwood, Works & Impact*. Reingard M. Nischik, ed. Rochester, NY: Camden House, 2000, pp. 202–213.

Kristeva, Julia. "Word, Dialogue and Novel" (1986). *The Kristeva Reader*. Toril Moi, ed. Oxford: Blackwell, pp. 35–61.

Mittell, Jason. *Complex TV: The Poetics of Contemporary Television Storytelling*. New York/London: New York University Press, 2015. E-book.

Ovid. *Metamorphoses*. Trans. A.D. Melville. Oxford: Oxford University Press, 1987.

Penny Dreadful. John Logan, creator. Showtime, 2014–2016.

Rich, Adrienne. "When We Dead Awaken: Writing as Re-Vision" (1971). *On Lies, Secrets, and Silence: Selected Prose, 1966–1978*. New York: W.W. Norton, pp. 35–49.

Stam, Robert. "Beyond Fidelity: The Dialogics of Adaptation." *Film Adaptation*. Ed. James Naremore. Brunswick, NJ: Rutgers University Press, 2000, pp. 54–76.

Woodcock, George. *Introducing Margaret Atwood's Surfacing. A Reader's Guide*. Toronto: ECW Press, 1990.

York, Lorraine. *Margaret Atwood and the Labour of Literary Celebrity*. Toronto: University of Toronto Press, 2013.

PART I

Atwood Adapts

"Atwood's *Hag-Seed* and *The Heart Goes Last*, a Generic Romp"

Marta Dvořák

> The mind is its own place, and in itself
> Can make a Heav'n of Hell, a Hell of Heav'n.
> *(Milton,* Paradise Lost, Book I. 254–255)

The Heart Goes Last (2015), like the *MaddAddam* trilogy and *The Testaments* that precede and follow it, delves into the utopia, a genre which not only represents another space-time but describes how a social ideal has become codified and standardized. *The Handmaid's Tale* first engaged with the utopian walled city, that urban paradise by definition designed to correct Nature and impose a regimented human order, in which politics, ethics, aesthetics, and metaphysics—all forms of utopian thought—are interconnected with the rational urban planning. The urban paradise gone wrong reappeared as *Oryx and Crake*'s loaded Paradice, then as *Heart*'s highly planned *sub*urban paradise, whose near future artificial intelligence

---

M. Dvořák (✉)
Limanton, France

and bio-and-neuro-technologies signal utopian or dystopian dynamics according to the standpoint considering the concept of the good—as my Milton epigraph (which Shelley subsequently quotes) suggests.[1] In addition, *The Heart Goes Last* uses the usual disaster ingredients to refract the discourse of a whole incorporated genre (as did *The Penelopiad*, which unlike monotextual pastiche recentered virile peripatetic Homeric epic on the waiting woman, transformed from patient—etymologically the one on whom action is performed—to agent). Grounded in intertextual dialogism, both *Heart* and *Hag-Seed* find themselves at different points on the transtextual axis which Gérard Genette has theorized in *Palimpsestes*.

For its experimental Shakespeare series, Hogarth Press commissioned *Hag-Seed: The Tempest Retold* (2016) by asking Atwood to write back to a specific Shakespearean hypotext of her choosing. Atwood's *Hag-Seed* is rooted not only in an original hypotext, Shakespeare's play, but also in a series of hypertextual spin-offs[2] which include Aimé Césaire's adaptation, *Une Tempête/A Tempest* (1969). Césaire's famously race-based postcolonial standpoint is also interestingly irrigated by a class-based critique of power politics which rocked both capitalism and the genre of the tragedy:[3] Arthur Miller's *Death of a Salesman*. The dialogic interrelation is manifest when Césaire's Caliban appropriates Willy Loman's "a man is not a piece of fruit" speech.[4] On the other hand, with *The Heart Goes Last*, rather than overtly writing back to a single anterior work, Atwood engages in a transformational replication structurally equating a text with a code or

---

[1] The women in Thomas More's *Utopia* who had 700 meals to prepare at the end of their day's work may have found their timetable and double labor less than idyllic. This is precisely Shelley's point when he famously claims, "All things exist as they are perceived; at least in relation to the percipient" (*A Defence of Poetry*, 1085) and goes on to quote the couplet by Milton.

[2] Prospero's avatar, Felix, who works incognito under the name of Mr. Duke, points out that "*The Tempest* spent the whole eighteenth century as an opera" (*Hag-Seed* 141), which allows him to persuade the convict players who are to perform it that it's a musical, a genre they understand.

[3] In his essay "Tragedy and the Common Man," Miller made a declaration that paved the way for Césaire's dark adaptation of Shakespeare's comedy, namely that "the common man is as apt a subject for tragedy in its highest sense as kings were" (Miller, *Theatre Essays* 3). Yet he acknowledges in "The Nature of Tragedy" that to differ from the merely dramatic or pathetic, the genre must bring us "knowledge or enlightenment" (*Theatre Essays* 9).

[4] Césaire's Caliban imagines Prospero exploiting him as squeezing the juice from an orange then tossing the rind away—an echo of Willy Loman protesting when dismissed that his employer "can't eat the orange and throw the peel away—a man is not a piece of fruit" (Miller, *Death of a Salesman* 64).

genre, its architext. Her endeavor involves a transformational rethinking of the whole architextual framework of the meta-utopia. The novel borrows from a hypotextual continuum of grand texts and narratives—ranging from Plato's *Timaeus* and Dante Alighieri's *Paradiso* to John Milton's *Paradise Lost*. These in turn dialogue syncretically with, on one plane, a gamut of material which Western society has assimilated as an operative part of its popular culture—a large share made up of pop-culture callbacks from the writer's youth. On another plane they dialogue with literary u-dys-topias ranging from *Gulliver's Travels*[5] to *Nineteen Eighty-Four*[6] and *Animal Farm*.[7] If *Paradise Lost* is the backbone of *The Heart Goes Last*, as I shall argue, the novel's cornerstone is undeniably Thomas More's *Utopia* (1516), which Atwood selects as the genre's early modern European prototype, incarnating what she has termed "the certain set of brackets" (Atwood, *Conversations* 193) around this particular art form.

The echoes of More's famously coined ou-topia or *nusquam* ("no place") in *Heart* inhabit the plot (notably the set timetables, identical houses and furnishings, rotation of living quarters and tasks, transfer of individuals, interchangeability of people within categories, communal meals, punishment of extramarital sex, and control of procreation through experimental technology, right down to the poultry). The nods to More's nowhere also inhabit the narration, which playfully begins with a chapter entitled "Where?" and ends with a chapter entitled "There." Charmaine fantasizes about the lover she meets in some vacant house, and about her willingness to do anything he wants "inside this non-house, inside this nothing space" (*Heart* 58). Stan is transferred to the top-security unit manufacturing prostibots (human replicas designed for sexual use, including kiddie-sexbots), is given "the tour," and thinks, "No one teleported in here would have a clue where he was—what city, what country even. He'd just know he was somewhere in the twenty-first century" (*Heart* 184).

---

[5] Calling up Gulliver's capture by the tiny Lilliputians, Atwood's protagonist Stan looks back on his life and "sees himself spread out on the earth like a giant covered in tiny threads that have held him down" (Atwood, *The Heart Goes Last* 150).

[6] Gesturing to Big Brother's surveillance via telescreens, Stan wonders, "What if the TV can see him?" (Atwood, *Heart* 82). Too numerous to mention here are the examples of Newspeak, such as the Positron Management's terms for killing someone off: "repurposing" via "Special Procedure" (*Heart* 129, 130).

[7] Summoning up Orwell's famous conceptual torsion (more equal), an Atwood character remarks, "Everyone's different," and another replies to general laughter, "But some are more different than others" (*Heart* 185).

The tour Stan is given corresponds in a distilled way to what Atwood in an address playfully labels the obligatory "tour of the sewage system" (*"The Handmaid's Tale*: A Feminist Dystopia?" 20)[8]: the part of the narrative which explains how the imaginary society functions. The writer also keeps what she identifies as the "just-so story"—the usual "historical overview of how things got that way" (20), which she remarks Orwell puts in the middle of *1984* in the form of a pamphlet, and which Atwood herself places at the end of *Handmaid* and *Testaments* and the beginning of *Heart*, mediated consistently through the partial knowledge of focalizers limited by their time and space. Throughout *Heart*, Atwood puts the accent on the compulsory ingredients of a u-dys-topian planned society, which provide the framework, boundaries, or brackets of the literary (anti) utopia. Indirectly lighting up the structural staples of *Heart*, then, the writer in her address points to how such a society regulates work, goods,[9] meals, clothes, and sex (*"The Handmaid's Tale*: A Feminist Dystopia?" 18–19). The genre's brackets then are those of constraint, and the story boils down to the issues of power, of freedom and control, as does, significantly, the story of *Hag-Seed* and of its Early Modern and contemporary hypotexts. *Heart*'s stress on sex, which certain reviewers (see Sarah Lyall) have found misplaced, is thus inherently political. As with Winston Smith in *Nineteen Eighty-Four*, sexuality is the privileged site of control and transgression.

Interestingly, one can detect an unresolved paradox regarding authorship which animates both works under scrutiny, as it does her recent generically oriented, oxymoronically titled story collection, *Stone Mattress* (2014). On the one hand, *Heart*'s postmodern *heterosemiotic* intertextuality (i.e. a profusion of allusions to other writers and texts like *Midsummer Night's Dream* and *All's Well that Ends Well* in addition to those already mentioned above), as well as *Hag-Seed*'s metatextual nods to other

---

[8] When *The Handmaid's Tale* was selected for France's 1998 Agrégation English language competitive examinations program, Atwood accepted my invitation to give a talk at the Université de Rennes, where I taught before moving on to the Sorbonne Nouvelle. Already interested in the issue of derivation and invention, I had asked the writer to address generic conventions and patterns of the (anti)utopia which she had chosen to keep for *The Handmaid's Tale*, and those for which she had moved the borders and expanded the brackets. She then kindly emended my transcript for publication.

[9] Atwood's dystopia demonstrates that the goods controlled include people, who are "hauled off to Positron to be processed in whatever way they process people there. Then into the chicken-feed grinder" (*Heart* 124).

Shakespeare plays such as *Macbeth* and *Hamlet*, in addition to texts by other writers ranging from Poe to Salinger and Beckett,[10] map an equally postmodern desire to explore, push back, and play with generic boundaries on the part of a widely read, theory-aware author. Atwood has notably remarked to Geoff Hancock that every art form has a certain set of brackets around it and that "some of the most interesting things happen when you expand the brackets" (Atwood, *Conversations* 193). In *Stone Mattress*'s story "Lusus Naturae," for instance, Atwood demonstrates that she understands the form of the vampire tale and sets out to turn it on its head. She notably twists certain conventions, such as making a little girl mutate into the vampire and giving it the voice and viewpoint in a pseudo dramatic monologue which produces an effect of immediacy and allows readers to put themselves in the monster's place. On the other hand, one can simultaneously discern a certain anxiety regarding shifting generic conventions. Other stories in the collection revisit genres which Northrop Frye has labeled "formula-writing" (Frye 234), only to express distress at their changing codes. In "The Dead Hand Loves You," the aging author of a horror classic finds himself patronized by "younger, sicker, more violent writers" who deem his novel

> tame by today's standards. Violet, for instance, did not get her intestines ripped out. There wasn't any torture, nobody's liver got fried in a pan, there wasn't any gang rape. So what's the fun of that? (*Stone Mattress* 190)

The structural irony rising from the shift in viewpoint and voice highlights an evolution on the time-and-value plane which equates "torture" and "fun"—an evolution with which the authorial mouthpiece is uncomfortable. "I Dream of Zenia with the Bright Red Teeth" metatextually boils down the classic ingredients of a vampire film in which "the music shifts to eerie, and eyes redden or yellow, and teeth elongate, and blood spurts like pizza sauce over everything in sight" (*Stone Mattress* 146). One used to know where one stood with vampires, predictably "smelly, evil, undead," deplores a focalizer who stresses that

---

[10] Felix, the theater director, muses that theater repertory rarely addresses the life of the belly, except in Beckett, who can always be counted on: "Radishes, carrots, pissing, stinky feet: it's all there, the entire human corpus at its most mundane and abject level" (*Hag-Seed* 119).

now there are virtuous vampires and disreputable vampires, and sexy vampires and glittery vampires, and none of the *old rules* about them are true any more. Once you could *depend on* garlic, and on the rising sun, and on crucifixes. You could get rid of the vampires once and for all. But not any more. (*Stone Mattress* 147, my emphases)

The nostalgic mode in both stories equating change with entropy is interestingly coterminous with, on a general plane, the utopian desire to control temporality, history, and memory (see Lapouge, Wunenburger)—remarkably encapsulated by George Orwell in the Party slogan which appears twice in *Nineteen Eighty-Four*: "Who controls the past controls the future; who controls the present controls the past." On a particular plane, the strangely elegiac mode is also coterminous with the Positron Management's Orwellian policy to arrest time, to use retro and vintage goods (which include Marilyn Monroe films and replicas) to freeze the walled community in the resuscitated 1950s, on the grounds that

The past is so much safer, because whatever's in it has already happened. It can't be changed; so, in a way, there's nothing to dread. (*Heart* 189)

This aporia between the classic desire to maintain the traditional texts and standards which have been passed down to us and the postmodern urge to unsettle them inhabits Atwood's *substitutive* intertextuality. I refer to a practice she borrows from the baroque period, meant to reinforce the truth effect and stature of her text by resting it on authoritative hypotexts which powerfully engage with her themes of necessity and choice, knowledge and freedom, such as More's *Utopia*, Shakespeare's *Tempest*, and Milton's *Paradise Lost*, to which I am drawing closer. The aporia is played out through the friction between matter and *manner*. Cultural theorists have pointed out that a prerequisite of art is the homologous relation between content and form, "between what a work represents or expresses or suggests, and the means it uses to do so" (Levinson, *The Pleasures of Aesthetics* 10). It escapes no one, however, that in both *Hag-Seed* and *Heart*, Atwood takes an elevated subject involving sublime, often grim, issues of life and death, and chooses to engage with it in a farcical low register in which a Shakespeare comedy paronomastically sinks to *Midsummer Night Scream* and its protagonist Titania morphs into "Tits Tania" (*Heart* 249). The systematic deflation is produced through equally systematic incongruity, and through the grotesque mechanics of the body, from Aurora's made-over face "stretched like a rubber bathing cap over a large bald head" (190) to the life of the belly, through the sex, food, and even dress which utopias regiment. In the utopian society of *The Heart Goes Last*, the Doris Day wife in the pinafore apron whose strongest profanity is "darn it to heck" (97) submits to her new lover's every desire, including trash talk and much more, suggested chiasmatically: "Sometimes she can't believe what comes out of her mouth; not to mention what goes into it" (*Heart* 54). Yet Charmaine enjoys her roast pork and Brussels sprouts after having been reduced by Max to melting toffee or even a grotesque "stepped-on blueberry muffin" (144). And as Chief Medications Administrator at Positron Prison, after having executed a prisoner through the Special Procedure of lethal injection, she eats up her blood-colored plum crumble, joins her trivially domestic knitting circle, and replies, yes, she has had a nice day. When she finds her own husband Stan (in charge of the poultry facility)[11] on the wrong end of the needle, she does her grim duty,[12] and wakes up back in her house, distressed: the distress stems from the fact that the outfit someone has replaced her uniform with has not been matched with the right blouse. The novel's grotesque realism includes the Elvis Presley look-alikes whose ranks Stan joins by gluing on fake lips (which fall off or dribble), eyebrows and sideburns (which tend to wander), bronzer tan (which smears), wig (which cooks his scalp), and jumpsuit (tight in the crotch). It includes the sexbots (punningly referred to as "slut machines" [178]) with flushable interiors whose rinse cycle calls up "the drain on a dishwasher," but which Stan deems preferable to the previous zoophilic "bonk-a-chicken racket" (109), which a vintage Atwood concrete simile renders even more grotesque. Worried about being a "chicken pimp" (66) but tempted to try, Stan reflects that "a man could look very undignified with a chicken stuck onto him like a marshmallow on a stick" (67).

---

[11] The chickens so important to More's investigation of advanced methods of procreation (incubators) are particularly plump and tasty in Positron Prison, thanks to the nutritious chopped-up remnants of the Special Procedure victims. Coupling black humor with the absurd, a new process is to lead to headless chickens nourished through tubes, shown to "decrease anxiety" (*Heart* 79).

[12] Charmaine notably dreads disfavor and prefers husband-erasing to being demoted once again to Towel-Folding. While cheating on her husband, moreover, she had contemplated eliminating him to avoid a violent fit of jealousy, and gave up the idea only because his heavy body would be too hard to cut up and too smelly to hide (75).

Atwood's low burlesque remake of *The Tempest* is naturally a prisoner of the play's most recent hypertext, Césaire's adaptation, which already set out to make the high style of the Early Modern text intelligible and relevant by transposing it into what Bakhtin has identified as the "common language" (in Césaire's case ebonics or black vernacular) expressing his contemporary audience's time-and-value plane or "going point of view" (Bakhtin 301). Atwood consequently differentiates her retelling through a double displacement: from low to lower, and from earnest to flippant.

"Was Lady Macbeth always bonkers, or did she go that way out of guilt?" (*Hag-Seed* 56) wonder the convicts in the prison literacy program Felix directs. When the Fletcher Correctional Players prepare to perform *The Tempest*, Felix recenters the Prospero that audiences since Césaire have loved to hate, by pointing out that the "castaway" (rather than "invader") Prospero (*Hag-Seed* 128) was kind to the young Caliban, but had to lock him up when he turned into "a testosterone-sodden thug who wants to rape [Miranda]" (143). Prospero's magic cape, which Felix in a postmodern desire to flaunt artifice has designed as de-stuffed plush animals sewn together, is defamiliarized as "an armful of skunks topped by a dead white cat" (25). When none of the inmates want to play Ariel, perceived as a fairy, Felix points out he is "not human" and has "superpowers" (102). With the inmates now ready to accept him as a trapped alien, like Superman or E.T., Felix emphasizes that Ariel also creates all the illusions, and today would be called "the special-effects guy" (104). (All hands now go up to play Ariel.) Needing to bring in an actress to play the innocent Miranda with the inmates, Felix chooses the gymnast Anne-Marie, capable of "making lasagna out of her ... male dancing partners" (112). Snake Eye, the inmate who plays Prospero's treacherous brother, Antonio (who casts the Duke and his baby daughter off to certain death in a leaky boat), interprets the role as "the most hardcore evil guy in the play" (251), but posits that always buried in his books of magic, "the stupid klutz" Prospero brought the usurpation down on his own head: "It was like leaving your car unlocked" (252, 251). Caliban's chant is presented as "an early example of rap" (*Hag-Seed* 119), and the inmates are allowed to rewrite sequences they feel need "updating" (142). The "contemporary vernacular" or even "trash talk" (142) engineers a parallactic perspective: readers ineluctably feeling that the art object, Shakespeare's last play, is speeding away from the direction the Renaissance playwright set it to follow. The novel's prologue is an analeptic filmed performance of the tempest and shipwreck staged by Felix and the Fletcher Correctional Players, mediated through a flatscreen showing stock shots of waves and rain. Shakespeare's text has become an anachronistically low oralized idiom structured on hudibrastic internal rhyme calling up contemporary rap: "What you're gonna see, is a storm at sea:/Winds are howlin', sailors yowlin'" (*Hag-Seed* 3). Still, it is useful to remember that the first scene of the original hypotext is also a carnivalesque confrontation between the noble passengers accustomed to command and the ship's crew trying to keep the vessel afloat. Similarly, Felix's choice to zoom in on a bathtub-toy sailboat tossing up and down on a blue fish print shower curtain undulating with the movement of hands is not far off from the postmodern Peter Brook production of the *Tempest* which I attended at the Paris Théâtre des Bouffes du Nord in 1990. Felix's artistic decision to throw water on the Boatswain from offscreen is arguably borrowed from Brook, who had an offstage pair of arms throw a pail of water over the sailors, and suggested death by drowning via an extra doing the crawl in a puddle. In turn, Brook's self-reflexive minimalist production may not have been far off from the often playfully self-conscious approach of the playwright who authored the iconoclastic love poem (Sonnet 130), "My mistress' eyes are nothing like the sun." For as Felix explains to his future players in the long subsequent flashback, "Shakespeare has something for everyone, because that's who his audience was: everyone, from high to low and back again" (*Hag-Seed* 84).

In her grotesque generic romp, Atwood certainly sinks from high to low (sometimes right down to the basement), but what about the "back again"? I argue that she changes the rules to sink, but that she also changes the rules to rise again. The Hancock interview once again throws light on her practice. She notably gives an interesting example of how to expand the brackets of an art form: Nova Scotia's Mermaid Theatre which unsettles puppet theater conventions by showing the live people running the puppets (Atwood, *Conversations* 193). I suggest that in *Hag-Seed* this is precisely what the author does: show us the ropes of the craft.[13] Rather like Al Pacino's multifarious *Looking for Richard* (1996), Atwood's retelling of *The Tempest* is multitiered,[14] and involves the process or *business* of

---

[13] These interestingly include the Japanese method of live puppeteers bathed in black light, Bunraku.

[14] Shakespeare's play on usurpation, legitimacy, and justice is overlaid by a contemporary, "real-life" version in which Felix is ousted, which in turn engineers a production of *The Tempest* as a means to shape or act on reality, including the interactive theater experience which interweaves the layers.

performance. The author escorts us behind the scenes, where we readers along with the neophyte actors grope toward an understanding of Shakespeare's characterization and of his plot's overarching sweep relevant to both his standpoint and ours—no mean feat. In a low burlesque but Socratic dialogue, the prison inmate players are given keys or rather tool boxes. These allow them to find answers to questions such as why and how Prospero replaces bloody revenge with a peace-making dynastic marriage. Interestingly, the subpremise maintained throughout plugs into the ideology of perfectibilism which reaches back to Godwin (who inverts Hobbes), utopians, and even Socrates (for whom humans do evil only out of ignorance). Now if we accept that humans can be perfected through education, we readers may assume along with Felix that the inmates will relate to the Early Modern artwork, which is "about prisons" (*Hag-Seed* 72). The convict actors are brought to realize that when they are not on stage in their major roles, they put on a mask and play the goblins, the law-enforcers required to keep the prisoners on the island space. Prisoners who are their own jailers, both "agents of control" and "enablers of vengeance and retribution" (131), is a paradigm they cheerfully endorse,[15] hinting that the rebellious individuals are on the way to acknowledging the legitimacy of a civil society. Axiological and deontic modalities unfurl before our eyes just as they do in Shakespeare's plays. What is goodness or badness, begin to wonder the medium-security prisoners (fraudsters, forgers, and con men rather than murderers); are they relative or absolute; what is permissible or reprehensible; are we agents or patients of prohibition and obligation?[16]

On another ascending plane, the tour of the original play which Atwood provides in her framing tale or over-story investigates the mechanics that transform a text into a production, notably what we can call the illusion-making machinery. Leaving aside publicity for the moment, the players, professional disguise artists in real life,[17] learn the how-tos of lighting, sound, props, costumes, music and choreography, tech special effects,

---

[15] "'Neat,' says 8Handz. 'I get it. Goblins 'R' Us'" (131).

[16] "Wisdom and goodness to the vile seem vile;/Filths savour but themselves," Albany tells Goneril (*King Lear*, 4.2. 38–39) while Hamlet makes a less value-loaded statement: "There is nothing either good or bad, but thinking makes it so" (*Hamlet*, 2.2. 255).

[17] In the vein of Shakespeare's "all the world's a stage" approach, Atwood gleefully points out that the "*real*" town that hosts Felix's former Shakespeare productions is quite *fake*, with its Inuit carving shops, Celtic woolen-goods outlets, English china boutiques, Thai nail bars, and pubs ornamented with "the heads of archaic poets and pigs and Renaissance queens" (29).

digital scenery, and the brains of the audience, for as Felix remarks about his Peter Brook-like set, "All you need is a few items: the brain completes the illusion" (165). As with *Moral Disorder*'s high school class, Atwood melds two planes of instruction.[18] Her pedagogical mouthpiece draws the listeners inside the story (the prison inmate players) into exegetic activity allowing the author by proxy to enlighten the extratextual audience (us readers)—even on puzzling fine points (such as "why Caliban smells like a fish" [139]) or unremarked ones (such as Miranda "heaving those logs around so Ferdinand didn't have to" [255]).[19] The stratified and mediated dialogic encounter between production and reception boils down to a central objective: making the Shakespeare play "more understandable to a modern audience" (85). *Hag-Seed*, then, is not a monotextual pastiche, grounded in the monovalent mode of mechanical correspondences. The novel belongs rather to what Linda Hutcheon has identified as the double-voiced bitextual synthesis of parody, a transcontextualized repetition with a difference which mixes playful offhandedness with homage (Hutcheon 32–33).[20] By offering readers an adventure in intelligent vulgarization which adheres to the classical functions of literature (to entertain and to teach), Atwood combats the current prejudices which have labeled Shakespeare's works irrelevant and boring, and installs in their place a new openness.

The Heart Goes Last, on the other hand, operates strongly in the imitative manner of monotextual pastiche. It does the splits by drawing attention to both a single intertext and to an architext and an interstyle (see Bilous), playfully replicating its stock forms and deflating the grand through the register of low burlesque and the low motifs of food and sex. I have also highlighted how Atwood deflates through counter-expectation, comic cleavage between opening topic and predicate, and anti-climactic punchlines whose grotesque realism carries the comic impact of graphic caricature reducing the complex to one quick trivial line or gesture. One last example will show her mastery of *gradatio*, one of the climbing figures

---

[18] On how Atwood exhibits an anxious dialogue with absent texts, in which exegesis becomes story and interpretation melds with plot, see Dvořák, "Rejoinders in a Planetary Dialogue" and "Metafiction and Ficto-Criticism, the Ultimate Subversions of Genre."
[19] When Atwood points out Miranda's incongruous strength, she spotlights the fun Shakespeare may well have provided his audience by underlining the fact that his delicate heroine was played by a muscular man.
[20] Hutcheon's heuristic definition rests on the etymology of the Greek *para* as "alongside" rather than "counter," in other words signifying accord rather than opposition.

(up or down) of replication and augmentation (which include parenthesis and enumeration), which we perceive as a crescendo. During his tour of the sexbots units, Stan is warned about the dangers of an error in Assembly: "Bits can come off," says Gary. "I mean bits of you" (*Heart* 186). The counter-expectation which substitutes a damaged customer for the initially implied robot moves into a tall tale strategy of escalation, the mounting referential *gradatio* resulting in Stan's and reader's acceptance of more and more extravagant terms (which I highlight below):

> One guy got clamped [1]. He was stuck like a trapped rat [2] for fifteen minutes, only it was more like a gyroscope [3]. It took an electrician [4] and three digital techs [5] to unplug him [6], and after that his dick was shaped like a corkscrew [7] for the rest of his life [8]. (*Heart* 186, my digits)

Now how can this grotesque romp downward possibly rise again? First, the hyperbolic sick humor actually uses sex to warn readers of how euphoric utopia (in this case "no condoms, no pregnancy woes" [186]) can morph into dysphoric dystopia. Second, it opens the issue of a possible error in the original Design. Though the author systematically debunks the grand, which on the surface amounts to denying transcendence, she aporetically plugs into the existential as well as ethical issues of free will, necessity, choice, and responsibility. She does this most strongly through her hypertextual dynamics which become visible when top dog Jocelyn, the strong right hand of the one who wields absolute power, Ed, mentions that she did her thesis on *Paradise Lost*. Stan of the dumbed-down culture first mistakes the title for a nightclub, then wonders if the book had been made "into an HBO mini-series" (110). But the antennae of Atwood's model readers quiver when Jocelyn asks Stan, "Do you believe in free will?" (*Heart* 119)—a concept anathema to utopias, which equate individual freedom with unpredictability and instability. The antennae quiver even more when Jocelyn later explains that she had foreseen that Charmaine would succumb to passion, and had even encouraged her husband to seduce her: Charmaine was deemed "Sufficient to have stood but free to fall" (129). The switch in register informs us that Atwood appropriates the speech of another, namely Milton's God. Milton's authoritative text, *Paradise Lost*, in turn speaks to that most authoritative Ur-creation story, *Genesis*, and gives it epic sweep. The full statement which Atwood partially ventriloquizes encapsulates the Reformation debate on free will and predestination framed by Erasmus (*On Free Will* [1524]) and Luther (*The Bondage of the Will* [1525]).

> It made him just and right,
> Sufficient to have stood, though free to fall.
> (Milton, *Paradise Lost*, Book 3 98–99)

One can note the strong medial pause in the chiasmus (sufficient/free; stand/fall), the comma spotlighting the cohabitation of two paradoxical truths regarding God's Design with respect to the human. Also ventriloquizing, Milton relegates speech to God himself so as to underscore that God gifted humans with free will, and that their fall, and all ensuing evil, was contingent on their own volition. I argue that Atwood builds her oppressive dystopia on Milton's ground to support the thesis of her speculative fiction, namely that humans are agents or authors of their own enthrallment, and that nothing is ineluctable.

> So without least impulse or shadow of Fate,
> Or aught by me immutable foreseen,
> They trespass, *Authors* to themselves in all
> Both what they *judge* and what they *choose*; for so
> I form'd them free, and free they must remain,
> Till they enthral themselves.
> (*Paradise Lost*, Book 3: 120–125, my stresses)

The under-text which inhabits Atwood's gives prominence to reason and choice[21] as well as their sustenance, knowledge. Charmaine, Atwood's exemplar, was led "astray" (*Heart* 129) like Eve, but could have chosen not to become a "fallen" woman. Anticipating Aunt Lydia in *Testaments* who, unlike Anita, chooses to be on the "right" or safe side of the guns, Charmaine could have chosen not to execute whoever the Management deems undesirable, including her own husband, and she bears the full responsibility of her acts.

Significantly, in this parabolic knowledge narrative governed by the operators of (im)possibility and necessity—the alethic modality—Charmaine

---

[21] Milton echoes his epic's God who emphasizes that "Reason also is choice" (PL 3: 108) in *Areopagitica*, in which he argues that when God gave Adam reason, "he gave him freedom to choose, for reason is but choosing" (Milton, *Complete Poems and Major Prose*: 733)—a nod to Aristotle's definition of reason as the power of choice (*Nicomachean Ethics* III.ii.6).

and Stan[22] forfeit the knowledge needed to choose. She never seeks to know what happens to the dead bodies, and brushes off the idea of "protein-enriched livestock feed" as impossibly "disrespectful": "whatever happens, it's bound to be useful, and that's all she needs to know. There are some things it's better not to think about" (*Heart* 70). In Milton's epic, man was "deceiv'd" (*PL* 130) by Satan, in Atwood's dystopia by Max (in the case of Charmaine as an individual) and by the propaganda-infested media (regarding the general "controlled population with a wall around it" [126]). In both cases the "*fraud*" (*PL* 152) which causes the individual to succumb is "join'd/With his own *folly*" (152–53, my emphases). Fraud and folly make the subject both patient and agent; in both cases the best guide, the "Umpire *Conscience*" (*PL* 195, original stress), requires knowledge and volition.[23] "Does loving Stan (obeying God, *PL*) really count if she can't help it?" (*Heart* 294), Charmaine wonders after a brain operation programs her to imprint on the first person she sees when she awakes, like a duckling. As in the numerous instances of malfunctions, mistakes, and flawed prototypes, Atwood leads readers to speculate if there was an error in design in the original Creation. Why did God/Christ need to "fix" things as does Christ's arguable avatar, Jocelyn, who declares, "I helped build this; I need to help fix it" (*Heart* 128). Being programmed to love her husband does not "seem right" to Charmaine, but it "*feels* right" (294, original stress). "Thank heavens she had that adjustment to her brain," she ends up thinking in her domestic contentment (303). One wonders, would Adam and Eve have been happier without all that free will? Stan, mandated to help Jocelyn "fix" the universe, also scolds himself for not being able to stop "thinking like a pre-human sex-crazed baboon for maybe just one minute" and conjectures, "it must be his hormones. Is he responsible for his hormones?" (228) Is the human perfectible without adjustments to the brain? When we get a second chance, with Jesus or Jocelyn, will we mess up once again?

---

[22] Stan abdicates responsibility for their fate when he signs on for the Positron Project for life having "barely even read the terms and conditions" (36).
[23] Believing her husband dead, Charmaine tells herself "it won't count as cheating" to go to bed with her lover, but is torn in a demonstration of Miltonian ethics at work: "You can't let yourself be swept away on a tidal wave of treacherous hormones. *Oh, please! Let yourself!* says her other voice" (191, original stresses).

Sublime issues of ethics, of responsibility, choice, guilt, right and wrong, and even being/human nature are central to both novels under scrutiny.[24] The Fletcher medium-security prison inmates in the framing tale of *Hag-Seed* have performed a play which cancels revenge and ends on forgiveness and "declares for second chances" (*Hag-Seed* 260). Will they be rehabilitated thanks to "the redemptive power of art" (199) and seize their second chance?[25] Convicted for embezzlement, Bent Pencil, who plays the benevolent counselor Gonzalo, discloses a profound interpretation of Shakespeare's play. He finds that it interrogates "the strength of goodness to resist evil" (*Hag-Seed* 260)—a kind of strength his own role does not display because Gonzalo never finds himself in the face of temptation. As this Atwood mouthpiece points out, "He doesn't have to say no to a sinfully rich dessert, because he's never offered one" (260). This is a modern way of saying what Milton said before in *Areopagitica*, namely that one can only know good by evil, its twin, so "what wisdom can there be to choose, what continence to forbear without the knowledge of evil?" (Milton, *Complete Poems* 728). In this speech to Parliament, Milton pleads for the liberty of unlicensed printing, arguing that books freely printed and freely read provide us with

> the knowledge and survey of vice [which] is in this world so necessary to the constituting of human virtue, and the scanning of error to the confirmation of truth. (Milton 729)

In the imaginary worlds Atwood has created, unfettered by our own, she takes on the role of demi-urge, like the blind Milton who prays that his illuminated mind "may see and tell/Of things invisible to mortal sight" (*PL* 3: 54–55). One can even say she plays the role of Milton's God, who authored the world, and who promises that frail humankind "shall hear [him] call, and oft be *warn'd*" (*PL* 3: 185, my stress). Or, perhaps more

---

[24] An existential questioning in *Heart* is manifest when Stan, fake lips and all, looks into the mirror and sees Elvis. "Is that all we are? he thinks. Unmistakable clothing, a hairstyle, a few exaggerated features, a gesture?" (*Heart* 215).

[25] Simultaneously, can one consider an ethical act of retribution the interactive theater experience Felix inserts into the *Tempest* performance, in which he (illegally) sequesters and drugs the Heritage, Justice, and Veterans Affairs Ministers who had (unethically) plotted to oust Felix and take power? And to boot, who during their sequestration sketch out a plot to drown the "real-life" counterpart of the King of Naples and smother his counselor with a pillow (a wicked wink to *Othello*).

humbly, like moralists and satirists throughout the centuries, she incarnates our Conscience, which judges according to the measure of enlightenment which it has received.[26]

The core issue of power and control is actually played out on the highest plane, that of authorship and authority, involving the notions of freedom and constraint in the writing and reading processes and that literary space created between the producer and the receiver. In a generic romp which proves to be grim as well as grotesque, Atwood engages in a deadly serious power game with the implied reader who, like her handmaid characters, is a "rat in a maze … free to go anywhere, as long as it stays inside the maze" (Atwood, *The Handmaid's Tale* 174). Calling up Nabokov whose increasingly intrusive mad editor persona, Kinbote, sends readers scurrying every which way in the textual maze of *Pale Fire*,[27] Atwood manipulatively scatters her texts with intertextual markers and indicators. Her heterosemiotic references are often cunningly disguised, through devices ranging from spoonerisms ("Time wounds all heels") and partial omission ("Vengeance is mine") to scrambling (Doré's *Inferno*, Dali's *Alice's Adventures in Wonderland*, Picasso's *Lysistrata*") (*The Testaments* 251, 316). Like the later wink at *Othello* when the revisited Aunt Lydia suggests that Vidala's "pillow [like Desdemona's] needs rearranging" (*Testaments* 392), signposted intertexts from Shakespeare's *Tempest* seep into *Hag-Seed*'s framing tale. So do partially digested and displaced quotes, from a range of Shakespeare plays, in the metatextual manner of Tom Stoppard's *Rosencrantz and Guildenstern Are Dead* (1966).[28] These participate in the various forms of frame-breaking[29] which can generate pleasure in readers familiar with the material, happy to decode what has been encrypted. Yet they also entrench the control of an authorial presence which guides readers toward a given interpretation. Or which even,

---

[26] Atwood's agenda also adheres to Shelley's affirmation that poets are "the unacknowledged legislators of the world" (*A Defence of Poetry*, 1087).

[27] Interestingly, *Pale Fire* itself is haunted by Shakespearean pre-texts ranging from *Timon of Athens* to *Hamlet* (Boyd).

[28] Stoppard's play is overtly inhabited by Shakespeare's oeuvre, but also—like Felix's radishes—covertly haunted by Samuel Beckett's seminal *Waiting for Godot* (1952).

[29] The device of frame-breaking involves points of intersection between different levels of narrative unexpectedly breaking through the logical established structure of points of view in the text.

elsewhere, more forcefully *goads* readers of lesser vigilance[30] toward an intended meaning, not through the logic of informational language, but by setting up sensations which affect the way we feel about the substance of the message.

One strategy that Atwood often deploys to make us pay attention is combining word sentences and single-sentence word paragraphs to close chapters dramatically, the technique amounting to sledgehammer emphasis. Readers are also dragged into the text through characters who represent their average profile, with whom they identify. While his coworkers justify distributing kiddybots complete with teddy bears to the international pedophilia market (age of tolerance, profitable, job generating), this is where Stan draws the line and the reader along with it with his categorical "It's not right" (*Heart* 202). Similarly, as Mary Shelley did with *Frankenstein*, Atwood makes sure we feel that tampering with brains exceeds our authority as humans, if only because a simple error in timing has made a female character imprint on a teddy bear—or, put with a bathos that wipes out any cute anthropomorphism, has made her fall in love "with knitwear" (*Heart* 263), which could be a sock. And just in case some of us readers have resisted being herded through to a conclusion privileging freedom over utopian equality, Atwood earnestly spells the message out for us through her mouthpiece, Jocelyn, in the last half page of the novel: "Isn't it better to do something because you've decided to? Rather than because you have to?" (306).

Playfully piggybacking on authoritative pre-texts, deploying a vexed dialogue between a low burlesque aesthetic agenda and a grim political and philosophical one, Atwood's postmodern novels display a fraught concern with classic, weighty issues, our relations with the world, and our conduct in life, consubstantial with Miller's conception of social drama which grapples with "the ancient question, how are we to live?" (Miller, *Theatre Essays* 57). One final example—an unsettling pastiche of Robert Frost's much-anthologized poem on choice and agency, "The Road Not Taken"—demonstrates how Atwood's works participate in postmodernity's lightness of being and emphasis on the individual good:

---

[30] Atwood is perfectly aware that her projected readers are not all ideal readers, and she takes into account the profile of the average reader likely to be in contact with the text through time.

Two roads diverged in a yellow wood, and I took the one most [*sic*] travelled by. It was littered with corpses; as such roads are. But as you will have noticed, my own corpse is not among them. (*Testaments* 66)

Atwood's art of sinking *both* pays tribute to the pre-texts that make up the underside of her novels' weave *and* treats their ethical issues of responsibility (in the above case Aunt Lydia's contribution to the littering) as one giant grim but grotesque romp.

WORKS CITED

Atwood, Margaret. *Conversations*. Ed. Earl G. Ingersoll. Willowdale, Ont.: Firefly, 1990.
———. *Hag-Seed: The Tempest Retold*. London: Hogarth, Penguin Random House, 2016.
———. *The Handmaid's Tale*. Toronto: McClelland and Stewart, 1985.
———. "The Handmaid's Tale: A Feminist Dystopia?" In *Lire Margaret Atwood: The Handmaid's Tale*. Ed. Marta Dvořák. Rennes: PU de Rennes, 1999, pp. 17–30. Web. https://books.openedition.org/pur/30511.
———. *The Heart Goes Last*. London: Bloomsbury, 2015.
———. *Moral Disorder*. Toronto: Seal Books/ Random House of Canada, 2007.
———. *Stone Mattress: Nine Tales*. London: Bloomsbury, 2014.
———. *The Testaments*. London: Chatto & Windus, 2019.
Bakhtin, Mikhaïl. *The Dialogic Imagination*. Trans. Caryl Emerson & Michael Holquist. Ed. Michael Holquist. Austin: U of Texas P, 1996.
Beckett, Samuel. *Waiting for Godot*. First published as *En Attendant Godot*, 1952. New York: Grove Press, 1954.
Bilous, Daniel. "Intertexte/Pastiche: L'Intermimotexte." *Texte 2, Intertextualité: intertextes, autotexte, intratexte*. 1984, pp. 135–160.
Boyd, Brian. *Nabokov's Pale Fire: The Magic of Artistic Discovery*. Princeton: Princeton UP, 2001.
Brook, Peter, dir. *The Tempest* by William Shakespeare. Performed at Théâtre des Bouffes du Nord, Paris, October 1990–February 1991.
Césaire, Aimé. *Une Tempête*. 1969. Paris: Editions Point/Poche, 1997.
Dvořák, Marta. "Metafiction and Ficto-Criticism, the Ultimate Subversions of Genre: Atwood's and Van Herk's Writings as Exempla". *Essays on Canadian Writing* 84, fall 2009, pp. 159–181.
———. "Rejoinders in a Planetary Dialogue: J.M. Coetzee, Margaret Atwood, Lloyd Jones, et al. in Dialogue with Absent Texts." In *Crosstalk: Canadian and Global Imaginaries in Dialogue*. Ed. Diana Brydon and Marta Dvořák. Waterloo, Ont.: Wilfrid Laurier UP, 2012, pp. 111–134.
Erasmus. *On Free Will*. 1524. *Desiderius Erasmus and Martin Luther: Discourse on Free Will*. London: Bloomsbury (Reprint edition), 2013. https://pdfs.semanticscholar.org/4318/ff6f297d5fe96224fa4d89cd6fb3c9c0608b.pdf.

Frost, Robert. "The Road Not Taken". 1916. https://www.poetryfoundation.org/poems/44272/the-road-not-taken.
Frye, Northrop. *The Bush Garden: Essays on the Canadian Imagination*. Toronto: Anansi, 1971.
Genette, Gérard. *Palimpsestes: la littérature au second degree*. Paris: Seuil, 1982.
Hutcheon, Linda. *A Theory of Parody*: Urbana & Chicago: University of Illinois Press, 2000.
Levinson, Jerrold. *The Pleasures of Aesthetics: Philosophical Essays*. Ithaca & London: Cornell UP, 1996.
Lapouge, Gilles. *Utopie et civilisations* [1973]. Paris: Albin Michel, 1991.
Luther, Martin. *On the Bondage of the Will*. 1525. https://pdfs.semanticscholar.org/4318/fff6f297d5fe96224fa4d89cd6fb3c9c0608b.pdf.
Lyall, Sarah. "Review: Margaret Atwood's 'The Heart Goes Last' Conjures a Kinky Dystopia". *The New York Times*, 29 September 2015. Web. https://www.nytimes.com/2015/09/30/books/review-margaret-atwoods-the-heart-goes-last-conjures-a-kinky-dystopia.html?_r=0
Miller, Arthur. *Death of a Salesman*. 1949. Harmondsworth: Penguin, 1972.
———. *The Theatre Essays of Arthur Miller*. Ed. Robert A. Martin. Harmondsworth: Penguin, 1978.
Milton, John. *Complete Poems and Major Prose*. Ed. Merritt Y. Hughes. Indianapolis/New York: The Odyssey Press, 1957 (14th printing).
More, Thomas. *Utopia*. 1516. Trans. and edited by Robert M. Adams. A Norton Critical Edition. New York/London: W.W. Norton & Co., 1992 (2nd ed.).
Nabokov, Vladimir. *Pale Fire*. 1962. London: Penguin, 2000.
Orwell, George. *Animal Farm: A Fairy Story*. 1945. Harmondsworth: Penguin, 1982.
———. *Nineteen Eighty-Four*. 1949. Harmondsworth: Penguin, 1979.
Pacino, Al, dir. *Looking for Richard*. Based on the play *Richard III* by William Shakespeare. Screenplay: Al Pacino, Frederic Kimball, William Shakespeare. Cinematography: Robert Leacock. Music: Howard Shore, 1996. Film.
Shakespeare, William. *The Complete Works of William Shakespeare*. London: Wordsworth Editions, 1997.
Shelley, Mary. *Frankenstein, or The Modern Prometheus*. 1818. London: Penguin, 2003.
Shelley, Percy Bysshe. *A Defence of Poetry*. In *English Romantic Writers*. Ed. David Perkins. New York: Harcourt, Brace & World, Inc., 1967, pp. 1072–1087.
Stoppard, Tom. *Rosencrantz and Guildenstern Are Dead*. First staged and published in 1966. London: Faber and Faber, 1968.
Swift, Jonathan. *Gulliver's Travels*. 1726. Harmondsworth: Penguin, 1971.
Wunenburger, Jean-Jacques. *L'Utopie ou la crise de l'imaginaire*. Paris: Jean-Pierre Delarge, Editions Universitaires, 1979. Digitized 2009.

"Negotiating with the Dead": Authorial Ghosts and Other Spectralities in Atwood's Adaptations

Ruby Niemann

From the early days of Margaret Atwood's career, all the way back to her early poetry, her books have been packed with ghosts, specters, and remnants of memory and history, overlaying and often actively commenting on the activities of the living. Her writing is haunted. While these spectral figures and moments appear in many of Atwood's works, her use of ghostly voice is a compelling lens through which to view her adaptations of the works of other writers. This chapter will look at the use of ghosts in three of these works—the book of poetry *The Journals of Susanna Moodie* (1970) and the novels *Hag-Seed* (2015) and *The Penelopiad* (2006)—in order to explore how these ghosts function as a metatextual commentary on the nature of adaptation and its ties to colonization through the lens of hauntology.

R. Niemann (✉)
Department of English, School of Humanities, University of Adelaide, Adelaide, SA, Australia
e-mail: ruby.niemann@adelaide.edu.au

These three texts are adaptations of pre-existing works that are, to greater or lesser extents, classics. *The Penelopiad* is a sardonic take on *The Odyssey* by Homer, and both this original text and its author are among the best known and foundational literary artifacts in Western history. Homer is seen by many as, as Adorno and Horkheimer put it, "the basic text of European civilisation", which positions the literature of European "civilisation" as one that is inherently tied to militarism and conquering (37). *Hag Seed* is a retelling of Shakespeare's *The Tempest*. Shakespeare is the crown jewel in the tradition of English literature, a byword for literary genius. *The Journals of Susanna Moodie* is also an adaptation, although the source material is less familiar to those outside of Canada. Within her adoptive homeland, however, Moodie was "Canada's foremost author of the 1850s" (Rukavina 37). Because of their roles in the narrative construction of colony, the inclusion of Moodie and *The Tempest's* Miranda indicates the importance of white women to the construction of the narrative of the colonial project. The role of white women in colony building both in practice and in the production of the colonial imaginary is an essential part of the history of literature and colony.

This paper explores the haunted nature of adaptation as a form. Moreover, using Atwood's adaptations, I explore the colonial project as a form of adaptation—a violent re-writing and erasing of the history of a continent—and the ways in which adaptations of colonial texts of proto-Western imperialism can use the specter as a way of making it explicit that the colonized country, like the adaptation, is a haunted space.

Adaptations always contain ghostly traces of the previous text, of the cultural reinterpretations of the work, or of the warring interpretations between author and audience. Saviour Catania writes that "adaptation is aesthetically haunted" and that "spectrality is the soul of adaptation". Haunted adaptations are troubled, complex adaptations. According to Esther Peeren, "the specter stands for that which never simply is and thus escapes the totalizing logic of conventional cognitive and hermeneutic operations. It cannot be reduced to a straightforward genesis, chronology or finitude and insists on blurring multiple borders" (10). Therefore, adaptations that highlight their haunted aspects—with the use of textual and literal ghosts—are more complex, less easily reduced to a comprehensible critical sphere.

In the case of Atwood's adaptations they are often haunted not only by the ghosts on the page, but also by the spectral traces of the original author. They are as much about the position of the author as a cultural figure, and therefore the cultural context in which the text was created, as they are about the texts themselves. The three works discussed in this chapter are reworkings of texts by authors who range from well-known to iconic in their respective literary spheres. As Michel Foucault writes, "unlike a proper name, which moves from the interior of a discourse to the real person outside who produced it, the name of the author remains at the contours of texts" and that when discourses are circumscribed by the name of an author "its status and its manner of reception are regulated by the culture in which it circulates" (305). According to Sarah Ahmed's reading of Foucault and Roland Barthes, writing "functions by cutting itself off from any supposed origin" and its opaqueness is "precisely the destruction of a point of origin, any true authorial voice" (Ahmed 121–122). The practice indicated by these theorists notes the primacy of the author as a figure but denies them credence in relation to their work—the author is always dead at the hands of their own writing.

"Writing back", "counter-discourse", "oppositional literature", and "con-texts" are terms that describe "a body of postcolonial works that take a classic English text as a departure point, supposedly as a strategy for contesting the authority of the canon of English literature" (Thieme 2). The process of writing back involves not a death of the author but a forcible reanimation by those who have not been allowed a voice—women, people of color, the poor, the colonized. Atwood foregrounds her acts of literary repetition and appropriation. Because Barthes's theories of authorship deny authorial identity to all authors unilaterally, including the disempowered, his narrative "represses certain contexts of writing", including women's writing and the writings of people of color (Ahmed 122). The disembodied masculine perspective identified by Ahmed is, in Atwood's adaptations, given a number of ghostly counterparts that both challenge the oppressive presence of the Author-God as a societal figure and prevent the ability of the "dead" author to escape culpability by being severed from their body of work. The author is therefore both dead and alive—the author is a haunting (Ahmed 122).

This process of "writing back" induces "a reconsideration of the supposedly hegemonic status of their canonical departure points, opening up fissures in their supposedly solid foundations" (Thieme 2). Because part of the project of postcolonial writing back is to break up this hegemonic view of canonical texts, "the ghost, as a figure of multiplicity" that "keeps turning up, turning into, and returning in unpredictable and not always easily demarcated ways, could inaugurate an alternative logic of the turn as something not necessarily definitive" (del Pilar Blanco and Peeren 32). In this way, we may view the "fissures in their supposedly solid foundations" as instead the walls through which ghosts walk (Thieme 2). This is complicated by the figure of the author as ghost. The author-figure as a societal figurehead is powerful. Through the symbol of the ghost the presence of the author becomes a haunting that is both formidable and vulnerable. The ghost has an "almost sovereign power—deriving from its ability to ignore material and metaphysical boundaries, its capacity to 'possess' the living" but this is "counterbalanced by vulnerabilities", due to its "incomplete and intermittent embodiment" that makes it "unable to affect the physical world directly or effectively" (Peeren 3).

It is also important to note the exact functions of authorial hauntings, particularly in the context of texts that engage with a postcolonial project of "writing back". To ignore the figure of the author ignores how authors of great cultural importance have been utilized to expand and reinforce colonialism throughout the world, and how these icons of literature are still, to this day, vestiges of Empire. Russell West writes that "the character of Shakespeare, as a cultural icon, has played a role that is by no means negligible in the maintenance of the ideologies underpinning colonialism in its nineteenth and twentieth century manifestations", and this cannot be ignored when considering the function of the author (5). Some of Atwood's most haunted works are adaptations and are also the works that deal most directly with colonialism. This is an important commentary on the persistent haunting of colonialism in settled countries like Canada, and also the uncomfortable role that the author—the written word in general—takes in the colonial project. Any adaptation is haunted by its source material, and Canadian, English, and Western literature in general are haunted by those considered to be the standard bearers of the art—Moodie, Shakespeare, and Homer among them.

Hauntology in the sense of Jacques Derrida "uses the figure of the ghost to pursue (without ever fully apprehending) that which haunts like a ghost and, by way of this haunting, demands justice, or at least a response" (del Pilar Blanco and Peeren 9), and Atwood's spectral appropriations trouble hierarchical systems of canonical power and allow the figures she raises from the dead to demand attention while also troubling doctrines of power between groups, particularly in regards to issues of gender and anticolonialism. By doing this Atwood is using the unstable figure of the specter to further the postcolonial project of fracturing and dismantling the official narrative as ordained by those in positions of power, opening the power of these narratives up to questioning. By introducing specters into her adaptation, Atwood eludes any chance of a totalizing reading of either the original text or her adaptation. The specter magnifies the fractured nature of the adaptation, and the totalizing role of the author in the cultural imagination and in the colonial project. Atwood's texts are haunted as much by Shakespeare and Homer as they are by Miranda and Penelope. Atwood's use of spectral figures as powerful counter-voices speaking back to canonical texts facilitates the destabilizing power of the con-text while also maintaining and reinforcing the "complex and ambivalent" relationship between the "con-text and the canonical pre-text" because "the ghost can be both a figure of sovereignty and one of disempowerment" (Thieme 2; Peeren 48). Thus the ghost, which "stands for that which never simply is", becomes a symbol through which to trouble the hegemony of the Western canon, which by its very nature relies on "the totalizing logic of conventional cognitive and hermeneutic operations", the same way as adaptations "reconceptualise the possibilities of meaning" (Peeren 10; Hutcheon 109).

Adapting History: *The Journals of Susanna Moodie*

The Journals of Susanna Moodie is a poetry collection based on the life and writings of Susanna Moodie, an English settler of Upper Canada (present-day Ontario). Moodie documented her experiences during an often-chaotic period of Canadian history, and was well-known in her era as a memoirist and writer of early settler narratives. Atwood's poetry takes elements of her life and work—as well as photos and drawings of both Moodie and the Ontario landscape—and using the necromancy of poetry explores the ways in which Moodie's constructs Ontario in her writings while at the same despising the land she lives on.

K.J. Verwaayen writes that "Atwood produces a defamiliarization that compels us to query the intertwining notions of biography and autobiography, intertextuality and historicity, the homage of 'giving voice' and the violence of its appropriation" (300). Verwaayen positions Atwood's adaptation as a difficult yet ultimately "ethical engagement with the responsibility of representation and the recognition of its always-potential violence", a violence that Verwaayen identifies as coming from "the homage of 'giving voice' and the violence of its appropriation" (302; 300). This violence of adaptation is seen in *The Journals of Susanna Moodie* as a haunting, one where Moodie—or Atwood, or Atwood-as-Moodie—haunts the text both textually and visually. Verwaayen points to an image found in *Journals* of "a blurred figure of a woman appears in the white space of outline ... against a backdrop of presumably Canadian bush. She hangs in the space of the page/scene; she is not anchored to the ground. She is *an apparition in/of text*" (303, italics mine). This apparition, this ghost in/of the text, is part of the spirit that haunts Atwood's adaptations, particularly this adaptation where she is using Moodie's voice to speak on Atwood's own thoughts on womanhood, poetics, and white Canadian identity. If appropriation of the voice of the Other is always an act redolent with potential violence, then it is this violence that creates the unquiet death that leads to a haunted text. The adaptation is metatextual and therefore not static, troubling Moodie's grave while also never allowing her a chance to speak her own words—the words on the page, after all, all belong to Atwood. Atwood's adaptation indicates the troubling nature of adaptation as a concept—writing back is not always (or should not always be) an attempt just to recontextualize and reclaim a text. It should be an activity that troubles the water of the original text.

In the *Journals*, Atwood links this violence of the appropriation of the Other to the palimpsestic haunting of the city of Toronto, a layered amalgamation of space and time, where remnants of geological time and pre-European contact space extrude between the glass wave of modern Toronto. Atwood's Moodie constructs Ontario at the same time as she is constructed by it, the colonized country and the colonizing woman feeding off of each other until Moodie is inextricable from it, becomes a ghost built into its foundations, asking in one poem "what will they do now/ that I, that all/depending on me disappears?" (Atwood, *Moodie* 53). Unlike both *Hag-Seed* and *The Penelopiad*, *The Journals of Susanna Moodie* is haunted by the authorial figure that it invokes, and she does not just haunt the text—she haunts the city of Toronto. While most of the poems in the collection are from the perspective of the living Moodie, the last four follow Susanna as a spectral figure haunting Canada and the Canadian literary landscape. In the final poem "A Bus Along St. Clair: December" Moodie speaks to the modern Toronto that has been built on top of her. She haunts the city of Toronto, saying:

> Though they buried me in monuments
> of concrete slabs, of cables
> though they mounded a pyramid

of cold light over my head
though they said, We will build
silver paradise with a bulldozer

it shows how little they know
about vanishing: I have
my ways of getting through. (Atwood, *Moodie* 60)

The modern city is no longer simply a collection of buildings and people. Atwood's version of Moodie's future-Toronto "becomes an alternative cosmos for collective identification, recovery of other temporalities and reinvention of tradition" (Boym 76). The "pyramid of cold light", the famous, tremendous wall of glass built on the shore of Lake Ontario, is "not merely [an] architectural metaphor" but is "also screen [memory] for urban dwellers, projections of contested remembrances" (Boym 77). Atwood puts Moodie in conjunction with the glossy surface of modern, post-boom Toronto to force cracks in the glass, highlighting the city (the center of a forest, the city-in-a-garden) as a site of contested pasts and uncertain futures, indicating that "cities ... are palimpsests of history, incarnations of time in stone, sites of memory extending both in time and space" and that, while Andreas Huyssen might see it as "too easy", "the spectres of the past now haunting modern societies ... actually articulate, by way of displacement, a growing fear of the future at a time when the belief in modernity's progress is deeply shaken" (101; 20). Atwood's resurrection of Moodie at a time when Canada's fragile unity was under threat by the Quebec separatist movement, among other things (the notion of a nation is reliant on the agreement that the nation exists), shows the ways in which both ghosts and adaptations can indicate the ways in which the fracturing of the present and the uncertainty of the future can lead to a reinspection of the past.

Spectral Reflexivity and Haunting the Text: *Hag-Seed*

The complicated meta-narratives in Atwood's adaptations are strikingly obvious in *Hag Seed*, in which the novel's Prospero—here called Felix—is an actor and prison-school English teacher trying to put together his own version of *The Tempest*. Felix is a reflexive Prospero, enacting the role of deposed duke in both the play and in real life, until the boundaries of both break down and bleed into each other in an acerbic act of performance art, literalizing the similar metatextual moment that happens at the end of *The Tempest*. This reflexive acknowledgment of the textual source creates a metatextual loop as Atwood writes an adaptation within an adaptation—several adaptations in fact. There is the prison play, the original stage-version the Felix is producing after his daughter dies and which ultimately results in his firing, and the liminal frame-performance of the prison play, in which the audience acts as members of the cast in the concurrently-running version of *The Tempest* that is Felix's life. Wound throughout this is the ghost of Miranda, Felix's daughter who dies as a toddler. Felix's first attempt at staging *The Tempest* is "a kind of reincarnation", an attempt to will his Miranda back to life by creating "an ornate mausoleum raised in honour of a beloved shade" (Atwood, *Hag-Seed* 15; 17).

Felix's *Tempest* becomes a hauntological space, a space in which Miranda can be allowed to return, and this is at least partially why he is so focused on eventually seeing it staged. It is only through keeping the dream of his *Tempest* alive, by holding onto his magical Prospero garment, that he can keep Miranda's ghost with him. The ghostly figure in *Hag-Seed* is that of Miranda, who Felix wills into being through the power of delusion. He is aware that she is not really 'real'—she is not even a straightforward ghost, as she ages at the pace of a living child—but she begins to impact his life anyway, as a ghost would. She even begins to interact with the world outside of Felix, hinting at a truly spectral nature behind what is supposed to be Felix's imagination. Miranda decides she is going to understudy 8Handz's Ariel, and at one point 8Handz tells Felix that he is "hearing this weird feedback thing. Like someone was saying the lines at the same time", which Felix and the reader understand to be Miranda—or, possibly, it is only the recording mic, as 8Handz suggests (Atwood, *Hag-Seed* 195). Either way, it becomes clear at the end of the novel that, whether or not Miranda's ghostly presence is a haunting or a crutch devised by Felix through his grief, the play has become her living tomb, her prison, and she must be set free from it. *Hag-Seed* ends with Felix's realization that his *Tempest's* "endgame" was not to "bring his Miranda back to life", but instead to release her (Atwood, *Hag-Seed* 291). Finally, he liberates her, telling her "to the elements be free" (Atwood, *Hag-Seed* 292). The book ends with Miranda's release from her spectral repetition, as if without the ghostly figure haunting the text and its protagonist there can be no book.

Fittingly for a ghost, Miranda's role in *Hag Seed* is ambiguous and difficult to quantify. The decision to replace both Ariel and Miranda with this adolescent ghost is a not-insignificant pivot from the original text. Tying Miranda's eventual disappearance with the end of the text indicates a relationship between Miranda and the narrative more integral than the relationship between protagonist Felix and the nested *Tempests* he functions within—it is Miranda, and not Felix, who becomes the central figure of the book, even though she is quite literally not in the text. Atwood invokes a ghostly figure to raise questions without answering them, spectralizing this knotted figure of colonialism and gender in a way that undermines the centrality of Felix to his own narrative and, in doing so, questions the authority and power of Prospero in Shakespeare's original play. *Hag-Seed* uses a fractured adaptation to playfully undermine the cohesive narrative of the original.

Hag-Seed's Miranda does not align "herself with the benefits and protection offered by the colonising father and husband" against the enslaved Caliban, nor is she constructed "as the sexual object of both the Anglo-European male and the native Other", as Laura Donaldson describes the original Miranda's situation (*Decolonising Feminisms* 17). Instead she gently yet firmly demands her freedom from her father, the self-created island prison of his play, and from the text itself. Miranda is exorcised from the novel but her haunting affect remains, as the ambiguity between her actual status—ghost or hallucination—continues. After this point the novel cannot continue, bringing to mind the fundamental ways in which Miranda "haunts" white women anticolonial authors, and in turn, how white colonial femininity haunts both this text and *The Journals of Susanna Moodie*. Atwood in these two texts "writes back" to the classics, adapting two works in order to surface the violence inherent in the original narratives. The use of Miranda as a ghost destabilizes *The Tempest* further, creating a narrative that cannot be reconciled. By surfacing the haunted and recursive nature of adaptation, Atwood's texts question the fundamental concept of a stable narrative, indicating the ways in which adaptation can be a form of counter-textual resistance.

ADAPTING AMBIVALENCE: *THE PENELOPIAD*

Atwood's third ghostly adaptation is *The Penelopiad*, a fractured version of *The Odyssey* told from the perspective of Odysseus's supposedly faithful and devoted wife Penelope. Like *Hag-Seed*, *The Penelopiad* is part of a commissioned series. The Canongate myth series tasked several well-known authors with producing their own novella-length takes on classic myths and legends. Unlike other retellings of myths, such as Madeleine Miller's novels *The Song of Achilles* and *Circe*, *The Penelopiad* is a metatextual narrative that relies on not only a knowledge of *The Odyssey* and the other poems and myths pertinent to the story of Penelope, but also the feminist reclamation of Helen and Penelope and the contentious position of Odysseus throughout history. Penelope continuously references "the official version" which turns her into "an edifying legend. A stick used to beat other women with", commenting on the creation and utilization of her own myth, which is, for her, separate from her actual self (Atwood, *Penelopiad* 2). There is an ambiguity to Penelope that sets Atwood's *Penelopiad* apart from more recent feminist adaptations of Greek myth, including Emily Wilson's translation of *The Odyssey* in which "she reduces [the] ethical ambiguity and ambivalence" of Homer's poem (Johnson np). Atwood's Penelope—and her Odysseus—is all ambiguity, however, opening up an adaptation that is both less faithful and yet sticks to the spirit of ambiguity that shrouds Odysseus and his tales. Later, during a short sketch depicting the trial of Odysseus, the Judge specifically refers to *The Odyssey*, leafing through it at the bench and calling it "a book we must needs consult, as it is the main authority on the subject" (Atwood, *Penelopiad* 179). This trial section is part of the intersecting narrative, made up of a series of sketches, songs, and monologues by the maids directed at Penelope, Odysseus, and their son Telemachus. With these sections, the maids undermine any kind of cohesive narrative or suspension of disbelief. The maids make it clear that the reader is being told a story, that Penelope is spinning a tale in the same way as she once spun threads for her father in law's shroud.

In *The Penelopiad*, Atwood creates a haunted adaptation. She describes it as such in the introduction to the book, noting that she has "always been haunted by the hanged maids; and, in *The Penelopiad*, so is Penelope herself" (Atwood, *Penelopiad* xxi). *The Penelopiad* is a novel "stained by time" (Fisher 21). Retellings are always haunted by their original text, always "fatal repetitions" that can introduce new twists and turns but always return to the same, salient facts (Fisher 21). Penelope superimposes her presence over what the reader knows about *The Odyssey* as Atwood superimposes her own vision over the mythic text, but she is also, literally, a ghost. She is a literal ghost haunting the text. She describes herself as such, reminding Helen that "We're spirits now, Helen ... Spirits don't have bodies" (Atwood, *Penelopiad* 153), and she opens the book by saying "now that I'm dead I know everything", telling the reader that she has achieved a "state of bonelessness, liplessness, breastlessness" (Atwood, *Penelopiad* 1). Her spectrality is central to the narrative, as is that of the maids, although Atwood demystifies Penelope's ghostliness. Penelope is petty and mostly powerless—she follows her opening pronouncement of omniscience with the admission that she knows "only a few factoids" that she didn't before (Atwood, *Penelopiad* 1). The duality of hauntings— Penelope haunting the text, the maids haunting Penelope—indicates "the ambiguity of the ghost's relationship to power: it may appear as a dominant, even sovereign being, but can also manifest as a figure of compromised agency" (Peeren 3). While *Hag-Seed* and *The Journals of Susanna Moodie* feature living characters—or landscapes—being haunted by ghostly figures, *The Penelopiad* centers on the struggle between ghosts. By turning both Penelope and the maids into figures of ambiguous power, Atwood uses the figure of the specter to explore the difficult question of lateral aggression between members of an oppressed class.

Penelope's choice to blame Helen supports the dominant narrative, particularly in regards to Helen. Penelope's refusal to sympathize with Helen or at least share blame for her actions props up the canonical story, which also holds Helen responsible for the Trojan War—she has been passed down through history as possessing the face that launched a thousand ships. By spectralizing these women and pushing men to the background—in the narrative space of Penelope's afterlife, Odysseus is present mostly in his absence, as he is continuously in the process of leaving Penelope—Atwood is furthermore using the ambiguity of power in the figure of the ghost to highlight inter-gender tensions between women.

Throughout these adaptations, Atwood pursues the spectral figure of the Author in a way that explores the author-figure in the modern hierarchy of canon formation and literary studies. Though the position of the author has been debated and deconstructed since the publication of Barthes's ground-breaking essay "The Death of the Author", the author as a figure has been, in modern literary criticism, not laid to rest but instead endlessly reanimated only to be banished once more. The author is not dead and gone, but is instead a specter. Atwood's works lead us to reinspect the author not as something *gone* but as something that is *always returning*—instead of the death of the author, the haunting of the text. Because of this, we are led to ponder the same question Derrida poses when he asks "what does it mean to follow a ghost? And what if this came down to being followed by it, always, persecuted perhaps by the very chase we are leading?" (10). When Atwood and Moodie finally catch up to each other at the end of *The Journals of Susanna Moodie*, Atwood's version of Moodie assures her audience that although she can be killed she cannot be destroyed, saying "it would take more than that to banish me: this is my kingdom still" (*Moodie*, 60) and any chase with her as its quarry will always result in the hunter becoming the hunted, as in Derrida's spectral metaphor.

By figuring Miranda, Penelope, and Susanna—two fictional women and one real authoress—as ghosts, Atwood unsettles the previously safe, almost inert women of literary history on whom they are based. Susanna, Penelope, and Miranda are "good" women of history, loyal and caring helpmeets to their husbands, fathers, and sons. Penelope is heralded across centuries for her loyalty as much as her cleverness, and it is her refusal to choose a new husband among the suitors that is greeted with the most approval both within the text of *The Odyssey* and without it. In *The Penelopiad*, her chastity is in doubt, and the maids assert that they were murdered in order to cover up Penelope's own dalliances. It is the maids themselves who introduce the notes of uncertainty into the previously agreed upon narrative, telling the reader "the truth, dear auditors, is seldom certain" (Atwood, *Penelopiad* 148). Miranda is a good girl in *The Tempest*, who cannot even escape her father's machinations through marriage. She falls in love with Ferdinand and through her marriage to him escapes both the island and her father's control, but in doing so cements her father's power as the returning Duke of Milan, tying her relationship to Ferdinand to her father's political power. Susanna Moodie is a more complex figure, but her position as a pioneer woman and the wife of a Sheriff and anti-rebel fighter makes her a symbol of a kind of Canadian colonial piety. Atwood troubles all of these assumptions, however. She makes Moodie something baleful, turning her into "the spirit of the land she once hated", speaking for the wilderness underneath Toronto as she once struggled furiously against it (Atwood, *Moodie* 64).

By spectralizing these "good" women, Atwood allows them to be duplicitous and slippery, untrustworthy mouthpieces with ulterior motives speaking in double speak. Atwood's haunted adaptations reopen questions of the past as a settled topic, and also of the power of both the narrator and the Author as the sole voice in the text and, in the case of Authors, in the narrative history of the various societies they become figureheads for. If the name of the author is inextricable from the contours of the discourse indicated by that name, and this discourse is "regulated by the society in which it circulates" (Foucault 305), then to raise their specters through the necromancy of "writing back" acknowledges the power of the role of the author while also undermining the authority of their discourses, in favor of allowing those previously voiceless to speak. It is this hauntological difference that allows Atwood to use her adaptations as multivocal, metatextual spaces in which to unsettle the frequently patriarchal control of narrative, art, and creation in Western literature.

Works Cited

Ahmed, Sara. *Differences that Matter: Feminist Theory and Postmodernism.* Cambridge University Press, 1998.
Atwood, Margaret. *Hag Seed.* Hogarth, 2016.
——. *The Journals of Susanna Moodie.* Oxford University Press, 1970.
——. *The Penelopiad.* Canongate, 2006.
Bess, Jennifer. "Imploding the Miranda Complex in Julia Alvarez's *How The García Girls Lost Their Accents.*" *College Literature*, vol. 34, no. 1, 2007, pp. 78–105, doi: https://www.jstor.org/stable/25115406. Accessed 4 March 2019.
Boym, Svetlana. *The Future of Nostalgia.* Basic Books, 2001.
Catania, Saviour. "Spectres of Film Adaptation: A Hauntology of Relational Hybridity." *Literature/Film Quarterly*, vol. 45, no. 2, 2017.
Dayan, Joan. "Playing Caliban: Césaire's *Tempest.*" *Arizona Quarterly: A Journal of American Literature, Culture, and Theory*, vol. 48, no. 4, 1992, pp. 125–145, doi: https://doi.org/10.1353/arq/1992.0020. Accessed 18 May 2018.
Del Pilar Blanco, Maria and Esther Peeren. "Introduction: Conceptualizing Spectralities." *The Spectralities Reader: Ghosts and Haunting in Contemporary Cultural Theory*, edited by Maria del Pilar Blanco and Ester Peeren, Bloomsbury, 2013, pp. 1–27.
Derrida, Jacques. *Specters of Marx: The State of the Debt, the Work of Mourning and the New International.* Trans. Peggy Kamuf. Routledge, 1994.
Donaldson, Laura E. *Decolonizing Feminisms: Race, Gender, & Empire-Building.* Routledge, 1992.
Donaldson, Laura. "The Miranda Complex: Colonialism and the Question of Feminist Reading." *Diacritics*, vol. 18, no. 3, 1988, pp. 65–77, doi: https://www.jstor.org/stable/465255. Accessed 4 March 2019.
Fisher, Mark. "What IS Hauntology?" *Film Quarterly*, vol. 66, no. 1, 2012, pp. 16–24, doi: https://doi.org/10.1525/fq.2012.66.1.16. Accessed 15 May 2018.
Foucault, Michel. "Authorship: What is an Author?" *Screen*, vol. 20, no. 1, 1979, pp. 13–14, doi: https://doi.org/10.1093/screen.20.1.13. Accessed 23 Jan 2019.

Goldman, Marlene. *DisPossession: Haunting in Canadian Fiction*. McGill-Queens University Press, 2012.
Horkheimer, Max and Theodore W. Adorno. *Dialectic of Enlightenment: Philosophical Fragments*. Trans. Edmund Jephcott. Stanford University Press, 2002.
Hutcheon, Linda. *The Canadian Postmodern: A Study of Contemporary English-Canadian Fiction*. Oxford University Press, 1988.
Huyssen, Andreas. *Present Pasts: Urban Palimpsests and the Politics of Memory*. Stanford University Press, 2003.
Johnson, Eleanor. "The Return of Homer's Women." *Public Books*, 2019. https://www.publicbooks.org/the-return-of-homers-women/?utm_source=PUBLIC+BOOKS+Newsletter&utm_campaign=49b61a7ab5-EMAIL_CAMPAIGN_2019_05_17&utm_medium=email&utm_term=0_d048c39403-49b61a7ab5-181021921.
Jones, Cecily. *Engendering Whiteness: White Women and Colonialism in Barbados and North Carolina, 1627–1865*. Manchester University Press, 2007.
Khalid, Saman and Irshad Ahmad Tabassum. "*The Penelopiad*: A Postmodern Fiction." *The Journal of Humanities and Social Sciences*, vol. 21, no. 1, 2013, pp. 17–28.
Peeren, Esther. *The Spectral Metaphor: Living Ghosts and the Agency of Invisibility*. Palgrave, 2014.
Perry, Adele. "'Fair Ones of a Purer Caste': White Women and Colonialism in Nineteenth-Century British Columbia." *Feminist Studies*, vol. 23, no. 3, 1997, pp. 501–524. DOI: https://www.jstor.org/stable/3178383. Accessed 4 March 2019.
Rukavina, Alison. "'Of the Irritable Genus': The Role of Susanna Moodie in the Publishing of *Roughing It in the Bush*." *Studies in Canadian Literature*, vol. 25, no. 1, 2000, pp. 37–56. DOI: https://journals.lib.unb.ca/index.php/SCL/article/view/12828.
Thieme, John. *Postcolonial Con-texts: Writing Back to the Canon*. Continuum, 2001.
Verwaayen, K.J. "Ethical Relations, Intertextuality, and the Im/Possibilities of an 'Intersubjective Third' in Margaret Atwood's *Journals of Susanna Moodie*." *Contemporary Women's Writing*, vol. 8, no. 3, 2014, pp. 300–318. DOI: https://doi.org/10.1093/cwwrit/vpt017.
West, Russell. "Césaire's Bard: Shakespeare and the Performance of Change in Césaire's Une Tempête." *Journal of Caribbean Literatures*, vol. 4, no. 3, 2007, pp. 1–16. DOI: https://www.jstor.org/stable/40986206. Accessed 18 May 2018.

Transforming the Human and the Novel: The Utopian Potential of Resilience in Margaret Atwood's *MaddAddam* Trilogy

Lena Crucitti

"We've just opened the great big gene-splicing toy box and people are going to be playing with that for years" (Atwood qtd. in Halliwell 260). This quotation about the burning issue of genetic engineering perfectly conveys the anxiety revolving around Margaret Atwood's *MaddAddam* trilogy. In the three novels constituting this work (*Oryx and Crake* [2003], *The Year of the Flood* [2009], and *MaddAddam* [2013]), Atwood imagines a post-apocalyptic world in which the last human beings have to coexist with strange hybrid animals, but also with Crakers, the new human species bioengineered by a hubristic scientist called Crake, who is also responsible for the Plague that decimated humankind. Crakers, who were technologically enhanced through the use of animal characteristics, represent a form of life that blurs the distinctive lines between animals, humans, and machines. This vision of posthumanism prompted fierce criticism among scholars. On the one hand, the emergence of Crakers as the future

L. Crucitti (✉)
Université Saint-Louis—Bruxelles, Bruxelles, Belgium
e-mail: lena.crucitti@usaintlouis.be

human race was interpreted as a rupture, representing humanity's demise and the triumph of a "fundamentally nonhuman", "fundamentally subhuman" (Parry 251) race. According to critics such as Gerry Canavan, the utopian potential of the trilogy does not involve human beings: there is "hope, but not for us" (138). Others perceive the rise of Crakers as a nonsensical vision of posthumanism. For instance, Stephen Dunning sarcastically wrote that it "is hard to take these purring, multi-colored, blue-bottomed, blue-penised, excrement-eating, perimeter-pissing, citrous-scented [sic] creatures seriously" (95). Whether they considered the emergence of the posthuman as the death of humankind or as an authorial joke, scholars systematically demonstrated a determination not to identify with Crakers. This chapter intends to challenge these responses which all betray a deep-rooted belief in human exceptionalism—the belief that human beings are essentially different from other forms of life. It also means to question the assumption that there are only dystopian scenarios concerning the fate of humanity in the trilogy. I will suggest that this profound need to discredit Crakers conceals a form of anxiety about our ontological status as human beings. My objective is by no means to prove that Crakers literally represent an ideal form of life, but to show that the depiction of this species sheds light on our own fears and possible misconceptions about human nature. Atwood's work suggests that the key to humanity's survival lies in the reconnection with our capacity to adapt to changing environments. The novels celebrate the resilience and monstrosity of the human subject whose evolution constantly involves internal transformations. This interpretation will be supported by the observation that the formal aspect of the trilogy mirrors a fragmented but resilient form of the human and thus expresses solidarity with the condition of humankind.

Transforming the Human

In order to discuss humanity's survival in the trilogy, my analysis will heavily rely on two notions: Dominique Lestel's definition of the human and Crawford Stanley Holling's concept of resilience. As pointed out by Lestel, the human is a concept that eludes definitions because it does not represent an immutable entity (Lestel 90).[1] The French philosopher and ethol-

---

[1] "En construction permanente, l'humain est toujours à définir, et une fois défini il n'est déjà plus ce qu'il était" (Lestel 90).

ogist assumes that the question of the human is intrinsically linked to the question of the animal. This consideration is particularly relevant to the *MaddAddam* trilogy, since Crakers are presented as perfect humans who have been improved through the use of animal features. Crake clearly drew his inspiration from animals to strengthen the human race. At some point, after having evoked his use of baboon and octopus DNA to improve the reproductive capacity of humans, the scientist praises the remarkable ability of animals to biologically adapt to changing environments: "Think of an adaptation, any adaptation, and some animal somewhere will have thought of it first" (*Oryx* 194). This can be read as an explicit invitation to draw a parallel between the transition from the human to the posthuman and the transition from the animal to the human, a concept called "hominisation". In an essay entitled *L'Animalité*, Lestel explains that this process of hominization, which represents a reassuring concept to apprehend human nature in a post-Darwinian era, is an illusion and that we have not become human by extracting ourselves from our animality but that this animality is still part of us (89–90).[2] Based on the idea that evolving means "assimilating" the Other, he elaborated a Darwinian definition of the human as a monstrous form that has managed to survive by "absorbing" the animal. According to Lestel, monstrosity is an essential part of humanity (Desblache 8).[3] From this perspective, it is possible to consider posthumanism as part of the process of human evolution. In the same way as there is no radical break from the animal to the human, the transition to the posthuman does not necessarily imply a rupture with the human.

In order to disentangle the mechanisms at work in this ontological transition, I will use the notion of resilience, which usually serves as a tool to describe the natural world but that I will apply to the human in the trilogy. My analysis relies on the assumption that the human can be considered as a microcosm whose mechanisms mirror the functioning of the ecosystem to which they belong. According to the model proposed by the Canadian ecologist Crawford Stanley Holling, resilience has to be defined in contrast with stability. This is a fundamental distinction: whereas

---

[2] "Nous avons pris le darwinisme tellement au sérieux que l'hominisation nous est apparue comme un processus idéal pour comprendre comment l'homme s'est arraché à l'animalité et pour mieux appréhender celle-ci. Mais il s'agissait d'une illusion. […] L'hominisation ne s'est pas produite *contre* l'animalité mais au contraire avec elle" (Lestel 89–90).

[3] "[…] il [Lestel] redéfinit l'être humain dans une optique darwinienne comme un monstre qui a réussi. Évoluer, c'est en quelque sorte assimiler l'autre en soi. Il envisage donc la monstruosité comme une part essentielle de l'humanité […]" (Desblache, 8).

stability refers to "the ability of a system to return to an equilibrium state after a temporary disturbance", resilience "determines the persistence of relationships within a system and is a measure of the ability of these systems to absorb changes of state variables, driving variables, and parameters, and still persist" (17). In other words, while a stable system is able to recover from a shock and return to its initial state, a resilient system adapts to the shock and absorbs it in order to continue to exist. A resilient system does not return to the previous state after the shock but evolves into something new. As highlighted by Dana Phillips, the new system might strike a new balance by including what she calls "unwelcome developments" (142) from a human point of view. For instance, at the level of an ecosystem, an unwelcome development could correspond to the proliferation of a specific type of insects. If we transpose the resilience theory to the human in the *MaddAddam* trilogy, resilience can be seen as the ability of the human to welcome change and to accept to be contaminated by unattractive but efficient animal features for the sake of survival. However, the human species in the novels tends to resist this change because it is seen as a threat to their ontology. Jimmy, the narrator in *Oryx and Crake*, epitomizes this attitude and can be considered as the guardian of human exceptionalism. He categorically refuses to be replaced by "a bunch of hormone robots" (*Oryx* 196). However, ironically, the way this representative of humanity as we know it today is depicted severely undermines the very concepts of human distinctiveness and superiority. Throughout the story, Jimmy is described as a nonhuman creature. The fact that he decides to call himself Snowman, after the mythical ape-like creature also known as the "Yeti", represents a first hint at the dehumanization process he experiences in the story. In *Oryx and Crake*, the protagonist believes that he is the very last human on earth and suffers from loneliness. He expresses his despair: "Why am I on this earth? How come I'm alone? Where's my Bride of Frankenstein?" (*Oryx* 199). This reference to the most popular monster story in the history of English literature is not insignificant. While we would expect Crakers to be portrayed as the monsters, it is Jimmy who paradoxically becomes the monster longing for a partner. Jimmy could have mentioned Mary Shelley's other canonical work *The Last Man*, a post-apocalyptic novel in which the desperate last survivor struggles to continue to live in a world ravaged by an unknown pandemic. However, Jimmy chose to identify with Frankenstein's monster instead, causing the reader to question whether Jimmy is human after all, and to reflect on what it means to be human in the context of this story. Moreover, this reference inevitably evokes the birth of the "Frankenbabies" when the two species meet at the end of the trilogy. Atwood consciously plays with the ambiguity of this allusion, which makes it impossible to assert that the monstrosity of the babies is only attributable to Crakers. As pointed out by Hilde Staels in "*Oryx and Crake*: Atwood's Ironic Inversion of *Frankenstein*", Jimmy's marginalization largely contributes to his transformation into the "Other", the "monster": "He is the sole remnant of what was once a human being with natural and normal human feelings and desires, yet he is afraid that to the children '[h]e is humanoid, he's hominid, he's an aberration, he's abominable'" (307). Later, the readers discover that there are other survivors, some of whom turn out to represent humanity at its worst. A group of criminals called the "Painballers" commit many terrible atrocities, which largely contributes to the blurring of the line between human and monster in the story. Jimmy's memories of the past imply that the Painballers are the inhuman product of a society dominated by violence and inequalities (human trafficking, child pornography, etc.).

Jimmy is depicted not only as a monster but also as an animal, that is to say, another nonhuman creature. For instance, one cannot miss the parallel that is drawn between Jimmy and the apes that Adam One, the leader of an eco-conscious religious group called the God's Gardeners, mentions in one of his homilies in *The Year of the Flood*:

> The Serpent is a highly charged symbol throughout the Human Words of God, though its guises are varied. Sometimes it is shown as an evil enemy of Humankind—perhaps because, when our Primate ancestors slept in trees, the Constrictors were among their few nocturnal predators. And for these ancestors—shoeless as they were—to step on a Viper meant certain death. (*Year* 278)

Jimmy is also reduced to the status of a shoeless creature that has to sleep in a tree to not fall prey to "pigoons" and other modern predators. At the end of the first volume, his life is at risk, not because he stepped on a Viper, but because he stepped on a piece of glass. Jimmy's vulnerability to his environment echoes what David Herman calls the "Creatural", which refers to "the status of being a creature, subject to the requirements of the surrounding environment, the vicissitudes of time, and the vulnerabilities of the body", a condition that "emphasizes the fundamental continuity between humans and other animals" (3). In the trilogy, humanity is depicted as regressing to a primitive, animal state and loses its status as a distinct species. As highlighted by Lee Rozelle, the human subject is re-inserted within the animal kingdom from the very first pages of the trilogy in which "Jimmy/Snowman's interactions include flicking a spider, urinating on grasshoppers, and rubbing ants off a mango". Jimmy becomes "a niche within an ecosystem concerned with predators and sustenance, his primary concerns not social but ecological" (64).

Beyond the fact that Jimmy is portrayed as a nonhuman being, a second element subverts the portrayal of humanity as a superior and distinct species: the fact that the human subject is described as a weak and non-adapted creature from a Darwinian perspective. Jimmy becomes ridiculous because he does not have the humility to accept that his behavior is no longer consistent with what has become the norm in this post-apocalyptic world. The text abounds in moments in which his patronizing attitude collides with reality. For instance, Jimmy mocks the fact that Crakers have been programmed to be able to recycle their own excrement by ingesting it and explicitly says that he finds this practice absolutely repulsive: "However you look at it, he'd said, what it boiled down to was eating your own shit" (188). As pointed out by Rozelle, "when we observe these traits in other species, they are understood as appropriate to specific adaptive functions" (68). It is the idea that those characteristics could contaminate the sacredness of the human that is seen as ridiculous and unacceptable. However, with hindsight, Jimmy can disdain this practice, but he is still the one who is literally dying of hunger: "Time to face reality. Crudely put, he's slowly starving to death" (*Oryx* 175).

In terms of survival, he can only rely on two very limited resources which represent leftovers from the civilization to which he belonged. The first resource corresponds to processed food from the old world. As Phillips ironically points out, "[t]hanks to an accident of history, the Sveltana sausages have become survival rations" (151). The same thing can be said of the "chocolate flavored energy bar scrounged from a trailer park' which Snowman "can't bring himself to eat" since "it might be the last one he'll ever find" (*Oryx* 4). Jimmy understands the unsustainable character of his method: each time he finds food, he only postpones the moment when there is nothing left to eat. He is described as a predator who cannot "live on clover" but who cannot satisfy his "beastly appetites" (*Oryx* 116) because he has never learnt how to kill. This is why he deceives the Crakers into believing that one of their missions is to hunt and prepare a fish for him every week: "[t]he people would never eat a fish themselves, but they have to bring him one a week because he's told them Crake has decreed it" (*Oryx* 116). Ironically, even though sacrificing an animal disgusts the Crakers, they obey because "[t]hey've accepted Snowman's monstruousness" (*Oryx* 116). This occasional offering is however not sufficient to keep Jimmy alive.

Jimmy's second resource corresponds to his encyclopedic knowledge, which is closely linked to his use of language. As a liberal arts graduate, Jimmy is the perfect example of a logophile. In Western cultures, language has often been interpreted as the distinctive human characteristic. Jimmy assumes that if he can save the words, then he can save humanity. In *Oryx and Crake*, he spends a considerable amount of time reciting list of words in his tree. He particularly focuses on the "[t]he odd words, the old words, the rare ones" (*Oryx* 78) which, he assumes, represent the quintessence of human culture: "Rag ends of language are floating in his head: mephitic, metronome, mastitis, metatarsal, maudlin" (*Oryx* 175). Jimmy clings to the words as one would cling to life: "'Hang on to the words', he tells himself" (*Oryx* 78). However, he soon realizes that in the same way that there will only be empty cans sooner or later, his words sound like forms emptied of their substance: "'I used to be erudite', he says out loud. Erudite. A hopeless word. What are all those things he once thought he knew, and where have they gone?" (*Oryx*, 175). In "'Hang on to the words': The Scarcity of Language in McCarthy's *The Road* and Atwood's *Oryx and Crake*", Oliver Völker argues that what Atwood and Jimmy have in common is that they both firmly believe in "the performative and restorative capacity of human language" (82). However, I would argue that on the contrary, they both invite the reader to question the power of "man's identifying characteristic par excellence" (Agamben 37) and to go beyond it. In contrast with Jimmy who feeds himself on lists of empty and presumptuous words, animals continue to thrive by speaking a raw and organic survival language. While observing birds flying in the sky, Jimmy reluctantly admits that their "list of words", though rude and primitive, is more appropriate than his: "He watches them with resentment: everything is fine with them, not a care in the world. Eat, fuck, poop, screech, that's all they do" (*Oryx* 174). Even though Jimmy shows contempt for them, he also recognizes that they use an efficient language that is able to impact reality and to answer basic needs. In the following extract, as Jimmy is trying to remember some basic survival techniques, an encyclopedia of useless words comes to his mind. His knowledge turns out to be too theoretical and completely disconnected from his immediate reality:

> The human body is ninety-eight per cent water, says the book in his head. This time it's a man's voice, an encyclopedia voice; no one he knows, or knew. The other two per cent is made up of minerals, most importantly the iron in the blood and the calcium of which the skeletal frame and the teeth are comprised. (*Oryx* 127)

Jimmy finally understands that he cannot survive if he continues to rely on his knowledge and resources from the old world. His tired and empty body feels the profound need to turn into something new: "He doesn't care about the iron in his blood or the calcium in his skeletal frame; he's tired of being himself, he wants to be someone else. Turn over all his cells, get a chromosome transplant, trade in his head for some other head, one with better things in it" (*Oryx* 127). Jimmy's body makes him acknowledge that technology and genetic manipulation might offer a solution in terms of survival strategy. As his human resources turn out to be useless in this new environment, the only way to survive is to absorb the change and to go beyond his limited and condescending vision of what it means to be human. He might be unconsciously starting to accept the fact that human beings have never been static forms. Just like any other living organism, they constantly have to adjust their biological functions to external conditions. As Rozelle points out, "The Crakers also help us to remember that as a species, humans are not exempt from adaptations and mutations that occur through processes of evolution, despite our various advances" (69). The story highlights the fact that we have not come to terms with our own animality yet, which also explains why we are not ready to face the rise of artificial intelligence and the frantic developments in neuroscience and genetic manipulation. In the *MaddAddam* trilogy, the survival of humanity involves the invasion of monstrous characteristics in the human and the recognition that Crakers are just a form of human adaptation. Resisting the change and aiming at stability instead of resilience is not an option as it would only mean signing humanity's death warrant. The story does not only re-embed the human within the continuum of organic life, it also hints at the possibility of the non-organic as the future of humanity. A parallel can interestingly be drawn between this portrayal of the human condition and the formal aspect of the trilogy. By mirroring the same monstrosity and complexity at various levels (generic, narratological), the three novels express solidarity with the human condition.

Transforming the Novel

In the same way the concept of the human exceeds categorization, theoreticians describe the novel as a genre that is difficult to apprehend. As pointed out by Terry Eagleton in *The English Novel*, "the novel is a genre which resists exact definition. [...] The point about the novel, however, is not just that it eludes definitions, but that it actively undermines them. [...] It cannibalizes other literary modes and mixes the bits and pieces promiscuously together" (1). Virginia Woolf characterizes this monstrous genre that can absorb the Other as "this most pliable of all forms" (77). The *MaddAddam* trilogy, which does not represent a perfectly homogeneous whole, can be considered as a laboratory in which this pliability is extensively explored. At least three different forms of transformation can be observed in this work. At a generic level, the trilogy fits into different categories. It can be considered either as a dystopia or as a post-catastrophe narrative, depending on whether the story refers to the past or the present. The text also includes fragments coming from many other genres such as homilies, hymns, radio broadcasts, and songs. Then, the three novels involve a variety of means of expression such as body language, animal language, silence, and music. For instance, the Gardeners reject writing and decide to memorize and transmit their knowledge through an oral tradition in order not to leave any traces: "Let us sing" (*Year* 15). Later, singing becomes too dangerous so they have to go one step further "for fear of being overheard": "Let us whisper" (*Year* 373). The Gardeners' means of communication tend to dematerialize as the story unfolds. This transformation occurs in response to the increasing number of dangers that the community members have to face. Finally, from a narratological point of view, the trilogy does not offer one traditional perspective on the story but stages a considerable diversity of voices. My hypothesis is that these formal transformations in the novel are dictated by the survival instinct of the protagonists. The text itself exhibits a form of resilience, since it is through the contamination of different genres, means of communication, and voices that the text is able to transmit the story. Because of the need to maintain a reasonably well-delimited focus of inquiry, this chapter limits itself to the investigation of transformation at the level of the narration.

From a narratological perspective, the most striking element is that the process of complexification is progressive and tends to intensify as the story develops. In *Oryx and Crake*, the form is not particularly challenging: the story is recounted through a third-person narration adopting the point of view of Jimmy/Snowman who believes that he is the very last human on earth. These are the very first lines of the novel: "Snowman wakes before dawn. He lies unmoving, listening to the tide coming in, wave after wave sloshing over the various barricades, wish-wash, wish-wash, the rhythm of heartbeat. He would so like to believe he is still asleep" (3). In terms of reliability, there are at least two aspects of Jimmy's account of the story that are problematic. The narrator's perspective is too limited: he belonged to the privileged class in the dystopian society preceding the apocalypse. His parents were scientists working in the Compounds, which means that Jimmy evolved in a favorable environment, far from the harsh living conditions of the Pleeblands. Moreover, beyond the fact his vision of the story is inevitably incomplete and biased, Jimmy is physically and emotionally unable to report on the events. As already mentioned, Jimmy suffers from loneliness and malnutrition. Furthermore, he is haunted by the murder of his lover and sees alcohol as the only solution to alleviate his pain. There is clearly a parallel between the weakness of his voice and the state of humanity as we know it today in the novel. Jimmy, who represents the advocate of human exceptionalism at the beginning of the story, soon has to question his convictions about human nature. At the end of *Oryx and Crake*, Jimmy's voice disappears as if he has capitulated. However, this change in the narration does not represent humanity's demise. Jimmy does not die; he loses consciousness. Metaphorically speaking, the withdrawal of his voice implies the deconstruction of the belief in human exceptionalism and the acknowledgment that he is too weak to continue as the narrator of the story. Jimmy's voice has to transform into something new in order to allow the story to be told.

In the second novel, *The Year of the Flood*, Jimmy's voice is supplanted by two other voices: a third-person narration through the perspective of Toby and a first-person narration as told from the point of view of Ren:

> In the early morning Toby climbs up to the rooftop to watch the sunrise. She uses a mop handle for balance: the elevator stopped working some time ago and the back stairs are slick with damp, and if she slips and topples there won't be anyone to pick her up. (3)

> *Beware of words. Be careful what you write. Leave no trails.* This is what the Gardeners taught us, when I was a child among them. (7)

These two women give their version of the story that Jimmy told in *Oryx and Crake* in a parallel timeline. In the society preceding the catastrophe, Toby and Ren both belonged to the lower class: They evolved in the Pleeblands and then became part of the God's Gardeners. The fact that they come from a totally different background means that their point of view substantially differs from Jimmy's. In Schmeink's words, "Whereas *Oryx* dealt with the male, privileged perspective of the Compounds, *Year* now interjects with the female, precarious perspective of the pleeblands" (74). Before the catastrophe, Toby and Ren had already developed the ability to adapt to a society that was hostile to them, which explains why they are more resilient than Jimmy. Interestingly, thanks to the diversification of perspectives on the same story, it is the communication of the story itself that becomes stronger and more reliable.

In the third novel, there is an amplification of the narrative polyphony and Crakers are finally given a proper voice. From the reader's point of view, there are at least three disturbing phenomena. First, some characters express their point of view via different pronouns. For instance, Toby's perspective switches from a first-person narrative to a third-person narrative. This phenomenon shatters the unity of the voice:

> In the beginning, you lived inside the Egg. That is where Crake made you. Yes, good, kind Crake. Please stop singing or I can't go on with the story. (*MaddAddam* 11)

> About the events of that evening—the events that set human malice loose in the world again—Toby later made two stories. (*MaddAddam* 17)

Then, the same stories are recounted through different perspectives. This phenomenon was already part of the first two novels with Toby and Ren revisiting Jimmy's version of the story, but crossovers between perspectives are taken to extreme lengths in the third novel. In *MaddAddam*, the different versions are literally juxtaposed. For instance, there are many episodes about the story of a Gardener called Zeb. As readers, we go from Zeb telling his story to Toby, to Toby "translating" it to the Crakers who are endowed with very limited abstract thinking. This textual repetition echoes the act of artificially replicating the human genome in order to make it more efficient. The text metaphorically becomes posthuman in order to be understood in the environment in which it is produced. To some extent, the ability of the new text to efficiently deliver the message compensates for its lack of literary quality. Finally, the last novel also features the rise of nonhuman voices. For instance, the pigoons develop the ability to communicate with Crakers in order to collaborate with the human survivors. Crakers become translators because the human subject has reached their limits in terms of communication. The voice of the Crakers is also increasingly present in *MaddAddam*. The very last chapters of the trilogy represent a climax as a Craker, a child called Blackbeard, becomes the first-person narrator of the story. The human subject is no longer able to tell the story: Humanity is too tired and not strong enough to carry on. The text absorbs change and adapts to the new narrator: "Toby cannot tell the story tonight. She is too sad, because of the dead ones. The ones who became dead in the battle. So now I will try to tell this story to you. I will tell it in the right way, if I can [...]" (*MaddAddam* 435).

Atwood's novels celebrate a diversity of voices and perspectives because it is precisely what allows the story to be communicated. All the different versions of the story interlock to render the text more resilient. In that respect, the fragmented aspect of the text expresses a form of solidarity with the condition of humankind. Interestingly, the text also has a strong performative dimension, since the reader also has to adapt to all these formal transformations. In the words of Phillips, "[t]o read the novel is to become culturally and environmentally literate, as if the reader also needs to adapt to the transformed world Atwood describes" (148). To some extent, the act of reading the *MaddAddam* trilogy mirrors a Darwinian process and sheds light on the fact that this state of constant transformation and adaptation is part of human nature. Atwood's *MaddAddam* trilogy had to be plural and monstrous to be able to transmit the story, which reminds the readers that it is their own monstrosity and fragmentation that have allowed them to survive in the animal kingdom.

Works Cited

Agamben, Giorgio. *The Open: Man and Animal*. Translated by Kevin Attell. Stanford, California, Stanford University Press, 2004.
Atwood, Margaret. *Oryx and Crake*. London, Virago, 2004.
———. *The Year of the Flood*. London, Virago, 2013.
———. *MaddAddam*. London, Virago, 2014.
Canavan, Gerry. "Hope, But Not for Us: Ecological Science Fiction and the End of the World in Margaret Atwood's *Oryx and Crake* and *The Year of the Flood*." *Lit: Literature Interpretation Theory*, vol. 23, no. 2, 2012, pp. 138–159.

Desblache, Lucile. *Écrire l'Animal Aujourd'hui*. Clermont-Ferrand, Presses Universitaires Blaise Pascal, 2006.
Dunning, Stephen. "Margaret Atwood's *Oryx and Crake*: The Terror of the Therapeutic." *Canadian Literature*, vol.186, 2005, pp. 86–101.
Eagleton, Terry. *The English Novel: An Introduction*. Oxford, Blackwell, 2005.
Halliwell, Martin. "Awaiting the Perfect Storm." *Waltzing Again: New and Selected Conversations with Margaret Atwood*, edited by Ingersoll, Earl, Ontario Review Press, 2006, pp. 253–264.
Herman, David. *Creatural Fictions: Human-Animal Relationships in Twentieth- and Twenty-First-Century Literature*. New York, Palgrave Macmillan US, 2016.
Holling, Crawford Stanley. "Resilience and Stability of Ecological Systems." *Annual Review of Ecology and Systematics*, vol. 4, 1973, pp. 1–23.
Lestel, Dominique. *L'Animalité, Essai sur le statut de l'humain*. Paris, L'Herne, 2007.
Parry, Jovian. "*Oryx and Crake* and the New Nostalgia for Meat." *Society and Animals*, vol. 17, 2009, pp. 241–256.
Phillips, Dana. "Collapse, Resilience, Stability and sustainability in Margaret Atwood's *MaddAddam* Trilogy." *Literature and Sustainability: Concept, Text and Culture*, edited by Johns-Putra, Adeline et al., Manchester University Press, 2017, pp. 139–158.
Rozelle, Lee. "Liminal Ecologies in Margaret Atwood's *Oryx and Crake*." *Canadian Literature*, vol. 206, 2010, pp. 61–72.
Schmeink, Lars. *Biopunk Dystopias: Genetic Engineering, Society and Science Fiction*. Liverpool University Press, 2016.
Staels, Hilde. "*Oryx and Crake*: Atwood's Ironic Inversion of *Frankenstein*." *The Open Eye*, edited by Moss, John, and Tobi Kozakewich, University of Ottawa Press, 2006, pp. 433–446.
Völker, Oliver. "'Hang on to the words': The Scarcity of Language in McCarthy's *The Road* and Atwood's *Oryx and Crake*." *RCC Perspectives*, no. 2, 2015, pp. 75–82.
Woolf, Virginia. *A Room of One's Own* (1929). Boston, Houghton Mifflin Harcourt, 1989.

Atwood's Protean Poetics: Adaptation in the Service of Survival

Nicole Côté

Survival has been a fundamental theme in Atwood's writing from the very start. Her perspective, however, is perhaps an unexpected one; as early as her discussion of environmental themes in *Survival* (1972), Atwood shows Canadian literature evolving from perceiving nature as monstrous to perceiving humans as monstrous toward nature.

A curious thing happens in Canadian literature once evidence starts piling up of what Northrop Frye calls the "conquest of nature by an intelligence that does not love it" (226). Sympathy begins to shift from the victorious hero to the defeated giantess, and the problem is no longer how to avoid being swallowed up by a cannibalistic Nature but how to avoid destroying her. Hence though the theme of survival is a sure thread running through Atwood's protean poetics, already in *Survival*, published fifty years ago, Atwood analyzes various Canlit works in which nature is considered endangered and in survival mode. This now Atwoodian theme finds its way in the *MaddAddam Trilogy*.

N. Côté (✉)
Université de Sherbrooke, Sherbrooke, QC, Canada
e-mail: Nicole.M.Cote@USherbrooke.ca

© The Author(s), under exclusive license to Springer Nature Switzerland AG 2021
S. Wells-Lassagne, F. McMahon (eds.), *Adapting Margaret Atwood*, Palgrave Studies in Adaptation and Visual Culture,
https://doi.org/10.1007/978-3-030-73686-6_5

In its very idea of nature, the *MaddAddam* trilogy (*Oryx and Crake*, *The Year of the Flood*, and *MaddAddam*) best exemplifies the organic relationship between survival and adaptation: It thematizes survival by showing humans and other species going through the most stark upheaval in history, from technologically highly evolved, late capitalist societies, to a postapocalyptic time seven years later, somewhere in the mid-twenty-first century,[1] where humans are nearly extinct, and new, genetically-modified species, both humanoids and animals, roam free, quickly adapting to their new existence.

The time after the "Waterless Flood"—a term coined by God's Gardeners, an eco-Christian sect, and which comes to mean an ebola-like virus that literally reduces humans into liquid—offers living conditions that are not much better than during the Neolithic Age. Just a handful of humans have survived, living alongside the humanoid Crakers, beings that were genetically spliced before the flood, and are better adapted to this world in ruins, a world which poses conditions of duress even for the genetically-enhanced animals and humanoids. Perhaps the most engaging aspect of the powerful novels is that for Atwood, speculative fiction concerns "things that really could happen but just hadn't *completely* happened when the author wrote the book".[2]

The trilogy shows adaptation as re-creation most obviously through its themes—death and regeneration or metamorphosis—but also through its reconfiguration of genres: speculative fiction—or "ustopia" (a mix of utopia and dystopia), as Atwood prefers to categorize it[3]—eco-fable, postapocalyptic narrative. Moreover, the trilogy harbors various subgenres, as it includes sermons and religious hymns, as well as ads: it is hybrid through and through. Mingling the poetic with the ironic, it also combines words, new and old, playing with assonance and alliteration in order to allude to a recreated reality.

Though the last book in the trilogy (*MaddAddam*) presents yet another social organization, a postapocalyptic one, where survival is possible only through interspecies mating (the Crakers and the remaining Sapiens), it is

---

[1] The dating is difficult to pinpoint, the Gregorian calendar having been obliterated in favor of a new postapocalyptic one (the entries of *The Year of the Flood's* two protagonists, Toby and Ren, reading Year 10, Year 25, for instance).

[2] Quoted in Alan Northover, "'Strangers in Strange Worlds': Margaret Atwood's *MaddAddam* Trilogy". *Journal of Literary Studies* 33:1, pp. 121–137, 2017, p. 122.

[3] See for example Atwood's *Dire Cartographies: The Roads to Ustopia*—The Handmaid's Tale *and the* MaddAddam *Trilogy.*

truly the upheaval and the world-making of the two first books which I would like to explore. I would like to give an overview of the various levels on which the narrative works, the world invented with evocative, musical language (poetic), the fun-making of human folly (ironic, satiric), and the suggestion that culture (material, symbolic) may be crafted through various means (performative), as is perhaps most obvious in the second and third books.

In other words, Atwood's titanic task—to show, from a distance, the dire consequences of reification at the ultimate phase of capitalism; to display the ongoing extinction of all species but human in the general disaffection before the Flood; to follow the evolution of the handful of humans and the genetically spliced non-human animals and humanoids—seems to be best exemplified by a frenzied adaptation of the material at hand, be it themes, genres, or words. I would thus like to explore a few Atwoodian idiosyncrasies that bear witness to creativity in the service of survival, covering both the trilogy's leitmotifs and its more formal devices.

COMMODIFICATION

One of the most salient themes in the trilogy is the commodification of Nature, animals and humans included, in a pre-apocalyptic world, where adaptation is prompted by profit. In *Oryx and Crake* (2003), Atwood shows the instrumentalizing that brought civilization and nature to the brink of collapse before a mysterious world pandemic hit. The characters, two young, and presumably white, men, Jimmy and Glenn, are shown mainly at home, in rich "Compounds". These are gated cities containing all services, including private schools, hospitals, and security firms owned by the corporations. The compounds were built so that the educated and rich do not ever have to venture into the polluted and dangerous pleeblands, at school and at work. The state of the world is mediated through the internet as the students—Glenn (aka Crake), and Jimmy (aka Snowman), the narrator-focalizer—watch and play video games together. This in itself is a comment on the homosocial friendship mediated through screens. On the same screens, they watch news or illegal filming as through a window onto a world that has lost its bearings, the objectification of life at all levels being rampant. The news and programs concentrate on the endless flow of events—real and fake—that shape the world, though the perspective is flattened by its very immediacy. However, the boys prefer videogames, and the games favored by Crake, the boy-genius, reflect mainly what is being, or has been, lost.

Extinctathon is the most blatant of these fictional games of loss, as it focuses on the vanished natural world, where the gamers have to learn all species and genus extinct since the dinosaurs. The list is impressive and will later somehow justify Crake's Paradice Project—the invention of a zero-trace humanoid race—since most of the losses are due to mankind's greed and its commodification of sentient beings, considering animal and plants as things to be used and abused.

In sequel *The Year of the Flood*, God's Gardeners learn by heart the extinct animals in order to bear witness, in remembrance of these animals they consider as their kin. The final tome, *MaddAddam*, discloses the schism between the two factions of God's Gardeners: the God's Gardeners and their founder, Adam One, think remembrance suffices, and that no violence should be used against the destroyers of the world; the MaddAddamites, most of them scientists who formerly worked for the corporations, believe immediate acts of targeted infrastructure destruction are needed to save the planet. Incidentally, a number of these were grandmasters at the game *Extinctathon*, and thus shared with Glenn/Crake the idea that mankind (and its commodification of Nature) needed to be stopped.

As for the historical videogames that Glenn and Jimmy play, they constitute a dire commentary on the arithmetic of gain and loss. Hence one of the games on culture, *Blood & Roses*, pits one horror (the Bergen-Belsen camp, for instance) against one great discovery (penicillin) or work of art (the Mona Lisa). The teenagers barter one horror for one marvel (like Beethoven's Ninth) every minute. Though this game at least opens perspectives, offering a balance sheet, a summary of sorts, for human civilization, it is nonetheless mired in ideas of commercial worth and equivalence, whereas these are obviously untranslatables, invaluable, like human life. These games, though they are windows onto the world, accumulate evidence of mankind's nearly total commodification of Nature but for the arts, and later give the reader an idea of Crake's motivation for the annihilation of the world's population through the BlyssPluss pill after he manages to advance his Paradice Project. This annihilation of humankind is an ironic reversal of its systematic commodification of Nature.

The various video games also act as windows on worlds that are (*Kwicktime Osama*), or that were (*Barbarian Stomp*), while the teenagers' comments act as strands weaving their friendship. As has been the case in our societies, their world is mediated through screens, screens acting as both mirrors of the world and as walls protecting from the worst and the best. Indeed, because of the distance they instill between subject and object, the screens enhance the emotional distance, and thus the commodification at play. Screens also reflect the loneliness of the boys left to themselves for their learning of society through natural and social history—school seemingly useless in informing on pressing issues.

The friends are also addicted to more dangerous games, games that are neither related to culture nor to events, but which nonetheless reflect a high level of commodification, this time of individual human beings, as mediated by the screen. Crake (Glenn) and Jimmy visit porn sites, including juvenile porn (*hottotts*) and snuff porn; they also visit online suicide sites (*nighty nite*). Various sites offer "live" viewings of deaths, where heads roll in dusty enclaves. Their parents of course know nothing about these games, as they are either terribly busy with work, have disappeared (Jimmy's mom), or are deceased (Glenn's father). *Oryx and Crake*'s parents seem disinvested in their progeny except when it comes to the salability of their talent, a sure sign of the widespread commodification of even the closest human relationships, and proof that "survival of the fittest" has become a commercial enterprise. Incidentally, all the novel's parents end up assassinated by the CorpSeCorps (the private security firm under the umbrella of the powerful corporations), mostly for having questioned the immoral goals of their corporation: Jimmy's mother, for example, having canceled her contract with her employer early on, manages to fight in the underground for years before she is killed (as Jimmy discovers through a video shown to him by the CorpSeCorps). Thus human life is uniformly presented as easily disposable, and commodified at every level.

The description of Glenn and Jimmy's life choices as they become young adults confirms the idea of adaptation run amok, where economic concerns trump humanity itself. Thus the young men's respective schools present an implicit critique of the dying humanities (in the decrepit standing of Jimmy's institution, the Martha Graham School for the Arts) and of the coopting of universities by and for Corporations (as with the Watson-Crick Institute, which specializes in genetic manipulation). The latter institution is where Glenn/Crake, a "number" student, will continue his studies. Even human relations are subject to commodification: While Crake finds that romance and sex distract from his studies, Jimmy uses the disappearance of his mother to attract women, though given his inability to commit, he accumulates short-lived affairs; both ultimately find their match through commercial exchange, when Crake places an order for a prostitute with Student Services. The human being offered for their "consumption" might very well be the girl they glimpsed a decade earlier on the porn site *Hottotts*, and they name their new acquisition "Oryx" after an extinct antelope.

Their professional lives confirm the mercantile bent of their education. After his degree, Jimmy ekes out a living writing fake ads for various dubious health products; that is indeed what his diploma prepared him for, words and literariness having been coopted to increase the salability of products. As for Glenn/Crake, he is recruited by a biotech company, RejoovenEssence, and is quickly given *carte blanche* to develop his Paradice Project. He tells his clients he is working on immortality, and, with a team of geneticists, secretly experiments to create a zero-carbon footprint humanoid race to replace Homo sapiens.[4]

In *Oryx and Crake*, Atwood lays bare the commodification that humanity has imposed on all of existence, both the animal kingdom and humankind itself (particularly women and children); this impulse creates a hierarchy—social, economic, sexual, biological (human vs. animals)—that Atwood implicitly critiques. Various means, amongst which the ubiquitous screens, establish a distance between the "us" and the "them", the "here" and "there", the "compounds" and "pleeblands". Satire (through exaggeration, reversal of points of views, etc.) and a pervading irony (contrasting what ought to be and what is) permeate the narrative, and these narrative distancing techniques make the compendium of horrors somewhat bearable. The humorous neologisms contribute to this general alleviation of reification's painful effects on sentient beings. Atwood seems to draw a parallel between the distancing techniques (namely the satire and irony Jimmy the narrator uses to keep his narrative bearable), and the distancing technique of the screen that the characters all use to make their own lives bearable.[5]

IRONY AND SATIRE AS ADAPTATION

Thus, against a gruesome background, satire and irony reign, and humor is paramount, be it in the characters' deadpan jokes, in the ironic juxtaposition of contrasts, or in the general satire achieved through the accumulation of gruesome details. Humor is also present in the neologisms that

---

[4] Vegan (they eat leaves) and without malice, uninterested in technology, created to be devoid of symbolic thought, and thus of the possibility of erecting religion, the Crakers will live without being a burden to the environment, Crake's foremost goal.

[5] There is a certain irony implicit in the use of screens as a distancing device, considering the sheer number of screen adaptations of Atwood's novels, perhaps suggesting that it is easier for people to watch a fictionalized truth.

please the mind through their invention and defamiliarize; they contain the past and a present that is not yet circumscribed.

Courtney Traub recently[6] discussed humor and the end of the human world in Atwood's trilogy, quoting Andrew Sear Green: "[W]hat a joy it is to see [...] Atwood taking such delicious pleasure in the end of the world", noting the "general cultural fatigue towards the pathos, gloom, and doom so prevalent in contemporary fiction about environmental risks" (86). Examining Atwood's "darkly funny climate fiction", Traub "discerns a variety of comic modes [...] that draw [...] attention to the ethical and epistemological quandaries raised by climate change" (86). She remarks that the trilogy style eschews jeremiads and the sublime, since they "tend to inspire a sense of paralysis at the immensity of the environmental crises that confront us" (87).

As for verbal invention, from which much of this humor derives, most of the neologisms are first presented in *Oryx and Crake*, echoing the diegetic concerns of the narrative, as the first volume is about creating new species from the old ones. In a sense, this is a comic amplification of a longstanding generic tradition, given that any utopia/dystopia offers a number of new words, or words whose meaning has drastically changed to describe a warped or strange reality.

These neologisms are presented from the point of view of Jimmy, the "word-man". They generally concern the spliced species, the trademarked vitamins, and the pricey beauty products. Their naming itself makes one rejoice in Atwood's seemingly infinite creative capacities, in the words' denotative and connotative power, as we have seen earlier: "pigoons", "liobams", and "rakunks", for instance, all born in labs, people the Earth after the Flood. The products being marketed before the Flood also bear stupendous names: "Anooyoo" (cosmetics) satirizes the clichéd depiction of women's dissatisfaction with their appearance; "Blysspluss" (the vitamin, sexual enhancer, and STD protection pill in which Glenn/Crake will hide the deadly virus) is a compound word that adds a "plus" to the seemingly ultimate sensation of happiness (to which is glued a third "s", which could suggest dollar signs), signaling the search for pleasure at all costs, as well as the marketing tendency toward verbal inflation. The HealthWyzer Corp adds viruses to its vitamins, thus boosting its sales of specialized medication for these particular viruses. The "CorpSeCorps", the

---

[6] "From the Grotesque to Nuclear-Age Precedents: The Modes and Meanings of Cli-Fi Humour", *Studies in the Novel*, Vol. 50, no. 1 (Spring 2018, 86–107).

corporations' special security Corps (replacing the government-run army and police forces) work exclusively for the benefit of the Corporations. In this compacted syntagma, the repetition of the word "corps" slides frighteningly from the rather illustriously connoted "corps" (in the army, the navy, or in other official groups) to the corpses the security forces create out of bothersome humans, soon to be transformed into "garboil" or "secret burgers". These neologisms create a humorous effect that offsets the dark realities they describe, insisting on the way that language can both create and adapt to these new realities. However, they also serve to defamiliarize the reader,[7] bringing both the fictional universe and its relation to our own world into sharp relief.

Frame Change

This defamiliarization is not limited to the word-play of the neologisms, however; another crucial form exists in the changing perspective of the narrative from one volume of the trilogy to the next, shifting the point of view, and relativizing the reliability of the until-then-narrator. The readers then are invited to reconsider what they thought was reality; like the characters in the novels, they too must adapt their worldview to accommodate this new framing of a familiar world.

Atwood's ability to adapt her point of view through characters is particularly obvious in the transition from the first to the second volume of her trilogy. Indeed, *The Year of the Flood* (2009), while keeping more or less the same temporal frame and the same panoramic plot, changes the frame or the angle of the narrative. Without warning, the narration has the previously recounted events unfold through the perspective of members of a sect who, in *Oryx and Crake*, had been presented by Jimmy's roommate Bernice as eco-extremists. Where in the previous entry two bright white boys from rich compounds had been at the center of action—one of them, Glenn/Crake, the boy-wizard, teaching the other, a "word person"—now in *The Year of the Flood* women of various ages and ethnic and social backgrounds are featured, living in the pleeblands and creating polyphonic voices (though Toby and Ren, an older and a younger woman, remain our primary narrators).

---

[7] "[D]efamiliarisation is expressed most clearly in the neologisms Atwood spins to describe the corporations, institutions, computer games, entertainment websites, and hybrid, genetically-modified animals that populate her fictional world" (Northover 123).

Hence the point of view shifts gender/sex, social class, and geography, giving the reader an inkling of the troubled terrain of the pleeblands, and suggesting what society looks like outside of the protected compounds. *The Year of the Flood* tackles diversity, offering a plural point of view, by locating various religious sects (Petrobaptists, Wolf Isahiahists, God's Gardeners) and ethnic groups (Asian Fusion, Tex-Mex, as well as single Black women working at menial and often dangerous jobs). Whereas in *Oryx and Crake*'s compounds there did not seem to be any older single females except for the few genius girls with varying degrees of Asperger's, and women were largely contained within hetero-patriarchal couples, in *The Year of the Flood*'s pleeblands, all the characters are shown as extremely vulnerable, whether because they are in trouble with the law (like Toby), undocumented workers toiling for fees much below the minimum wage, or sex workers (like Ren), especially women and children. Yet these women and children show great resiliency, and are able to fight for their lives, to regroup and form communities linked by beliefs or ethnic backgrounds. These groups help each other, even the children, who haunt the streets in gangs, as can be seen with Toby's rescue from the Secret Burger's by God's Gardeners while the children were acting as distraction.

Indeed Atwood's power of adaptation to, and investment in, this totally new frame for the same story—with a similar to-ing and fro-ing of temporal frame—is mirrored in utterly adaptable characters who eke out a living in a dangerous geography. These pleeblands, though a far cry from the quiet and clean compounds, are controlled by the same corporations through the CorpSeCorps, which coerce the undocumented workers to do the illegal, "dirty work" for them, including pharmaceutical testing without consent, drug dealing, sex marts, human organ trafficking, murder, and the disposal of human bodies through the local mafia. The so-called SeksMarts and the Scales and Tails clubs (where girls are dressed in biosuits of glittery scales and feathers to mimic rare animals) run by the CorpSeCorps point to the underbelly of the elusive "feminine ideal" as represented by Asian character Oryx and other girls "imported" from unnamed underdeveloped countries to feed the endless need for dancers and prostitutes. Ren once mentions that Scales and Tails offers the "painballers"[8] undocumented sex workers when they manage to win their

---

[8] These are repeat offenders who are let loose in a forest to fight for their lives with corrosive paint ball guns, while the general public can view the televised "competition". The term is of course a play on "paintball".

freedom and spend an evening at the club—girls that Ren never sees again. The girls are often found dead in the back alley in the morning, their kidneys missing. The frame change from *Oryx and Crake*'s University Student Services, which offer "clean" sex to male students through prostitutes, is dramatic.

The Year of the Flood foregrounds narrative multiplicity: Toby's narrative is presented in the third person, whereas younger Ren's narrative flows from the first person; both voices narrate in the present. Even within Toby's narrative, Toby's narrative maintains two perspectives (agnostic and gnostic): Toby believes and yet does not quite believe in the God's Gardeners' creed. She is analytical, yet shows empathy; she is an excellent judge of character and situations, yet begins to get an inkling of a spiritual world. When she witnesses old Pilar's dealing with the bees and the hallucinogenic mushrooms, her ability to elicit dreams that will provide a solution, Toby's rationality is put to test. The novel suggests that the character's hard-won, no-nonsense rationality ultimately does not allow her to fully grasp the new world God's Gardeners offers.

Ren's first-person narrative highlights her youth and inexperience, focusing on decisions made under the sway of immediate emotions or centered on the self. Like the previous volume's similarly naïve narrator Jimmy, Ren attended the Martha Graham Academy (in dance and gymnastics), but will foreground the vulnerability of female characters (and the implicit privilege in Jimmy's narrative) when she ends up at Scales and Tails, a high-end night club offering sex services.[9] The fact that both women end up in menial jobs confirms the first volume's depiction of the low status of the humanities, but also points to the double standard exerted on women in this fictional universe.

Thus *The Year of the Flood* as a whole can be seen as an adaptation of its preceding volume, reworking the initial narrative events (the years preceding the apocalyptic event of the Waterless Flood and its immediate aftermath), but adopting a change in perspective that allows for a fuller understanding of the now-familiar world. Atwood insists on the subjectivity of the narrative and points to the variety of experiences for the different

---

[9] One could perhaps see Ren and Toby as representative of Innocence and Experience, the former being characterized as impulsive and optimistic, with youthful ideals of friendship and love, while the latter is described as solitary and skeptical toward what she sees and experiences: the third-person narrative she uses (free indirect speech, limited point of view) is indicative of Toby's character, highlighting the distance between narration and character.

characters, most notably through contrast in this novel's representation of the female population of the pleeblands, as compared to *Oryx and Cake*'s depiction of the male (and screen-mediated) perspective of Compounds with Glenn and Jimmy. That the men are protected by Compound walls and the women have to survive the direst circumstances out in the open and unsafe pleeblands is another of Atwood's ironic twists.

Defamiliarizing the Human

MaddAddam's world is similar enough to our own to see the latter through a defamiliarizing lens, forcing us to reconsider stances which are naturalized through habit and general consensus (as promoted by global corporations). The ability of the characters to acknowledge the ongoing defamiliarization, notably through a critical appraisal of their own objectification, is a sure step toward adaptation, as it allows them to change, even to use mimicry in order to hide and thus to survive.

Probably the most obvious example of this is the widespread use of changing perspectives. Alan Northover's work on this aspect of the trilogy is central here: He notes that its most extreme example in the novels is Atwood's use of the animal gaze, since through it humans become decentered subjects (132). This posthuman perspective is made more effective through repeated use of defamiliarization: Northover notes that "Atwood naturalizes [...] scenes and scenarios that most contemporary readers will find outrageous or scandalous, for instance, the impunity with which the strong prey upon the weak" (123), thus "[...] explor[ing] the objectification and instrumentalization of life forms for corporate profit" (125 note 2). Indeed, the predator-prey relationship that humans have systematized through agribusiness and which, in *Oryx and Crake*, reaches a peak with genetic splicing, is reversed once the plague of the Waterless Flood has hit, as the human population declines and is deprived of the advanced technology that protected it. Northover suggests that defamiliarization is foregrounded in this shift of perspective, namely the "ousting [of] humanity from a position of power that most people take for granted today, where animals are reduced to mere tools for human use and are processed out of sight of the general public on animal farms, in slaughter houses and in laboratories" (127). He posits that Atwood's prose foregrounds what

Carol J. Adams (2003) terms the "absent referent",[10] that is, the meat's origin, the conditions under which the animals that we eat spend their lives or die. *Oryx and Crake* dramatizes this cultural desensitizing through Jimmy, who as a child is sensitive to the plight of animals, only to become inured to it in adulthood—until a fundamental shift after the Flood, when he is hunted by pigoons (127).

Perhaps equally defamiliarizing is the fact that the extreme objectification of animals is a treatment also extended to women and children: "Several critics have noted Atwood's depiction of women as 'meat' in *The Year of the Flood* and have discussed the implicit cannibalism. Bouson (12–13) and Wright (517) briefly mention Carol Adam's concept of the absent referent to expose a hidden exploitation at work" (Northover 126). Toby is a case in point; having had to forego her papers for fear of being sued by the very corporation which put her family in debt, she must now find work without identification: "Toby's having to sell her hair and ovaries is part of Atwood's critique of the commodification of the female body" (Northover 128). Once these traditional or biological markers of the female are no longer available for sale (an infected needle ends her ability to harvest her ovaries for money), Toby symbolically moves down a notch in the hierarchy from human to animal, obtaining employment as an animal impersonator in a "furzoot" (a suit of fake fur). She is incognito, but prey to fetishists, and with her view limited by her costume, she becomes a living metaphor of the situation of young women in the pleeblands. Then comes her job at SecretBurgers, where her boss Blanco (an ironic name) expects his girls to use their thirty-minute lunchtime for his sexual satisfaction. They have become meat, both literally and metaphorically, as those who refuse become refuse, are disposed of, and might end up as hamburgers. According to Botta, SecretBurgers meat-grinders "destroy any subjective feature and homogenizes the matter into a shapeless mass recall[ing] the 'absent referent'" (123). Defamiliarization (and the insistence on dehumanization) is thus common for female characters, and especially poor and minority women.

Atwood contrasts society's reification of living beings (animals and women), with individual female characters learning agency through God's Gardeners. Thus Toby's increased independence follows her acceptance of the precepts of the group: Adam One, their leader, tells her to act as if she

---

[10] According to Adams, "The absent referent was what enabled the interweaving of the oppression of women and animals" (in Northover 126).

believed, seemingly inspired by Pascal's precept that if you fall on your knees and pray, faith will follow. Toby, having lost her family to corporations, and having been traumatized by her experience with Blanco—that is, after the deeply defamiliarizing/dehumanizing experiences she suffers—is happy to oblige the Gardeners' vegan creed, and vows not to eat her kin, the animals; in so doing, as Northover suggests, she obtains "her liberation from the dominant patriarchal 'text of meat' that objectifies women and animals, thereby justifying their oppression". (129).

The character of Ren presents as much younger and seemingly weaker, but the narrative allows her to also achieve agency through understanding, empathy, and female friendship, even while working at Scales and Tails. Like the other girls in this high-end club, she is associated with the consumption of exotic animals. Here again, Atwood establishes a link between our carnivorous tendencies, and financial and sexual predation, for as Northover and several other Atwoodian critics note, in *MaddAddam*, "flesh eating is linked to corporate capitalism" (132).[11]

As we have seen, defamiliarization in these novels becomes dehumanization, with women being considered by men as animals, who can be further transformed into meat, be it metaphorically or literally. This is counterbalanced by the other extreme example of defamiliarization and decentering in the narrative, that is, the animal gaze and its view of humanity. Here again, the bioengineered animals released after the Flood consider humans as mere meat, an ironic reversal of the traditional (human) attitude toward animals, which negated their bond with (farm) animals, and relegated them to enforced captivity and cruel deaths. This extreme inhumanity toward the animal kingdom is dramatized through the genetic manipulations of *MaddAddam*'s animals, where scientists "play God" to various ends, be they religious ("liobams"), medical ("pigoons"), or food-related ("chickienobs"). Nobody, not even their creators, knows what these animals will become. In the post-flood era, this sense of uncertainty is intensified for the humans, who have become beasts of prey expecting the unexpected from these hybrid monsters. This is an ironic take reframing ongoing discussion of the value of life, both human and non-human, and is perhaps the most extreme form of defamiliarization in these novels.

---

[11] Northover adds that the great critic Berger points out that "the nineteenth century [...] saw the beginning of a process, today being completed by corporate capitalism, by which every tradition which has previously mediated between man and nature was broken" (132).

Mimicry as Adaptation

The commodification in view of maximum profit, at the expense of sentient beings, and especially of women and animals, leads to the necessity of camouflage and mimicry. Giuseppina Botta focuses on this aspect of the fiction, suggesting two possibilities allowing characters to hide in plain sight: "Invisibility can be attained [...] through an assimilation to the environment in order to blend [...] or through the assumption of a different shape so as to pass as someone else" (116). The latter of these two strategies, "passing as someone else", is a form of adaptation that enacts "performative strategies which lead to the reconstruction of their selves" (116). According to Botta, protagonists in *Oryx and Crake* and *Year of the Flood* either wear disguises or "undergo physical manipulations and transformations" (116), which corresponds to a deeper, and permanent disguise.

We have seen that both Toby and Ren—and indeed most of the MaddAddamites and God's Gardeners in one guise or another—regularly adapt to face the rapidly changing circumstances that lead to the demise of their world. Once her father commits suicide to avoid his creditors, Toby knows the CorpSeCorps will come after her, and so must forego all official documents, be they diplomas or identity cards. She saves her life by becoming invisible, and earns a living handing out flyers as an animal impersonator. In so doing, she adapts Crake's creation myth from the preceding volume, wherein Crake, the Creator of the new humanoid race, offers the title of "mother of animals" to the colored, diminutive female "Oryx", a refugee from a poor, nondescript Asian Country—but because this novel is in the same timeframe as its predecessor, her actions also suggest that Glenn/Crake is ultimately adapting his reality to a mythological narrative: women, the reader is given to understand, are so closely associated with animals that, as in Toby's case, dressing as one in the Pleeblands is an easy camouflage, a way *not* to attract attention. As Zeb had taught God's Gardeners' children in "Urban Bloodshed limitation", to avoid turning into prey, you must "see [...] without being seen", "hear [...] without being heard" (*The Year of the Flood* 165). In the animal kingdom, both prey and predator need the camouflage and mimicry, but for the prey the consequences are more immediate: thus Ren, as a high-end dancer and sex worker in the Scales and Tails club, wears a biosuit that is covered with sequined feathers, offering the men who pay for sex the exotic feeling of being made love to by a bird, a serpent or a lizard, while hiding her own identity.

Likewise, when Toby is informed that Blanco, her ex-(psychopathic) boss at SecretBurgers, is out of prison and back into the neighborhood of

Edencliff Garden, Zeb drives her to a clinic where her facial features are modified, her camouflage made permanent: her voice is lowered, her eyes slanted, her cheekbones are made prominent, her skin color darkened, and the hair of a spliced lamb sutured onto her scalp. To take on these different markers of minority ethnicity, Atwood suggests, is to become invisible to the authorities, to better blend in to the majority population in the pleeblands. With new ID papers and her ethnicized body, Toby now can work as the manager of the AnooYoo spa, and will cease being prey. The subtext is that any woman living without means to make herself invisible, without the help of a powerful organization in the pleeblands, is ultimately doomed. However, as Giuseppina Botta contends, this adaptive reflex may come at the expense of self, given that it is "indissolubly connected with corporeity [... and thus] every change on her body contributes to a fragmentation of her identity" (117). Botta convincingly argues that the first two volumes of the *MaddAddam* trilogy suggest "the disanimalization of the animal body and the animalization of the human body. Both processes develop in terms of the relationship between prey and predator" (123). Once again, the dramatization of the adaptation process in the narrative suggests a biological imperative—one that parallels the author's own need to adapt her fiction to highlight the similarities between her fictional ustopia and the reader's reality.

Atwood, inverting the relation between the expected and the unexpected, creates worlds by fashioning new words, new narrative syntaxes. Critics have mentioned the necessity to create a new lexicon for new realities, and with *MaddAddam*, as De Fontenay says "the [...] figures of animality [...] are so new they appear monstrous enough to call for a change of name" (13). Botta argues that Atwood creates "an appropriate vocabulary which replays in the linguistic level the laboratory species' hybridization" (124).

Moreover in the *MaddAddam* trilogy, the unsettling mixture of horror and humor particular to satire to describe an almost entirely commodified world clashes to produce an exalted feeling of newness, a form of adaptation to a changing world, especially as a frame change is effected with the second book. Defamiliarization itself shocks with the same underlying tragedy, but in a comic mode that humorously obliges the reader to adapt, to come to terms with this brave new world. This defamiliarization paradoxically forces the most vulnerable to adapt by either mimicry or camouflage.

Atwood's *MaddAddam* trilogy shows an exceptionally protean poetics, mingling the freshness of vision with the horrors of a planet reified for maximum profit. The trilogy shows her narrative power at its best, creating a fictional world that expands our own.

Works Cited

Adams, Carol J. *Pornography of Meat*. Brooklyn, Lantern Books, 2003.
Atwood, Margaret. *Dire Cartographies: The Roads to Ustopia*—The Handmaid's Tale *and the MaddAddam Trilogy*. New York, Vintage, 2011.
———. *Oryx and Crake*. Toronto, Vintage, 2003a.
———. *The Year of the Flood*. Toronto, McClelland & Stewart, 2003b.
———. *MaddAddam*. Toronto, McClelland & Stewart, 2014.
———. *Survival. A Thematic Guide to Canadian Literature*, ©1972, 7.
Beran, Carol L. 'Strangers Within the Gates. Margaret Atwood's *Wilderness Tips*', in *Margaret Atwood*. 'Bloom's Modern Critical Views', New York, Interface editions, 2009, Pp. 67–78.
Botta, Giuseppina. "Body Assemblages at the Time of the Apocalypse." *Alicante Journal of English Studies* 26, 2013, pp. 113–127.
Bouson, J. Brooks. "A 'Joke-filled romp' through endtimes: radical environmentalism, deep ecology, and human extinction in Margaret Atwood's eco-apocalyptic *MaddAddam* Trilogy." *Journal of Commonwealth Literature*, 2016, vol. 51 (3) 341–357.
De Fontenay, Elizabeth. *Without Offending Humans. A Critique of Animal Rights*. 2008. Minneapolis: Minnesota University Press, 2012.
Frye, Northrop. *The Bush Garden: Essays on the Canadian Imagination*. 1971. Toronto: House of Anansi Press Inc., 2017.
Northover, Alan. 'Strangers in Strange Worlds': Margaret Atwood's *MaddAddam* Trilogy. *Journal of Literary Studies* 33:1, 2017, pp. 121–137.
Traub, Courtney. "From the Grotesque to Nuclear-Age precedents: The modes and meanings of cli-fi humour". *Studies in the Novel*. Vol. 50, no. 1 (Spring 2018, pp. 86–107).

Feminist Adaptations/Adaptations of Feminism: Margaret Atwood's *The Penelopiad*

Penny Farfan

In *A Theory of Adaptation*, Linda Hutcheon describes adaptation as a "palimpsestic" art that acknowledges the source text but is also inevitably a departure from it. An adaptation is thus double in nature: "process and product" (9); interpretation and creation; persistence and change; "repetition without replication" (7). Approaching "adaptations *as adaptations*" (4), Hutcheon proposes, entails engaging this "double nature" and recognizing that adaptations pay homage to but may also contest their source texts (6).[1] "[T]hink[ing] of narrative adaptation in terms of a story's fit and its process of mutation or adjustment, through adaptation, to a particular

[1] This research was supported by the Social Sciences and Humanities Research Council of Canada. The essay was originally written as a chapter for Penny Farfan and Lesley Ferris, eds., *Critical Perspectives on Contemporary Plays by Women: The Early Twenty-First Century*

P. Farfan (✉)
School of Creative and Performing Arts, Faculty of Arts, University of Calgary, Calgary, AB, Canada
e-mail: farfan@ucalgary.ca

© The Author(s), under exclusive license to Springer Nature Switzerland AG 2021
S. Wells-Lassagne, F. McMahon (eds.), *Adapting Margaret Atwood*, Palgrave Studies in Adaptation and Visual Culture, https://doi.org/10.1007/978-3-030-73686-6_6

cultural environment," Hutcheon notes that stories "are not immutable over time"; they "travel to different cultures and different media," and "adapt just as they are adapted" (31). In *Adaptation and Appropriation*, Julie Sanders observes further that adaptations are often motivated or influenced "by movements in, and readings produced by, the theoretical and intellectual arena as much as by their so-called sources" (13), and she lists feminism among other critical developments informing contemporary adaptations. In this chapter, I take Hutcheon's and Sanders's insights as a premise for considering feminist adaptations but also adaptations of feminism, focusing on Margaret Atwood's 2007 play *The Penelopiad* and also its relation to and difference from the recent television adaptation of her iconic 1985 dystopian novel *The Handmaid's Tale*, which similarly features a wife and her maids. The example of *The Penelopiad* in relation to *The Handmaid's Tale*, I suggest, clarifies the usefulness of approaching adaptations as adaptations, but also the feminist potential of writing for the stage.

Commissioned by Canongate Books as part of its Myths series, for which leading contemporary writers were invited to create short works reimagining myths from a range of cultures, Atwood's 2005 novella *The Penelopiad* and her later dramatic adaptation of it revisit the myth of Odysseus and his wife Penelope. Homer's *Odyssey* centers on Odysseus's journey home from the Trojan War while the faithful Penelope holds off the suitors who want to take his place by promising that she will choose one of them after she has finished weaving a shroud that she then secretly unravels to delay its completion. When Odysseus eventually returns, he kills the suitors and orders his son Telemachus to kill the maids who consorted with them.[2] In *The Penelopiad*, Atwood revisits the mythic terrain of *The Odyssey* by way of the female figures at the margins of the heroic male-centered epic, giving "the telling of the story to Penelope and to the twelve hanged maids" (xv), whom she imagines as having aided Penelope in her ruse to hold off the suitors.

In *Women & Power*, Mary Beard identifies a moment early in *The Odyssey* when Telemachus chastises Penelope for speaking publicly as the "first recorded instance of a man telling a woman to 'shut up'; telling her that her voice was not to be heard in public." For Beard, Penelope

(University of Michigan Press, 2021). Items from the Margaret Atwood Papers in my Works Cited list are courtesy of Thomas Fisher Rare Book Library, University of Toronto.

[2] Emily Wilson, the first woman translator of *The Odyssey*, uses the words "girls" or "slave girls" to refer to the maids.

exemplifies "how deeply embedded in Western culture are the mechanisms that silence women, that refuse to take them seriously, and that sever them [...] from the centres of power" (3, x–xi). Beard's Penelope is not Atwood's, however. Drawing on *The Odyssey* and other ancient and modern sources,[3] Atwood's novella and play chart the formation of Penelope's character from her childhood experience of near-drowning by her father, through the influence of her water naiad mother, to her competitive relationship with her more beautiful cousin Helen. These formative experiences and relationships determine the dynamics of Penelope's marriage, causing her to delay telling Odysseus of her enlistment of the maids to aid her in her deception of the suitors, and of their rape in the course of their service to her, because she is reluctant to wound his pride by letting him know that she recognizes him through the disguise he wears on his return. In the opening line of the play, Penelope declares, "*Now that I'm dead I know everything,*" including, she adds, "some things I would rather not know" (3; italics in original). She then proceeds to narrate her story from the underworld, where she is eternally haunted by the maids and comes to recognize her role in their rape and murder, in part through their reenactment of key moments in her story. In this way, Atwood revises the myth of the ideal wife, foregrounding her silent compliance and choice not to make a choice.

In giving voice to the maids in her novella, Atwood drew inspiration from the use of the chorus and alternating episodes and choral odes in Greek drama, as well as from the burlesque qualities of the satyr plays that accompanied ancient performances of Greek tragedies. These conventions were retained in her stage adaptation, but in the course of being condensed from the original novella to a suitable theatrical length, her play took shape as a tragedy. According with crucial Aristotelian elements of tragic form—reversal, recognition, suffering—it does so, however, via modern revisions of the intersection of gender and tragedy, as exemplified in such works as Ibsen's *Ghosts* (1881) and *Hedda Gabler* (1890), in which the tragic arises not from women's contravention of conventional gender norms as in ancient Greek tragedy but, rather, from their compliance with such norms. Unlike Sophocles's Antigone and also unlike the Penelope that Mary Beard invokes as the foundational example of women's exclusion from power, the tragic reversal of fortune of Atwood's protagonist is

---

[3] On Atwood's sources, see her "Notes," *The Penelopiad*, 197–98 and "Author's Introduction," *The Penelopiad: The Play*, v.

not the result of an unfeminine incursion into the male-dominated public sphere or of forcible silencing, but, rather, of her own failure to speak.

In *Negotiating with the Dead*, Atwood describes Hell as "possibly [...] the place where you are stuck in your own personal narrative forever" (174); and at the end of *The Penelopiad*, Penelope suggests the personal hell of her life in the underworld when she laments of the hanged maids she is unable to forget, "They never talk to me, down here. They never stay. I hold out my arms to them, my doves, my loveliest ones. But they only run away. *Run* isn't quite accurate. Their legs don't move. Their still-twitching feet don't touch the ground." In the play's final image, "*The Maids dance away in a line, with their ropes around their necks, singing,*" their accusatory song haunting Penelope into eternity (82). The anachronisms of Atwood's novella are mostly gone in her stage adaptation, but the colloquial tone remains, extending Penelope's eternity into our present moment and beyond into the future.[4]

Referring to the embedded layers of adaptation in the stage version of *The Penelopiad*, including *The Odyssey* and other sources, earlier dramatic forms and conventions, and her own 2005 novella, Atwood has described her play as "an echo of an echo of an echo of an echo of an echo of an echo" ("Author's Introduction," v). The play itself continues to echo, however, resonating particularly with the recent television adaptation of *The Handmaid's Tale* through its focus on an elite wife and the women who serve her, including scenes of rape and possible mass hanging that echo the fate of Penelope's maids.[5] The television series generated high praise in its first season for its dystopic vision of women's disempowerment and victimization not only by men but by other women and for its timeliness in relation to the election of Donald Trump and the rise of the #MeToo movement. Its second season, however—inspired by but not directly drawn from Atwood's novel—generated significant controversy

---

[4] In an article about the RSC/NAC production of *The Penelopiad* in 2007, Nicole Estvanik recounts a phone conversation with actress Penny Downie, who was playing Penelope: "Other souls choose to be reincarnated, but Penelope remains in Hades, reclaiming her history, but also perhaps atoning for her behavior. 'Why won't she allow herself to forget?' Downie asked rhetorically."

[5] The links between Atwood's two works seem to have been apparent at the time of the premiere of *The Penelopiad* at the NAC, "where the drink to drink" at the opening night reception "was an Atwood-inspired tropical cocktail called the Hanged Maid" (Phillips). Also, one section of Coral Ann Howell's 2006 essay "Five Ways of Looking at *The Penelopiad*" is entitled "The Handmaids' Tales" (12).

for its relentless depiction of extreme violence against women. Anna Silman, for example, described it as "a ceaseless cavalcade of grisly feminist torture porn to rival our greatest misogynist auteurs: horrifying, nauseating, and uncannily familiar in equal measure."[6] The show also fetishized women's bodies and reproductive functions while at the same time intending to resist and critique such fetishization and objectification in Gilead, formerly the United States, where environmental contamination has resulted in decreased birthrates and fertile women's reproductive capacities have been commandeered by a ruling male elite and their high-status wives. Critics noted, for example, the series' "endless close-ups" on lead actress Elisabeth Moss as Offred/June (Gilbert, "*The Handmaid's Tale*"; see also Paskin), and in one widely reproduced still photograph from Season 2, Moss gazes upward with doe-eyes, her mouth encased in a leather muzzle.[7] The facial close-ups that pervade both seasons were, moreover, increasingly matched in Season 2 by close-ups of Moss as Offred/June clutching and caressing her belly as her pregnancy advances, intensifying what Hank Stuever has described as the series' "almost manic attention to the afflictions of motherhood."

Much of the controversy surrounding Season 2 had to do with the fundamental nature of the television series form. In critic Alison Herman's view, moving into a second season implied that "[showrunner Bruce] Miller and his team were choosing to expand *The Handmaid's Tale* [...] because they had something to add." For many critics, however, Season 2 simply intensified the violence against women while also repeatedly thwarting Offred/June's chances at freedom, thus raising questions about the feminist politics of continuing to watch. Sophie Gilbert argued that "[t]he task for a show like this one is to offer not just more of the same, but some sense that women have the capacity to enact change" ("*The Handmaid's Tale*"), while Lisa Miller objected that "[i]n an infuriating and grotesque reversal, Atwood's feminist allegory has turned instead into a showcase of female abuse." The final episode of Season 2 inspired further outrage when Offred/June chose to stay in Gilead, thus—crucially—setting the premise for a third season. For Gilbert, this ending was "incomprehensible" and "infuriating," "def[ying] logic" ("A Maddening Season Finale"). Margaret Lyons described the series as "part hair shirt,

---

[6] See also Lisa Miller on Season 2 as "torture porn."
[7] See, for example, Bernstein, where this image of Moss in the muzzle serves as an illustration.

part commodification" and dismissed the Season 2 finale as "the same repackaging and commercialization of women's ideas and women's suffering as everything else, just another story we've heard before." From the feminist moment that Season 1 seemed to tap into so powerfully, Season 2 ultimately seemed to adapt feminism for the purposes of profitably renewable mass entertainment. Perhaps not surprisingly, while feminists began to adopt the handmaids' red cloaks and white bonnets for activist purposes—for example, at demonstrations in support of Planned Parenthood and to protest the U.S. Supreme Court confirmation of Brett Kavanaugh—the television series also inspired designs for sexier versions of the iconic uniform by lingerie and adult costume retailers, as well as a line of wines named for Offred, Ofglen, and Serena Joy and characterized with sexualized descriptions. The pinot noir named for Offred, for example, was marketed as "so beguiling it seems almost forbidden to taste" (qtd. in Nevins). These product tie-ins met with considerable criticism, causing retailers to abandon their plans to capitalize on the high visibility of the television series and tap into its ambivalent status in relation to feminism.

Atwood's own stance on the label "feminist," along with that of Moss and other women in the cast, was part of the media controversy about *The Handmaid's Tale* (Bradley; Schwartz). Responding during Season 1 to the question of whether her original novella was feminist, Atwood replied,

> If you mean an ideological tract in which all women are angels and/or so victimized they are incapable of moral choice, no. If you mean a novel in which women are human beings—with all the variety of character and behavior that implies—and are also interesting and important, and what happens to them is crucial to the theme, structure and plot of the book, then yes. ("Margaret Atwood on What 'The Handmaid's Tale' Means")[8]

---

[8] Atwood also resisted categorizing *The Penelopiad* as feminist. Reporting on a press conference in 2006 to announce the RSC/NAC co-production, Brianna Goldberg noted that RSC associate director Deborah Shaw described Atwood's novella as "a feminist take on *The Odyssey*" that was appealing to the RSC for its "leads for women," given all the "blokes in Shakespeare" (qtd. in Goldberg). Goldberg then quotes Atwood as having expressed amazement that "anytime you do something from the point of view of a woman, it's automatically called feminism" and as having noted that *The Penelopiad* does not present "empowered or idealistic women."

She also described her own response to a scene in Season 1 in which she herself made a cameo appearance and which involved the handmaids being made to slut-shame one of their own:

> I found this scene horribly upsetting. It was way too much like way too much history. Yes, women will gang up on other women. Yes, they will accuse others to keep themselves off the hook [...]. Yes, they will gladly take positions of power over other women, even—and, possibly, especially—in systems in which women as a whole have scant power: All power is relative, and in tough times any amount is seen as better than none. ("Margaret Atwood on What 'The Handmaid's Tale' Means")

For Sarah Ditum, Atwood's statement was "not really so much of an answer as a slipping between two straw feminisms. Feminism is neither the claim that women are perfect, nor is it anything that happens to be about women: it's a movement to dismantle a system in which men systematically hold power over women and exploit them economically, sexually and [...] reproductively. Part of that movement," Ditum adds, "has always been what's called 'consciousness raising.'" *The Penelopiad* may serve to clarify Atwood's seemingly ambivalent stance toward feminism not only through its foregrounding of the women on the margins of Homer's epic but through its staging of the tragic consequences of Penelope's error in judgment for the maids she harmed and also for herself.

Looking at Atwood's dramatic adaptation of *The Penelopiad* in relation to *The Handmaid's Tale* as adapted for a multi-season television series may also serve to clarify some key distinctions between and potentialities of the mediums of theatre and television. *The Penelopiad* had its first performance iteration in October 2005, shortly after the publication of the novella and amid the publicity campaign to promote the work. A collaboration between Atwood and UK director Phyllida Lloyd, who had directed an opera version of *The Handmaid's Tale* in 2002, this initial performance was a 30-minute staged reading of the first part of the novella that was held in St. Mark's Church, Piccadilly, with Atwood herself reading the part of Penelope and three actresses standing in for the twelve maids and all the other characters. For Atwood, the staged reading of the novella was "dipping a toe in the theatrical waters out of which it came in the first place" in that "Penelope's opening speech presupposes an audience. She's speaking from the world of the dead to the world of the living. She wants to tell 'you' that she's not what people thought." Atwood also likened the structure of the novella to that of Greek tragedy "in that the central characters' stories are told in quite long monologues, then the chorus comment on the action" ("She's left holding the fort"). The novella's inherent theatricality thus invited its development in performance, while the shoestring budget that limited the cast for the reading to Atwood and three actresses in turn led to the larger all-female cast which became a crucial and distinctive feature of the full stage adaptation that was subsequently developed in collaboration with the Royal Shakespeare Company (RSC) and that premiered at the Swan Theatre in Stratford-upon-Avon in July 2007 in a co-production with Ottawa's National Arts Centre (NAC), where the play received its Canadian premiere in September of that same year. In addition to its all-female cast of thirteen British and Canadian actresses, most of the other members of the RSC production team were women, including the producer, literary manager, dramaturg, director, set and costume designer, lighting designer, and movement director. The transatlantic co-production was, moreover, sponsored by nine Canadian women donors who became known as the Penelope Circle, and this feminist-inflected financial support was replicated in subsequent productions at Alberta Theatre Projects in Calgary in 2010 (Program; Worden) and at Nightwood Theatre in Toronto in 2012 (Wright 32).[9] Such financial support was linked to Atwood's high profile in the Canadian and international literary scene, which generated extensive interest in the play and its key productions in Canada following its UK premiere.[10]

In approaching adaptations as works that are "second without being secondary," as "derivation[s] that [are] not derivative" (9), Hutcheon moves beyond a more traditional and hierarchical approach that evaluates adaptations in terms of their fidelity to their literary source texts. At the same time, however, she notes that commercial interests often make adaptations appealing to producers and that different representational modes

---

[9] On these productions, see Penny Farfan with Kelly Thornton and Vanessa Porteous, "Staging *The Penelopiad*" in this volume.

[10] The NAC press release asserted that the RSC/NAC co-production would provide "an opportunity for Canadian culture to make a significant mark on the world stage" (Mazey). Zita Cobb, one of the original "Penelope Circle" donors, explained: "I think Margaret Atwood is a national treasure, and if (she) has something we can put on the international stage, it's a wonderful way for Canada to express to the world who we are" (qtd. in Lin). Kailin Wright notes that Nightwood Theatre's advertising campaign for its production of *The Penelopiad* "capitalized on Atwood's wide appeal by extending its regular ads in *Now* and the *Globe and Mail* to also include billboards in the Toronto subway and booths at book fairs" (227).

entail different processes and techniques for transcoding. Bethany Wood, moreover, has demonstrated the significance of material concerns and commercial contexts for the representation of gender in inter-industrial adaptation processes and products in both theatre and film. Connecting Hutcheon's insights to Wood's observations, it is worth considering the circumstances of the television adaptation of *The Handmaid's Tale* as distinct from those of the stage version of *The Penelopiad*. Notably, although Atwood was a consulting producer on Season 1 in 2017 and made a cameo appearance in one episode, she stated in the context of the controversy over Season 2 in 2018 that she had no control over the series "because of the history of the rights that were acquired by the distributors of the 1989 film" version of the novel.[11] She also commented on the impact of the television series form on the adaptation of her work: "It's a television series. If you're going to have a series you can't kill off the central character and you also can't have the central character escape to safety in episode one of season two" (qtd. in Brown). Hutcheon observes that sequels and prequels are not really adaptations (9), but although Season 2 goes beyond where Atwood's novel ends, the series maintains her title and showrunner Bruce Miller has described himself as "a guy adapting one of the great feminist works of forever." Indeed, Miller has confessed that he "want[s] to grow up to be Margaret" and also that he "spent 35 years thinking about Season 2, since [he] read the book." His comments somewhat unsettlingly foreground the ambivalent duality of adaptation that Hutcheon describes. Miller has stated that he initially envisioned ten seasons of *The Handmaid's Tale* (Wigler); at the time of this writing (November 2019), Season 3 has aired and Season 4 has been announced.[12] Hulu and MGM have also announced that Atwood's own sequel to *The Handmaid's Tale*—entitled *The Testaments*, published in September 2019,

---

[11] Atwood has, however, been consulted in relation to story development throughout the series. See, for example, Feldman, in which she is quoted as having told Miller that he could not kill off Aunt Lydia, who is a central character in Atwood's own recently published sequel, *The Testaments*. See also Wigler for Bruce Miller's description on consulting with Atwood about Season 2.

[12] The critical response to Season 3 was mixed. In a review of the first three episodes, for example, Sophie Gilbert wrote, "June—trapped in her sequence of shock, rebellion, rinse, repeat—doesn't feel like a person anymore. She's the empty embodiment of female rage, perpetually denied meaningful release" ("The Growing Paradox"). Hillary Kelly suggested that the finale redeemed the season and opened up new possibilities for future directions, but she also argued that it was time for the series to kill June off (see "*The Handmaid's Tale* Season Finale Recap" and "It's Time for *The Handmaid's Tale* to Let June Die").

and set fifteen years after the ending of her original novel and of Season 1 of the television series—will also be developed for television. Miller has been reported to be in discussion with Hulu and MGM about *The Testaments*, but it remains to be seen whether the television version of Atwood's sequel will be incorporated into or an extension of what Miller had already planned for Season 4 and beyond, or whether it will be a separate work (Feldman).[13]

In the meantime, following my detour into the controversy surrounding Season 2 of the television series, I will conclude by returning to *The Penelopiad* as a feminist adaptation of the Odysseus and Penelope myth, of classical dramatic forms and conventions, and of Atwood's own novella, and in distinction from *The Handmaid's Tale* as adapted for a multi-season and still-ongoing television series. Against the serial elongation that contributed to the features of Season 2 that so many critics found objectionable, the stage version of *The Penelopiad* is distinguished by tragic compression and crystalline concision. Against the televisual realism of *The Handmaid's Tale* despite its dystopic fictional setting, *The Penelopiad* foregrounds theatrical transformation, requiring a minimal set and an ensemble cast that plays multiple roles. Against the essentialist reduction of women to their reproductive functions not only within Gilead but through the camera's lingering focus on Offred/June's pregnant belly, *The Penelopiad* foregrounds the performance of gender, requiring members of its all-female cast to step out of their roles as members of the chorus of maids to perform the male roles required for their telling of the story. Against the graphic violence against women that appalled viewers of *The Handmaid's Tale*, *The Penelopiad* stylizes and distances the violence at its core without mitigating its horror, so that, for example, for the hanging scene in the RSC production, the actresses simply went up on their toes (Taylor), a staging choice that gestically captured the essence of their eternal dance on the periphery of Penelope's consciousness and conscience. Against the camera gaze that fetishizes women's bodies and suffering and positions viewers as consumers of the objects of that gaze, *The Penelopiad* offers spectators the freedom to choose where to look. Against the cliffhanger open ending of the television series that works to create the desire for more of the same, *The Penelopiad* offers closure—not the cathartic release of classical tragedy but the closure of the protagonist's recognition of her betrayal of the maids and her own eternal suffering in light of that

---

[13] *The Testaments* is narrated by three women connected to Gilead: Aunt Lydia and Offred/June's two daughters, Agnes and Nicole, as they are named in the television series.

recognition. In addition, then, to exemplifying the usefulness of approaching adaptations as adaptations, *The Penelopiad* suggests the critical potential of feminist writing for the stage through its differences from an extended television series on related subject matter that aims to be feminist while at the same time functioning as popular entertainment for a mass audience.

Works Cited

Atwood, Margaret. "Descent: Negotiating with the dead: Who makes the trip to the Underworld, and why?" *Negotiating with the Dead: A Writer on Writing.* Cambridge UP, 2002, pp. 153–80.

———. "Margaret Atwood on What 'The Handmaid's Tale' Means in the Age of Trump." *New York Times*, 10 Mar. 2017, https://www.nytimes.com/2017/03/10/books/review/margaret-atwood-handmaids-tale-age-of-trump.html.

———. *The Penelopiad.* Alfred A. Knopf Canada, 2005.

———. *The Penelopiad: The Play.* Faber and Faber, 2007.

Atwood, Margaret, and Phyllida Lloyd. "She's left holding the fort" [interview with Lisa Allardice]. *Guardian*, 26 Oct. 2005, https://www.theguardian.com/stage/2005/oct/26/theatre.classics.

Beard, Mary. *Women & Power: A Manifesto.* Profile Books/London Review of Books, 2017.

Bernstein, Arielle. "The future isn't female enough: the problematic feminism of The Handmaid's Tale." *Guardian*, 8 May 2018, https://www.theguardian.com/tv-and-radio/2018/may/08/the-future-isnt-female-enough-the-problematic-feminism-of-the-handmaids-tale.

Bradley, Laura. "Why Won't the *Handmaid's Tale* Cast Call It Feminist?" *Vanity Fair*, 22 Apr. 2017, https://www.vanityfair.com/hollywood/2017/04/handmaids-tale-hulu-feminist-elisabeth-moss.

Brown, Mark. "The Handmaid's Tale: Margaret Atwood tells fans to chill out." *Guardian*, 28 May 2018, https://www.theguardian.com/tv-and-radio/2018/may/28/the-handmaids-tale-margaret-atwood-tells-fans-to-chill-out-about-tv-divergences.

"Canadian, U.K. theatres plan co-production of Atwood's Penelopiad." *CBC CBC Arts*, 18 Dec. 2006, https://www.cbc.ca/news/entertainment/canadian-u-k-theatres-plan-co-production-of-atwood-s-penelopiad-1.588224.

Ditum, Sarah. "Never-Ending Nightmare: Why Feminist Dystopias Must Stop Torturing Women." *Guardian*, 12 May 2018, https://www.theguardian.com/books/2018/may/12/why-the-handmaids-tale-marks-a-new-chapter-in-feminist-dystopias.

Estvanik, Nicole. "Stratford-Upon-Avon, England, and Ottawa, Canada: 'The Penelopiad.'" *American Theatre*, July–Aug. 2007, p. 74.

Feldman, Lucy. "Exclusive: Hulu and MGM Are Developing Margaret Atwood's *The Testaments* for the Screen." *Time*, 4 Sept. 2019, https://time.com/5668056/the-testaments-hulu-margaret-atwood/.

Gilbert, Sophie. "The Growing Paradox of *The Handmaid's Tale*." *The Atlantic*, 5 June 2018, https://www.theatlantic.com/entertainment/archive/2019/06/the-handmaids-tale-season-three-review-hulu/590992/.

———. "*The Handmaid's Tale* and the Suffering of Women." *The Atlantic*, 25 Apr. 2018, https://www.theatlantic.com/entertainment/archive/2018/04/the-handmaids-tale-season-two/558809/.

———. "A Maddening Season Finale for The Handmaid's Tale." *The Atlantic*, 11 July 2018, https://www.theatlantic.com/entertainment/archive/2018/07/a-maddening-season-finale-for-the-handmaids-tale/564884/.

Goldberg, Brianna. "Atwood Acted: The Penelopiad Takes to the Stage." *National Post*, 19 Dec. 2006: AL2, Margaret Atwood Papers, Thomas Fisher Rare Book Library, University of Toronto.

Herman, Alison. "The Diminishing Returns of 'The Handmaid's Tale.'" *The Ringer*, 25 Apr. 2018, https://www.theringer.com/tv/2018/4/25/17278604/handmaids-tale-season-two-review.

Homer. *The Odyssey*. Translated by Emily Wilson. W. W. Norton, 2018.

Howells, Coral Ann. "Five Ways of Looking at *The Penelopiad*." *Sydney Studies in English*, vol. 32, 2006, pp. 5–18.

Hutcheon, Linda, with Siobhan Flynn. *A Theory of Adaptation*. 2nd ed., Routledge, 2013.

Kelly, Hillary. "*The Handmaid's Tale* Season Finale Recap: A Talent for Ruthlessness." *Vulture*, 14 Aug. 2019, https://www.vulture.com/2019/08/the-handmaids-tale-season-3-episode-13-recap-mayday.html.

———. "It's Time for *The Handmaid's Tale* to Let June Die." *Vulture*, 14 Aug. 2019, https://www.vulture.com/2019/08/the-handmaids-tale-season-3-cliffhanger-june-must-die.html.

Lin, William. "Women make donations to back Atwood play." CanWest Service, *Cranbrook Daily Townsman*, 8 Mar. 2007, Margaret Atwood Papers, Thomas Fisher Rare Book Library, University of Toronto.

Lyons, Margaret. "'The Handmaid's Tale' Season 2 Is Brutal and Not Much Else." *New York Times*, 11 July 2018, https://www.nytimes.com/2018/07/11/arts/television/handmaids-tale-season-2.html.

Mazey, Steven. "Atwood's Penelopiad being adapted for the stage." CanWest News Service/*Edmonton Journal*, 21 Dec. 2006, Margaret Atwood Papers, Thomas Fisher Rare Book Library, University of Toronto.

Miller, Bruce. "'The Handmaid's Tale' Showrunner Wishes the Show Was Irrelevant" [interview with Emma Gray]. *HuffPost*, 25 Apr. 2018a, https://www.huffingtonpost.ca/entry/handmaids-tale-season-2-bruce-miller_n_5adf9210e4b07be4d4c58f3e?ec_carp=3338026819237773938.

Miller, Lisa. "The Relentless Torture of *The Handmaid's Tale*." *The Cut/New York Magazine*, 2 May 2018, https://www.thecut.com/2018/05/the-handmaids-tale-season-2-review.html.

Nevins, Jake. "Is The Handmaid's Tale wine collection the worst tie-in ever?" *Guardian*, 10 July 2018, https://www.theguardian.com/tv-and-radio/2018/jul/10/is-the-handmaids-tale-wine-collection-the-worst-tie-in-ever.

Paskin, Willa. "The New Episodes of *The Handmaid's Tale* Suggest It Should Have Ended After Its First Season; But it's still as good as ever at making you feel bad." *Slate*, 24 Apr. 2018, https://slate.com/culture/2018/04/the-handmaids-tale-season-2-reviewed.html.

Phillips, Carolyn. "Atwood's Tale Surfaces Nicely." *Ottawa Citizen*, 24 Sept. 2007, https://www.pressreader.com/canada/ottawa-citizen/20070924/282024732886521.

Program for Margaret Atwood's *The Penelopiad* at Alberta Theatre Projects, Calgary, Canada, 10 Sept.–9 Oct. 2010, p. 5.

Sanders, Julie. *Adaptation and Appropriation*. Routledge, 2006.

Schwartz, Alexandra. "Yes, 'The Handmaid's Tale' Is Feminist." *New Yorker*, 27 Apr. 2017, https://www.newyorker.com/culture/cultural-comment/yes-the-handmaids-tale-is-feminist.

Silman, Anna. "The Most Traumatizing Moments From *The Handmaid's Tale* Season Premiere." *The Cut*, 25 Apr. 2018, https://www.thecut.com/2018/04/scariest-moments-from-the-handmaids-tale-season-2-premiere.html.

Stuever, Hank. "In 'Handmaid's Tale' and 'Homeland,' two heroines judged by their devotion to motherhood." *Washington Post*, 24 Apr. 2018, https://wapo.st/2sRPFuM.

Taylor, Craig. "Twelve Angry Maids." *The Walrus*, 7 July 2007, https://thewalrus.ca/twelve-angry-maids/.

Wigler, Josh. "How 'The Handmaid's Tale' Will Remain Relevant in a Trump and #MeToo World." *Hollywood Reporter*, 15 Jan. 2018, https://www.hollywoodreporter.com/live-feed/handmaids-tale-season-2-bruce-miller-interview-1074657.

Wood, Bethany. "Gentlemen Prefer Adaptations: Addressing Industry and Gender in Adaptation Studies." *Theatre Journal*, vol. 66, no. 4, 2014, pp. 559–79.

Worden, Peter. "Rise of the Maids: Female footnotes from an ancient myth – reanimated in Alberta." *Alberta Views*, 1 Sept. 2010, https://albertaviews.ca/rise-of-the-maids/.

Wright, Kailin. "Dispublics: Popular Yet Political Spectatorship in Margaret Atwood's *The Penelopiad* and Erin Shields's *If We Were Birds*." *Theatre Journal*, vol. 69, no. 2, 2017, pp. 213–34.

PART II

Atwood Adapted

The Unreliable Female (Narrator) in Mary Harron's Miniseries *Alias Grace*

Anne-Marie Paquet-Deyris

Part of the reason why Mary Harron's miniseries *Alias Grace* holds such a curious fascination for the viewer has to do with the way in which the narrative unfolds, never fully reaching either a definitive truth or any form of closure. The serial format makes this absence of closure all the more palpable, as each of the six episodes' endings provides screenwriter Sarah Polley and showrunner Mary Harron with new possibilities of toying with open-endedness. In this sense, the series is rather a mystery tale about the inscrutable personality of the "celebrated murderess" Grace Marks, as nineteenth-century author Susanna Moodie calls her in *Life in the Clearings*, than a formulaic murder mystery (Basbanes qtd. in Wisker 129).

Grace's baffling and enigmatic figure takes center stage in this intricate web of open-ended narratives, but understanding the character also involves a better grasp of the complex structure of these multi-layered tales and their sometimes contradictory strands. Thus, to fully represent the complexity of Grace's persona, it needs to be observed from the

---

A.-M. Paquet-Deyris (✉)
English Department, University Paris Nanterre, Nanterre, France

© The Author(s), under exclusive license to Springer Nature Switzerland AG 2021
S. Wells-Lassagne, F. McMahon (eds.), *Adapting Margaret Atwood*, Palgrave Studies in Adaptation and Visual Culture, https://doi.org/10.1007/978-3-030-73686-6_7

perspective of these enmeshed tales whose potent impact upon others she also fully grasps. As the original core of all the narratives, Grace herself is framed as the mistress-weaver who toys with deceptive, superimposed discourses only partly revealing "[herself] behind [herself] concealed" (to paraphrase Emily Dickinson's poem "One need not be a chamber to be haunted"). Harron and Polley chose stanza 4 of Dickinson's poem "One need not be a chamber to be haunted" as the first episode's epigraph. It both replaces the source novel's first epigraph from William Morris's poem, "The Defence of Guenevere," and indirectly echoes the novel's second epigraph, "I have no tribunal," in which Dickinson's I-centered persona refuses to be judged by men. It also operates as the visual sign announcing the manipulative autobiographical pact the heroine makes with Doctor Jordan for after all, as she says early on, "A lot of it is lies" (Atwood, *Alias Grace*, 30; E1). The latter unfolds as some ongoing game in which actress Sarah Gadon's masquerading body and narrative quilt forever reformat the truth—if there is any.

Uncharacteristically then for the genre and format, each episode manufactures a muddy story which doesn't truly advance toward any form of revelation and obsessively asks the question: What kind of narrative is Grace telling and in which voice(s)? As they become the vectors of various transformative subjectivities, the voices also send us back to our own decoding practices in the restrictive and highly codified space of the series. They force us to encompass and accept the multiplicity of interpretations at the heart of the fictional universe while constantly questioning the narrator's stances.

The Tales Grace Tells: "Through a glass, darkly" (St Paul, Corinthians 13:12)

From the outset, even before Grace's actual first-person account starts, the spectator gets an immediate sense that she's toying with the various versions of her story while experimenting with the different facets of her personality. She is first framed in close-up watching herself in some off-screen mirror, as if trying to check on the different images she can project (Figs. 1 and 2).

In their relentless search for a cinematic translation of Atwood's prose, poetry, and mastery of first-person narration, Sarah Polley and Mary Harron design a mesmerizing, although brief, opening scene. Allegedly,

Figs. 1 and 2 E1: The mirror scene. Grace is "[a]ll these different things" at once

the narrator or central character's inner voice is one of the most difficult dimensions to successfully inscribe on screen. Polley and Harron had to erase this often insurmountable barrier so as to expose Grace's most private thoughts. In Atwood's novel, the texture of this voice held in check for so long is paramount and the narrative is almost entirely structured around it as it freely unfolds in Grace's secret mindscape:

> So I've read what they put in about me. [The governor's wife] showed the scrapbook to me herself, I suppose she wanted to see what I would do; but I've learned how to keep my face still, I made my eyes wide and flat, like an owl in torchlight, and I said I had repented in bitter tears, and was now a changed person […]. (Atwood, *Alias Grace*, 30)

In the series, camera movements, close-ups, and exchanged glances bring to the foreground the intensity of the character's stream of consciousness in a manner which somehow turns the viewers into ultimate voyeurs. From the very first shots onward, they are invited to get a peek at the ceaseless flux of her mental states which contrasts with her rather carefully guarded appearance, but matches the external turmoil over her case. In these introductory shots, the boundary between the mirror and the camera is erased as these silent photograms precede by a few seconds Grace's comments in voice-over which echo almost word for word the same mirror scene in the novel. Grace's mental *camera obscura* is eerily exposed as it coincides with the actual camera representing her interior monologue in the manner of the infinitely expressive faces in a silent film's photograms:

> I think of all the things that have been written about me. That I am an inhuman female demon. That I am an innocent victim of a blackguard forced against my will and in danger of my own life. That I'm too ignorant to know how to act and that to hang me would be judicial murder. [...] That I am cunning and devious. That I am soft in the head and little better than an idiot. And I wonder, how can I be all these different things at once? (E1)

This liminal scene is the key operative one in the entire series: it materializes the moment when we the viewers are officially invited to the show and turn into what could be called "acceptable voyeurs," who get to witness the seemingly infinite capacity Grace has of informing what we—along with Doctor Simon Jordan—perceive to be one of the facets of a complex reality. Although Grace isn't actually addressing anyone in particular, her rehearsal is a very physical one, one which very much depends on her alluring face and body. She puts her acting performances to the test and flaunts her mastery of composition as she is about to launch into her own recreative process and active game of seduction. From the onset, telling one's life story is therefore clearly identified as being mainly a manipulative and unreliable exercise. The scene also depicts the moment when Grace starts taking charge of the narration, deliberately fostering the type of ambiguity key to maintaining the series' distinctive tone. But even though she eventually gets to tell her own stories, there's a disturbing ring to the mirror shots as the apparent game of pretense aligns the numerous diverging external accounts of her own personality with a potential multitude of selves. Ironically, the close-ups give the illusion that Grace is literally a breath away and hence within our reach to be fully deciphered at any moment. But the camera captures her embodying a whole array of different characters as if haunted. As the introductory poem by Emily Dickinson suggests, she also willfully maintains an essential ambiguity.

In the tradition of the best psychological thrillers, the aura of doubt created around Grace's personality and accounts is compounded by the disjunction between the voice and the images on screen. Instead of an *either/or* equation, she seems to be successively and even simultaneously lost in the midst of various competing external and internal versions. What the series' initial mirror scene achieves is precisely to alert the viewer to the fact that she's an expert manipulator of these pluralized representations. The obvious reference haunting our collective memory here seems to be the final shots of Norman Bates's composite face as he looks straight at the camera at the end of Hitchcock's film *Psycho* (1960). The mother's voice-over and skull are famously superimposed on Norman's face at the end, fusing several personalities but also several stories that do not match. Hence, they provide an unreliable narrative and frame.

Grace is also quickly identified as a story crafter and insists self-consciously that she may not be telling the truth: "Perhaps I'll tell you lies" (E1). Very early on in the first episode, the camera frames her in medium close-up shots confronting Doctor Jordan and asserting her right to lie. Telling lies therefore becomes one of the structuring devices of a serial narrative unfolding in sometimes contradictory directions. Grace Marks deliberately points at the fact that her words no longer function as authentic markers of reality (Grace qtd. in Moos and Kozakewich 122), which Simon Jordan readily accepts as being part of the agreement—or rather the game here, as he replies, "[t]hat is a chance we'll have to take" (E1 8:02-8:17). The very nature of the narrative voice is clearly highlighted as problematic and its inscription on screen involves playing with the intradiegetic and extradiegetic viewer's gaze (Scheckels 128). As her Toronto lawyer points out to Simon Jordan in episode 6, Grace willfully engages in an endlessly destabilizing Scheherazade-like verbal game. The depth of the trouble she generates in the "good doctor" is of course also a measure of the unease she visits upon the viewer. The intercutting between the 1843 murder scenes, the earlier clips of the traumatic sea voyage, of Grace's early days as a servant, and of the 1859 interview, provides the necessary frame for such an intricate work of reconstruction: the narrative is so fractured and saturated with competing texts and contexts that very early on it clearly hints at its own unknowable and unsolvable essence. The excess of material somehow hinders the hermeneutic process at work from the start, leading to utter interpretative frustration on all fronts.

In *Margaret Atwood and the Female Bildungsroman*, Ellen McWilliams insists that,

> As she sits quietly sewing, Grace's own narratives, the crafting of her own Bildungsroman, prove far more compelling than anything a second-hand reflection of the world might have to offer. Grace is a progenitor of texts, both in the stories that she tells and in the stories that are told about her. Like Zenia, she is an empowered muse, capable of adding footnotes and corrections to the narrative of her life. (McWilliams 93–94)

In the TV series however, the visual shock caused by the often abrupt and unmediated juxtaposition of different time periods and dimensions of

Grace's narrative forces the viewer to confront head-on the extreme complexity and deviousness of the voice. It reflects but also exacerbates the manipulative aspect of the literary narrative. It highlights both Grace's virtuosity and the showrunner's own skillfulness at manipulating nonsynchronous parallel editing when inscribing on screen brief insights into the murder scene for instance. The various snippets Harron tantalizingly offers each time are emblematic of an overall scheme of endless reformatting. The series consistently stages this corrective dimension over the course of the six episodes. It literally turns Grace's character into a metaphor for its own serial simulation strategy.

THE CORRECTIONS: MASQUERADING BODY AND NARRATIVE QUILT

The notion of performance—and more specifically the performance of a female voice which had so far been silenced—is pivotal to the serial format as the voice's many incarnations come to structure the overall narrative. In chapter 45 of her novel, Atwood chooses to quote from Longfellow's 1858 poem, "The Courtship of Miles Standish" (Atwood, *Alias Grace*, 429). Polley and Harron use the lines as an inscription to episode 2:

> ... for it is the fate of a woman
> Long to be patient and silent, to wait like a ghost that is speechless,
> Till some questioning voice dissolves the spell of its silence.

The quote actually works in both contexts since the "questioning voice" is both the voice of the lead investigator eliciting the tale from his patient—and the voice(-over) of Grace who starts her narrative with a question, then keeps interrogating the legitimacy of the various stories about herself while toying with her own versions of the facts. Through minute facial expressions and minimal body postures and by modulating her natural and internal voice, Gadon succeeds in giving actual physical weight and identity to the narrating voice. Thanks to this tight interaction between text and image, her own voice also eventually fully incarnates the "questioning voice [which] dissolves the spell of its silence" from Longfellow's seminal poem. Adding corrections for her means taking the liberty of reshaping these accounts and therefore superimposing her own voice and projecting her own body onto the "master" (narrative). The suggestiveness of Grace's story mirrors her own body's. The screenwriter and the director are in turn intent on highlighting the indissoluble connection between articulating one's own stories and reappropriating one's confiscated female body. The intrinsic linkage between the two in the process of reappropriation has been discussed many times by critics of Atwood's literary works but it becomes the founding principle of the serial process. Each new episode is predicated on Grace's voice literally rising from the past and resurrecting the dead.

In "Margaret Atwood's female bodies," Madeleine Davies underlines for instance how the author chronicles power relationships by focusing on female bodies telling their own tales and insists that no reader could "fail to be aware of the various ways in which the body becomes associated with shape-shifting, masquerade, crisis, or play in these novels [as it] is linked with metaphors of disembodiment, a failure to be completely there, or with the occupation of liminal territories which mark uneasy gaps between 'real' and 'other'" (Davies in Howells 58).

Such a protean quality and play with presence and absence are also at the heart of the serial format. Grace's power to conceal and reveal is artfully materialized on screen by Harron's *mise en scene*. When the camera focuses on Doctor Jordan trying to psychoanalyze the young woman or any other person attempting to gain access to her thoughts, the notion of displacement ironically starts applying to the outsider. It seems to increasingly characterize Jordan himself as he's gradually subjugated and held *captive* (which happens to be the French title of the series) by his patient's words. As a direct consequence, he becomes increasingly cut off from the rest of the group of reformers petitioning the court to free Grace. Cinematographer Brendan Steacy captures his innermost illusions of getting romantically involved at regular intervals in the series. He does so by inserting similar shots of his fantasized intimacy with Grace in various episodes (Fig. 3).

The haunting shots of his embrace of Grace's white face and quasi-spectral body keep resurfacing at different moments in the series and materialize some sort of visual seepage of Grace's image into his own psyche. She turns into a dramatic illusion, the chief locus of all his obsessions. In the opening to episode 2, even as she proves to be a figment of his imagination after the analyst has woken up, the very fact that she should be physically present before him immediately afterward causes him to take a dangerously empathic road from which he won't be able to deviate. Her physical being imposing itself, "her slight graceful figure" (Moodie 21) takes center stage in the penitentiary yard while her

Fig. 3 Visual seepage: the obsessive image of Grace's desired body in virtually identical shots in E2 and E4

voice-over never pauses as it articulates the various strands of her story. With this simple visual trick, Mary Harron forcefully inscribes in the frame the multifaceted storytelling process at work.

The recurrence of virtually identical shots at the beginning of episode 4 also foregrounds the way in which Grace's tale and life stop being relegated to the margins of society. Feeding off the good doctor's fascination in a subtly predatory way, her presence and image contaminate and colonize his mental space challenging his prescriptive, male-centered discourse. Steacy's visual grammar represents the character being progressively taken over and receding into the background as he becomes another figure in Grace's tale. At the end of episode 2, the camera focuses in a smooth point-of-view shot on the trap door and the cellar where the murder of

Nancy the governess has been committed while Grace keeps commenting in voice-over on the forbidden "knowledge of [her Simon] crave[s]." While innocently looking straight at him, she muses in voice-over: "You want to go where I can never go. See what I can never see inside me. You want to open up my body and peer inside. In your hand, you want to hold my beating female heart" (E2). Even after the straight cut to the governor's house, the voice keeps going. As the camera frames Jordan watching Grace being roughly brought back to the penitentiary by the guards, the oblique-angle shots and the final fade to black already inscribe the doctor's increasingly dysfunctional relation to his patient, once again materializing on screen the spell he is under (Fig. 4).

The camera alternately shows the trap door to the cellar and cuts to the present time in the next episode. The caesura between episodes 2 and 3 proves to be instrumental in staging such a strategy of interrupted disclosures. Shots and comments alike foreshadow the radical inversion between the two characters' situations. Having been denied the "knowledge gained through the descent into the pit, [...] with a lurid glare to it" (E2), just like Iris Chase in Atwood's novel *The Blind Assassin*, Simon Jordan in turn becomes "as a blank space or page encoded by others: with no autonomy over [his] own body [he] has no rights over the words written onto it and no access to them anyway since they are inscribed in a code to which [he] does not hold the key" (Davies in Howells 61). The words apply to Atwood's literary piece but they also aptly characterize the way in which the doctor's subsequent vacuity is captured at the end of the series. Harron's representational strategy toys with the notion of ironical reversal. Jordan too then fails "to be completely there" (Davies qtd. in Howells 58) and ends up as an empty shell with unknowable thoughts in the care of his mother in the end sequence of episode 6 (Fig. 5).

Fig. 4 Ending of E2: oblique-angle shots of Jordan as visual signs of dysfunction

Fig. 5 Ending of E6: Simon becoming in turn "as a blank space or page encoded by others" (Davies qtd. in Howells 61)

The discrepancy between the soundtrack and the image track and the treatment of the voice-over in general consistently highlight Grace's strategy of reclaiming both text and social coding very early on in the TV series. Using Dr. Jordan as the unsuspecting tool of her patient work of rebuilding her identity, she keeps steering the conversation in particular directions, or stopping short when she doesn't want to reveal anything. In episode 4 for instance, when questioned about becoming pregnant at the asylum, she immediately asks whether they could change the subject. This mimetic strategy of arrested disclosures operates as so many intraepisodic cliff-hangers. Mary Harron alternates the moments when the trap door is about to be opened in Grace's mental flashbacks with straight cuts abruptly taking the spectator back to the time of the diegetic conversation, thus materializing on screen both the viewer's and the good doctor's deep frustration. The (mostly) impassive features Grace maintains paradoxically provide her with a useful mask she can modify at will, literally on her own terms, all the while wondering "what [Jordan] will make of all that"

(Atwood, *Alias Grace*, 328). Hence the editing technique is a substitute for Grace's literary narrative voice which flaunts the fabricated nature and artificiality of its own discourse. Polley and Harron repeatedly emphasize this pick-and-choose dimension of "the truth" by focusing repeatedly on the verbal (and actual) quilting technique numerous critics have already underlined. What is truly fascinating in the series however is the way in which the plurality of narrative strands is patched together and articulated, sometimes in the same scene, in a plurality of voices. The very hesitation of the voice, its own idiosyncratic glossolalia functions as the show's distinctive signature. As it prevents the series from ever reaching a definitive form of truth, closure is eventually erased.

CREATIVE TRUTH: TOYING WITH THE UNDECIDABLE

In the final episodes of the series, the heroine's voice and body no longer occupy liminal territories but become central sites for the negotiation of new memories and identities. Memory here is to be understood in the sense Toni Morrison confers upon it in her essay, "The Site of Memory" (Morrison qtd. in Zinsser 82):

> Like Frederick Douglass talking about his grandmother, and James Baldwin talking about his father, and Simone de Beauvoir talking about her mother, these people are my access to me; they are my entrance into my own interior life. Which is why the images that float around them the remains, so to speak, at the archeological site—surface first, and they surface so vividly and so compellingly that I acknowledge them as my route to a reconstruction of a world, to an exploration of an interior life that was not written and to the revelation of a kind of truth. (Morrison qtd. in Zinsser 95)

In episode 5, the ambiguities of the voice are playfully materialized on screen and pave the way for a different kind of truth to emerge in the final episode. In the first half of episode 6, Polley and Harron ask the viewer to focus on a version of the truth possibly rooted in some other-worldly dimension, hence recycling some of the supernatural film genre's conventions. During a voyeuristic séance she's forced to attend, Grace's voice suddenly changes register and nature, resembling some fantastic and monstrous voice from beyond the grave which is not supposed to resurface. Such an uncanny phenomenon very much resembles what Michel Chion calls the "acousmatic voice" in *The Voice in Cinema*. In both cases, it originates from some unknown, unassignable point behind a curtain and in this case, a veil, and eerily "sees" it all while sounding clearly malevolent (Fig. 6).

The director and screenwriter design a scene which subsumes all other manifestations of a voice which is, once again, oddly reminiscent of the terrifying low-pitched range of Mother's voice in *Psycho*.[1] Covered in a black veil, Grace is the center of attention of an intradiegetic audience and starts speaking in (hellish) tongues. The whole process has an obvious metafilmic dimension as it can also be associated with the very nature of the adaptation, transposing the words of others into a foreign context, and exposing a previously unrealized truth. With this session of

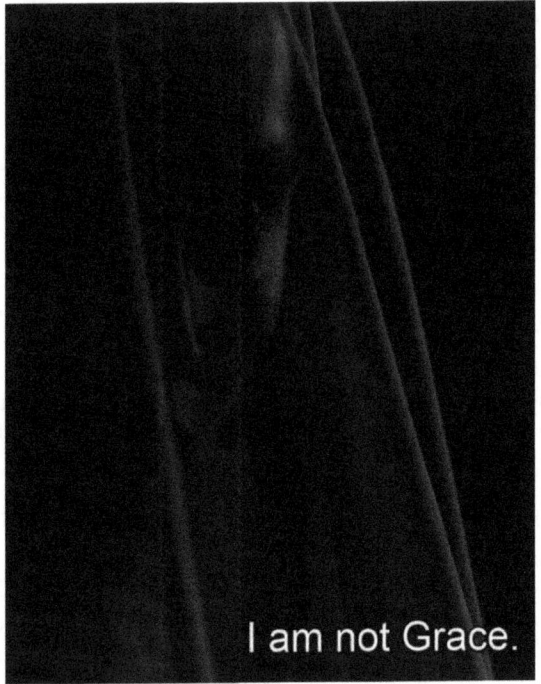

Fig. 6 Episode 6: Grace speaking in tongues during the session of neuro-hypnosis

[1] Its blood-curdling tessitura has achieved a cult status over the years. See: https://www.youtube.com/watch?v=dYDxxHrlmUg.

neuro-hypnosis, the crudeness of the discourse and the bluntness of the tone are no longer the voice-over's prerogative: though unascribable and truly unverifiable, the words are finally fully articulated in some eerie displacement of Grace's voice onto the voice of another—possibly her dead friend Mary Whitney's. The very fact that they are merely spoken out loud only puts an end to the voice's indecisiveness and unwillingness to choose between viewpoints and partially true or untrue memories. Hence it playfully erases its own indecision when wondering which version of the truth to select earlier on, "What should I tell Dr. Jordan about this day?" (Atwood, *Alias Grace*, 341). Even though neither the intradiegetic nor the extradiegetic spectator can still clearly see the contours of the overall design or of each reconstruction of the past, the voice is shown gaining extra narrative agency. It's captured being given some leeway in the way it has so far been recorded in the series and has formatted its own production of meaning.

In an article on poetic indetermination in the source novel, Jennifer Murray quotes Frank Davey on the modes of production of meaning:

'The realization over the last three decades that meaning ... is a product of the language in which events are recorded, that it may change even as writer and reader perform their interrelated tasks, has given the writer who works with historical materials much more freedom' (Davey 130). (Murray 2003, 310)

It is this type of creative freedom that Grace Marks seems to be claiming in the final shot of episode 6. She is looking straight at the camera as if challenging the viewer to find any satisfactory narrative closure. Actress Sarah Gadon's simple attire and seemingly innocent face devoid of any makeup function as a blank page onto which the viewer may recreate his own version of the truth (Fig. 7).

Like the enigmatic final shot from Edwin Porter's *The Great Train Robbery* (1903) when cowboy Broncho Billy looks straight at the camera, the last photogram foregrounds the undecidability of Grace's many "truths." What interpretative patterns must the spectator follow? How can he possibly translate a story which is by essence undecidable and whose narrator constantly flaunts her own essential unreliability?

Throughout the miniseries, Grace Marks is framed working on various quilt patterns. The highly codified and literally binding quilting technique she had to follow for her employers gives way to her own intensely

Fig. 7 End shot of Episode 6, Grace looking straight at the camera: undecidable

pleasurable, intimate, and evolutive creative process. It finally inscribes itself in the full-blown, liberating, and hybrid patchwork design at the end which both demonstrates and transcends the series' basic tenet that "[a] lot of it is lies" (Atwood, *Alias Grace*, 30; E1) as Grace comments on the numerous stories about her (Fig. 8).

As Theodore Scheckels underlines in "The Political in Margaret Atwood's Fiction," Grace's whole life seems to revolve around how well she can stage her own persona when caught in the web of a social system and dependent on its modes of commodification (Scheckels 130). Her survival is actually conditioned by the degree of freedom with which she can impose revisions on the various plots and designs at her disposal. Deeply aware that her fate has always been literally in someone else's hands, she knows that "choosing from among the truths she could offer"

Fig. 8 Episode 6: A narrative quilt of her own: the modified pattern, "all [of them] together" in the end

(Scheckels 131) is her only chance of finally producing a (narrative) pattern, whether partially true or untrue—on her own terms.

In many ways then, Grace operates as a serial narrator acknowledging the unreliability of her own voice and, as for history and meaning, the unattainability of truth. Until the very last photogram, she stages herself as some kind of enigma machine whose encryption cannot be broken, leaving the viewer—intradiegetic and extradiegetic—to his own conclusions, struggling with an elusive, undecidable, supposedly objective truth. In this sense, the series is profoundly destabilizing as Grace's personality remains forever out of anyone's grasp, hidden behind the fragments of a multitude of voices, and disseminated into the folds and the "modified" pattern of her quilt. Not only do the inventiveness and intricacy of the design reflect the artifice of fictional constructs and (serial) representation in general, they also point at Grace's mastery of the game as she ends up being a craftier player than either Doctor Jordan or the viewer, caught up as they are in the trappings of objective truth and their own subjectivities.

Fig. 9 Episode 6, end sequence: the gaps in the overall design/story/series

Her art of composition is by essence an art of deception, one that—as Margaret Atwood perversely underlines—sends us "right back [to] our own uneasiness about the trustworthiness of memory, the reliability of story, and the continuity of time" (Atwood 1998, 1515). The close shots of the quilts and of Sara Gadon's impassive features tauntingly remind the viewer that Grace's power of invention and ingenuity when fashioning adaptable truths can only thrive as it feeds off the gaps left unfilled (Fig. 9).

Works Cited

Alias Grace. Created by Mary Harron and Sarah Polley, CBC Television, 2017.
Atwood, Margaret. *Alias Grace* (1996). Virago Press, 2017.
———. "In Search of Alias Grace: On Writing Canadian Historical Fiction." The American Historical Review, Vol. 103 No. 5, Dec. 1998, pp. 1503–1516.
Davey, Frank. *Post-National Arguments: The Politics of the Anglophone Canadian Novel since 1967*. Toronto: University of Toronto Press, 1993.
Hammill, Faye. "'Death by Nature': Margaret Atwood and Wilderness." *Gothic Studies*, Vol. 5 Issue 2, Nov. 2003, pp. 47–63.

Howells, Coral Ann. *The Cambridge Companion to Margaret Atwood*. Cambridge UP, 2006.
Kay, Jeremy. "Sarah Gadon on starring in 'Alias Grace': 'I was completely consumed.'" *Screen International*, 15 June 2018, N_A.
Mcwilliams, Ellen. *Margaret Atwood and the Female Bildungsroman*. Ashgate, 2009.
Moodie, Susanna. *Life in the Clearings versus the Bush*. Jefferson Publication, 2015. http://www.public-library.uk/ebooks/21/63.pdf. Accessed 7 Jan. 2018.
Morrison, Toni. "The Site of Memory." *Inventing the Truth: The Art and Craft of Memoir*, 2nd ed., edited by William Zinsser, Houghton Mifflin, 1995, pp. 83–102. https://blogs.umass.edu/brusert/files/2013/03/Morrison_Site-of-Memory.pdf. Accessed 21 Dec. 2018.
Moss, John, and Tobi Kozakewich. *Margaret Atwood: The Open Eye*. University of Ottawa Press, 2006.
Murray, Jennifer. "Historical figures and paradoxical patterns: The quilting metaphor in Margaret Atwood's 'Alias Grace.'" *Studies In Canadian Literature-Etudes En Litterature Canadienne*, Vol.26, no. 1, 2001, pp. 65–83.
———. "History as poetic indetermination: the murder scene in Margaret Atwood's Alias Grace." Études anglaises, Vol. tome 56 (3), 2003, pp. 310–322.
Scheckels, Theodore F. *The Political in Margaret Atwood's Fiction. The Writing on the Wall of the Tent*. Ashgate Publishing Company, 2012.
Wynne-Davies, Marion. *Margaret Atwood*. Northcote House Publishers, 2010.
Wisker, Gina, *Margaret Atwood: An Introduction to Critical Views of Her Fiction*, Palgrave Macmillan, 2012.
Zarum, Lara. "The Steely-Eyed Ferocity of 'Alias Grace.'" *The Village Voice*, 4 Dec. 2017, https://www.villagevoice.com/2017/12/04the-steely-eyed-ferocity-of-alias-grace/.
Zinsser, William, editor. *Inventing the Truth: The Art and Craft of Memoir*, 2nd ed. Houghton Mifflin, 1995, pp. 83–102.

The Figure of the Objectified Servant, from the Silent Biblical Maid to the Twenty-First-Century Web TV Rebel

Ingrid Bertrand

Mainstream popular interpretations often tend to overshadow this fact, but the Bible, the Word of the Judeo-Christian God, is full of silences, especially when women are involved. As Christina Büchmann and Celina Spiegel remind us, "[m]any of the women in the Bible are especially sketchy figures, surfacing for a moment or two to perform a significant action, then sinking back under the text, leaving us to guess at the larger story" (xi). Such an invitation to enter into dialogue with the Bible could not be missed by an author like Margaret Atwood. As the following epigraph indicates, her bestselling dystopian novel *The Handmaid's Tale* revisits the biblical character of the maid Bilhah who, in the Book of Genesis, is used as a surrogate mother by sterile matriarch Rachel:

I. Bertrand (✉)
Université Saint-Louis—Bruxelles, Bruxelles, Belgium
e-mail: ingrid.bertrand@usaintlouis.be

> *And when Rachel saw that she bare Jacob no children, Rachel envied her sister; and said unto Jacob, Give me children, or else I die.*
> *And Jacob's anger was kindled against Rachel; and he said, Am I in God's stead, who hath withheld from thee the fruit of the womb?*
> *And she said, Behold my maid Bilhah, go in unto her; and she shall bear upon my knees, that I may also have children by her.*—*Genesis, 30:1–3* (Atwood, *Handmaid* 9)

In the Bible, Bilhah has no voice. Utterly objectified, this figure of the female servant embodies silent submissiveness and passivity. Transposing this ancient story of forced surrogacy to the twentieth and twenty-first centuries, respectively in the form of a dystopian novel (1985) and a web television series (2017–), *The Handmaid's Tale* challenges the silencing of the maid. Through the protagonist's first-person narration in the novel, and the heroine's voiceover narration combined with the ubiquitous, extreme close-ups and shallow focus in the series, we are given access to the servant's perspective. In and through her testimony, the maid strives to redefine herself as a subject. This chapter will demonstrate that from the novel to the series, the silencing of the figure of the maid keeps receding thanks to the surrogate mother's growing rejection of her objectification. To prove this point, the dystopias' plaything imagery will be analyzed.

Silenced into Doll-Like Submissiveness

In Atwood's novel, June uses doll comparisons to refer to her objectification by Gilead. When, following the coup d'état, Offred loses her job, her financial independence and most of her basic rights, she expresses her frustration and enforced helplessness in physical terms: "I felt shrunken, so that when ... [Luke] put his arms around me, gathering me up, I was small as a doll" (Atwood, *Handmaid* 191). The narrator uses the same plaything imagery when describing her submissive attitude during her first meeting with the Wife, whose questions she invariably answers with a "Yes, Ma'am" or "No, Ma'am": "They used to have dolls, for little girls, that would talk if you pulled a string at the back; I thought I was sounding like that, voice of a monotone, voice of a doll" (Atwood, *Handmaid* 26).

The Hulu series also suggests such a comparison in the fourth episode of the second season, entitled "Other Women." After being blamed by Aunt Lydia for the death of Omar, the man who helped her during her second failed escape attempt, June collapses emotionally. In this state of apparent depression and total submission to the regime, she shuns all forms of genuine communication. Walking past her lover Nick on her way to her compulsory shopping, she hides behind prescribed Gileadean formulas that she keeps repeating like a broken doll:

> NICK. Hey! Look, I'm sorry. I tried everything to get you out.
> JUNE. We've been sent good weather.
> NICK. June ... June!
> JUNE. We've been sent good weather. ... We've been sent good weather. ... We've been sent good weather. ... We've been sent good weather. (S2E4 49:24–50:42)

If such doll comparisons convey the Handmaid's sense of being subjugated and manipulated by Gilead, they are also used by Offred to describe the tragic fate met by rebels. For those who refuse to be the toys of the theocracy, the string at the back often becomes a rope around the neck. The talking dolls give way to silent "dolls on which faces have not yet been painted; [...] scarecrows" (Atwood, *Handmaid* 42) hanging from a hook on the Wall or the wooden posts of a Salvaging. Bruce Miller's television series repeatedly foregrounds those faceless dolls, reinforcing thereby the atmosphere of impending doom, as when Aunt Lydia forces the heroine to face Omar's body hanging from the Wall (S2E4 36:49–38:24), or in "After," the seventh episode of season two, in which June, through the curtained window of the Birthmobile, has to face the ghastly vision of streets lined up with shrouded Marthas, Wives and Commanders hanging from trees or gutters after a raid by the Eyes (05:43–05:49), or, again, in the third season when, as she is reflecting on the recklessness she showed as she helped a Martha escape, the protagonist keeps staring at hanged Marthas with hessian bag heads displayed in the middle of the street (S3E3 01:09–02:35).

In Atwood's dystopia, such frightening doll-like figures are perceived by Offred as performing a macabre dance. The narrator for instance pictures her predecessor, who was found hanged in her bedroom, "swinging, just lightly, like a pendulum" or "turning in mid-air under the chandelier" (Atwood, *Handmaid* 223, 305). She also describes the victims of the Salvaging as "feet [that] dangle, two pairs of red shoes, one pair of blue. If it weren't for the ropes and the sacks it could be a kind of dance, a ballet, caught by flash-camera: mid-air" (Atwood, *Handmaid* 289). The television series emphasizes this association between the dolls and dancing, through the pervasiveness of shots foregrounding the executed—or, more specifically, their feet—gently swinging to and fro in the wind. For instance, the scene in "Useful" that shows June standing in the middle of the circle formed by hanged Marthas immediately conjures up the eerie dance performed by the dead bodies through a J cut that features the ominously familiar sound of the rustling ropes before we can even see them (S3E3 01:09–02:35).

Such dancing dolls evoke the motif of the "red shoes." This motif, which recurs throughout Atwood's work (Bouson 139; Wilson 121; Rigney 9), is found in Powell and Pressburger's 1948 film *The Red Shoes* that Atwood saw as a young girl and that "momentarily traumatized" her, as Rosemary Sullivan explains in her biography of the author (55). In this film, a ballerina acted by Moira Shearer is torn between her career as the lead dancer in the ballet *The Red Shoes* and her love for a young composer. She eventually commits suicide, seemingly under the influence of her red ballet shoes. As Sharon Rose Wilson points out, this film revolves around "the either/or choices for women" (122), who can either be and express themselves, or love and be loved, but cannot have both.

In *The Handmaid's Tale*, Atwood critically revisits this "paradigmatically female story," as J. Brooks Bouson calls it (139). The status of Handmaid and the associated red shoes which, as Offred points out, are "not for dancing" (Atwood, *Handmaid* 18), immediately rob Offred of both love and freedom. The only choice left to her is a choice between impossibilities: accepting her silencing to survive, or expressing herself at great risk to her life. In other words, Handmaids like Offred can choose to be the regime's puppet, or to rebelliously dance their own dance, either to death, like Offred's ominous toy doubles at the Salvaging, or to at least some form of mutilation. Offred's best friend Moira—who, as Barbara Hill Rigney points out, "is surely intended to recall Moira Shearer who dances herself to death in 'The Red Shoes'" (117)—learns this to her cost when her feet are whipped with "steel cables" as a punishment for her escape attempt, and she cannot walk for a week.

Such a scene again echoes the film *The Red Shoes*, but also Hans Christian Andersen's fairy tale of the same name on which it is based, for both center around the image of female amputation, as Wilson remarks (122). In the 1948 film, amputation is purely symbolic. It refers to the drastic limitation of the heroine's possibilities, which leads to her tragic death. In Atwood's *The Handmaid's Tale*, Offred denounces the severe infringements on her most basic rights in similarly physical terms. When she is relegated to the domestic sphere by the newly set up theocracy, she feels "as if somebody cut off my feet" (Atwood, *Handmaid* 188). She also describes the illicit conversations exchanged with her fellow Handmaid through the headgear of her uniform as "[a]mputated speech" (Atwood, *Handmaid* 211). But in *The Handmaid's Tale*, amputation or mutilation can also be frightfully literal, as in Andersen's *The Red Shoes*. This fairy tale portrays a young girl named Karen, who is so obsessed by her pair of beautiful red shoes that she neglects her family and religious duties. An angel appears to her and punishes her for her vanity by condemning her to dance continually:

> "Dance thou shalt," said he; "dance on, in thy red shoes, till thou art pale and cold, and thy skin shrinks and crumples up like a skeleton's! Dance thou shalt still, from door to door, and wherever proud, vain children live thou shalt knock, so that they may hear thee and fear! Dance shalt thou, dance on—" (Andersen 20)

In a desperate attempt to end her torment, the young Karen has an executioner cut off her feet with the red shoes. Even then, the red shoes continue to dance, with the girl's amputated feet inside them, and to torment her, until the angel eventually gives her the mercy she begged for, and her soul ascends to Heaven.

As in Andersen's fairy tale, in Atwood's dystopia, mutilation is the price women are often sentenced to pay for daring to dance to their own tune, for daring to leave their submissive, doll-like posture to express themselves. As Offred remarks when describing Moira's punishment: "It was the feet they'd do, for a first offence. [...] After that the hands. They didn't care what they did to your feet and hands, even if it was permanent. Remember, said Aunt Lydia. For our purposes your feet and your hands are not essential" (Atwood, *Handmaid* 102). In Miller's series, the visual medium reinforces the impact of this threat, which the authorities keep carrying out. Mutilated female bodies are omnipresent, from one-eyed Janine or Emily and her genital mutilation, to the second Ofglen's cut tongue and Serena Waterford's amputated finger in season two or the ring-pierced mouths of the Washington Handmaids in season three.

The Servant's Subversive Dance: From a Tentative Solo to a Rebellious Collective Ballet

Despite the threat of the dancing doll or mutilation, the figure of the servant in *The Handmaid's Tale* strives to symbolically dance her own dance to counter her silencing objectification. In Atwood's novel, Offred's resistance first takes the form of a testimony to suffering and survival. Thanks to this, the protagonist can conjure up an addressee through which she is again more than a doll with a string at the back, and pass on the stories of women whose frontal rebellion against Gilead turned them into forever silent dancing dolls, like the previous Offred, Ofglen, or even—as Offred seems to think—Moira. The Handmaid also rebels against Gilead's elimination of desire through her affair with the chauffeur Nick. In the novel, the first physical contact between the two revealingly involves Offred's red shoes. In this scene, the assembled household is waiting for the Ceremony to begin, and Nick starts playing footsie with Offred beneath the folds of her dress: "He's so close that the tip of his boot is touching my foot. Is this on purpose? Whether it is or not we are touching, two shapes of leather. I feel my shoe soften, blood flows into it, it grows warm, it becomes a skin" (Atwood, *Handmaid* 91). Through the power of physical attraction, the symbol of Offred's fallen state and dehumanizing servitude seems to Offred to acquire an organic quality. It becomes the very organ through which physical contact is possible—a skin—, and thereby foreshadows the crucial role that the relationship with Nick will play in Offred's deliverance.

If the protagonist is seen to resist her objectification, toward the end of the narrative however, the image that she projects is of a maid who seems to be paralyzed by her fear of becoming a dancing doll. After being told that her shopping partner hanged herself when she saw the Eyes' black van coming for her, Offred is relieved that, unlike Ofglen, she never really joined the resistance: "I haven't done anything, ... not really. All I did was know. All I did was not tell" (Atwood, *Handmaid* 297). She then thinks:

> I'll sacrifice. I'll repent. I'll abdicate. I'll renounce. ... I don't want to be a dancer, my feet in the air, my head a faceless oblong of white cloth. I don't want to be a doll hung up on the Wall. ... I resign my body freely, to the uses of others. ... I feel, for the first time, their true power. (Atwood, *Handmaid* 298)

As Marta Dvořák points out, the narrator's "allusion to the death dance shows how she has off(e)red herself up to the dominant ideology" (150). In a state of apparent lethargy, Offred passively waits in her bedroom for the coming punishment from which she ultimately escapes thanks to Nick and the resistance. If in *The Testaments*, the sequel published more than thirty years after *The Handmaid's Tale*, Offred is described by the main characters as a "renegade" who smuggled out her baby daughter and as a "terrorist" (331) whom Gilead tried to eliminate twice, at the end of *The Handmaid's Tale*, the readers are left with the impression that, as often in "an Atwood text, transformation has just begun" (Wilson 21): "Whether this is my end or a new beginning I have no way of knowing: I have given myself over into the hands of strangers, because it can't be helped. And so I step up, into the darkness within; or else the light" (Atwood, *Handmaid* 307).

While Miller's heroine expresses her fear of becoming a dancing doll in the same words as in the novel, the scene comes much earlier than in Atwood's dystopia, indicating in this way that June's transformation will not be delayed in the series. The scene is situated in the third episode of the first season, "Late," when June is interrogated for failing to report to the authorities a conversation in which her shopping partner mentioned that she was gay. June's attitude moreover is very different from Offred's in Atwood's novel, for when Aunt Lydia reduces the Beatitudes to an exhortation to submissiveness, the heroine answers back to show that she is not fooled by the Aunt's tampering with the biblical text, and to reaffirm her solidarity with her peer:

EYE: Why didn't you report the conversation?
JUNE: Because she was my friend.
AUNT LYDIA: Remember your Scripture. Blessed are the meek.
JUNE: And blessed are those who suffer for the cause of righteousness. For theirs is the Kingdom of Heaven. I remember. (S1E3 29:21–30:21)

This scene is emblematic of the maid's attitude in the series, and of her difference with her literary predecessor. To compare the two, using the dance metaphor of the red shoes again, one could say that Atwood's maid resists her silencing by symbolically dancing a secret, individual—or even individualistic—dance in a tentative way. The Handmaid of Miller's series, by contrast, emphatically rejects her doll-like status and dances her rebellious dance in a more confident and collective way.

The Ballerina in the Box

The difference between Atwood's and Miller's maids is also emphasized through the original addition to the plaything imagery in the series: a musical box that June receives as a gift from the Wife in episode eight of the first season, "Jezebels." As the heroine opens her present for the first time, a close-up shows its little pirouetting ballerina superimposed on Offred's reflection in the mirror inside the lid (S1E8 44:55–45:01). The music played by the box, the Swan Lake theme, further strengthens the link with the red shoes motif, for in Powell and Pressburger's film *The Red Shoes*, it is precisely thanks to her trial performance of *Swan Lake* that the heroine gets a starring role. By evoking Tchaikovsky's famous story of a woman who falls prey to an evil man, is separated from the man she loves, and is trapped in an identity she has not chosen, the tune moreover immediately establishes the connection between June and the little ballerina. June herself instantly perceives the dancing "girl trapped in a box" as her double:[1] "She only dances when someone else opens the lid, when someone else winds her up" (S1E8 45:27–45:37), like the doll in Atwood's novel, who only speaks when someone pulls the string at the back.

A proleptic sign of the toy ballerina's function as June's double can be found in the fourth episode of season 1, in which flashbacks show the heroine being tortured at the Red Centre after her failed escape attempt. As June is dragged back to her dormitory, her bandaged mutilated feet look like ballet shoes (S1E4 42:42–42:54). But unlike the dancing girls in the fairy tale and in the film *The Red Shoes*, Miller's maid does not dance herself to death. On the contrary, this dance is associated with the protagonist's symbolic rebirth as a rebel supported by female solidarity, for at the Red Centre the other Handmaids pay tribute to June's bravery by offering her stolen food scraps and reverently standing in front of her bed.

Such solidarity is also evoked when June transports us back to her present in the same episode. As she is banished to her room for failing to be pregnant, the protagonist conjures up the spirit of her predecessor, whose hidden message—"Nolite te bastardes carborundorum"—she has just

---

[1] The musical box can also be interpreted on a metanarrative level as a reference to the series itself, with the female figure of Elisabeth Moss dancing when the "idiot box"—as television is sometimes disparagingly referred to—is switched on. In the same way as June chooses to embody resistance in a regime that rests on the dehumanization of women, so has Moss become the symbol of the series' denunciation of women's objectification in today's media and society.

discovered in the cupboard, to manipulate the Commander during one of their Scrabble sessions. After asking for the meaning of the Latin message, June evokes the possibility of her following her predecessor's example—that is, committing suicide in her bedroom. She therefore uses the Commander's own fear of the dancing doll to persuade him to end her banishment. As she celebrates her small victory and walks out of the Commander's house for the first time in days, June honors the previous Offred as the one who put her on her feet again: "There was an Offred before me. She helped me find my way out. She's dead. She's alive. She's me. We are Handmaids. Nolite te bastardes carborundorum, bitches" (S1E4 48:36–49:02). These words are pronounced by a June leading a formation of Handmaids walking down the street in their red uniforms and brown shoes. Revealingly, in Miller's series, Handmaids have swapped their red shoes for red-brown boots that look more like army boots than delicate ballet shoes. This difference between the novel and the series represents more than an aesthetic detail. It suggests that the heroine and her peers will dance a very different kind of dance. This point is made clear through the many shots of processions of Handmaids in the red uniforms, whose military-like quality June points out at the beginning of the tenth episode of the first season when she muses: "They should've never given us uniforms if they didn't want us to be an army" (S1E10 05:48–05:56).

Unlike her literary ancestor, Miller's servant seems to be able to transcend her fear of the dancing doll on the Wall. As she tells Nick just before receiving the musical box, she will not let him put an end to their relationship, even if they could end up on the Wall as a consequence, because existing as a subject, even for a short time, and being remembered as such is preferable to a longer life lived without love: "[A]t least ... at least, someone will remember me ... in this place. At least someone will care when I'm gone. That's something. That is something" (S1E8 42:46–43:17). The doll on the Wall is preferable to the dancing ballerina of the musical box.

This similarity that June perceives between her position in Gilead and the ballerina of the musical box urges her to accumulate seditious gestures through which she can reclaim her humanity. The Handmaid's first move after receiving her box is to use its key to engrave her own message of solidarity and resistance in her cupboard—the words "You are not alone"—before she conjures up her imaginary addressee and forcefully asserts her refusal to be reduced to her miniature double: "If this is a story I'm telling, I must be telling it to someone. There's always someone, even when there is no one. I will not be that girl in the box" (S1E8 45:39–46:15). Moving from words to deeds, June joins Mayday at the beginning of episode nine. The object of her first mission, a package that has to be smuggled out of the theocracy, precisely becomes associated with the musical box in the first season's finale, "Night." The scene starts with a shot that stresses June's seclusion and her likeness to the ballerina once more, as the heroine's head and the open musical box are shown through the partially open window of her bedroom. Spurred to action by the tune of her musical box, June opens the package to find dozens of clandestine testimonies hastily scribbled down on scraps of paper. When reading these messages, June comes to embody a polyphony of voices who have defied the ban on writing to ask for help and be remembered, which they eventually are in season two, when the letters are made public thanks to June's connections.

Driven by her decision to not be the ballerina in the box, June publicly displays her dissident side when she sabotages her fellow Handmaid Janine's staged stoning. If, after dropping her stone to the ground to indicate her refusal to be complicit in murder, the protagonist utters the traditional apology "I'm sorry Aunt Lydia" (S1E10 46:44–46:45) like a child who has just been caught doing mischief, it is to better beat the elderly woman at her own power game, as June's offensive, triumphant smile unmistakably betrays. As a chorus of Handmaids follows June's example, the repetition of the prescribed formula, in this context, is no longer associated with the image of a broken doll, but with that of the first collective rebellion against the regime, a rebellion that, when the Handmaids walk back home in their military-like procession led by a determined-looking June, heralds the new dawn, new day and new life sung by Nina Simone in the score.

In the second season, the musical box reappears when female bonding takes a most unexpected form and Serena, the very embodiment of female sacrifice and unconditional acceptance of the either/or choices for women, starts shaking the foundations of Gilead to protect her future baby from the authorities' heavy-handed response to Ofglen's bomb attack. Addressing June, not as the "walking womb" that she usually considers her to be, but as a professional editor, she asks the Handmaid to join forces with her behind the Commander's back to forge official documents scaling down security measures while he is in hospital. At the issue of their fruitful collaboration, Serena gives June back her musical box as a thank-you gift. Although June's decision to help the Wife might be interpreted as complicity, it is primarily its subversive character that is foregrounded, through June's description of their work as "an offence to God," as heresy through which Serena will join her Handmaid on the "naughty list" (S2E8 01:28–01:29, 01:39)—and for which she will be whipped by her husband—, but also through the way in which the scene is shot. The unmistakable parallelism between June's flick of the thumb in "After," as she is about to start writing with the red pen she has carefully selected to revise Serena's text (S2E7 51:16–51:31), and Ofglen's own thumb movement as she detonates the bomb that blows up the brand new Rachel and Leah Center in the previous episode, "First Blood" (S2E6 53:53–54:03), suggests that June's act—and, more generally, her progressive empowerment through clever alliances—could threaten the Commander's authority and Gilead as a whole as severely as the bomb attack that killed twenty-six Commanders.[2]

The musical box, which June accepts, thinking "[i]t was nice working with you too" (S2E8 08:33–08:34), comes to symbolize the possibility of—albeit limited and temporary—understanding and alliances between June and the Wife when both women share the same goal: protecting their daughter from Gilead.[3] In the first season already, the toy was connected with both June's future baby and her first daughter, Hannah, for in a scene following the revelation of June's second pregnancy, June is shown to remember her first pregnancy while listening to the musical box. In June's memory, the future parents go into raptures over their daughter's kicking fist or foot, which they interpret as a sign that "[s]he's a fighter like Mommy" (S3E1 11:56–11:57).

When in the second season, June gets a stolen picture of Hannah from the Commander, she places it inside the box. By superimposing Hannah's image on her own reflection in the mirror, June symbolically adds a third girl, a third ballerina, to the original duo. Like her mother, Hannah is trapped in Gilead. June is painfully aware of the fate her child faces if she grows up in the theocracy. She will be married off to an older man to bear children for the republic. The musical box therefore helps June remember

---

[2] In the third season, the dangerousness of the writing tool is most literally stressed, for it is precisely with the help of a pen that June commits her first murder, by stabbing Commander Winslow to death when he tries to rape her in the eleventh episode (S3E11 35:08–35:27).

[3] This alliance, which culminates in Serena's decision to allow June to smuggle Nicole out of Gilead in season two's finale, is however broken in season three when, after briefly seeing the baby in Canada, Serena has a change of heart and decides to do whatever it takes to be reunited with her.

what, but also who she is fighting for. It emphasizes that June's struggle against objectification is not an individual or individualistic struggle. It is a struggle that she wages for herself and both her daughters, to make sure that they do not grow up to become dancing ballerinas trapped in a box. If in the second season's finale, June eventually decides not to get into the van that could lead her to freedom in Canada, and instead chooses to stay behind after putting her baby in Emily's care, it is because, as she already formulated it at the end of the first season, she wants "to make things better for Hannah. Change the world, even just a little bit" (S1E10 51:59–52:08).

From what Emma Dibdin calls the "vaguely superhero-esque final shot" of the second season's finale, in which June puts up the hood of her cloak before slowly raising her head to stare at the camera with a grim, defiant look and disappearing into the night, to the first shot of the protagonist in the third season, which only shows her swirling cloak and running feet in their familiar brown boots as the Handmaid declares via voiceover "I'm sorry, baby girl. Mom's got work" (03:31–03:35), the transformation of the heroine into a freedom fighter determined to destroy Gilead from the inside in season three is unequivocally heralded. As Julie Kosin puts it, "[t]he third season of the Emmy-winning show swaps its depictions of emotional and physical torment for a tone of empowerment and rebellion." If the dancing dolls of the executed dissidents still loom in the background, the trapped ballerina of the musical box has been left behind, both literally—the box having most probably been reduced to ashes through Serena's arson—and symbolically, to give way to the figure of the resistance leader with a ruthless will to federate around her those "[w]ho can be turned, ignited, to burn this shit place to the ground" (S3E4 01:45–01:53) and rescue dozens of children from Gilead's dehumanizing terror.

From the Bible to Margaret Atwood's dystopian novel and then Hulu's television series, the figure of the maid forced into surrogacy has evolved from complete silence to resistance and even outright rebellion against her objectification. But the protean transformation of the figure of the maid still is an ongoing process, for the series has been renewed for a fourth season. As in 1985, when Atwood's *The Handmaid's Tale* came out, in today's society, which is increasingly seen as turning the nightmarish visions of dystopias into a concrete reality, the character of the Handmaid strikes a chord with many readers and viewers, who see in her struggle a symbol of female empowerment.

Works Cited

Andersen, Hans Christian. *The Red Shoe*. Translated by Jean Hersholt, Read Publishing, 2015.
Atwood, Margaret. *The Handmaid's Tale*. 1985. Random House, 1996.
———. *The Testaments*. Random House, 2019.
Bouson, J. Brooks. *Brutal Choreographies: Oppositional Strategies and Narrative Design in the Novels of Margaret Atwood*. U of Massachusetts P, 1993.
Büchmann, Christina, and Celina Spiegel, editors. *Out of the Garden: Women Writers on the Bible*. Fawcett Columbine, 1995.
Dibdin, Emma. "*The Handmaid's Tale* Season 2 Finale Offers a Light in the Darkness." *Harper's Bazaar*, 11 July 2018, www.harpersbazaar.com/culture/film-tv/a22105741/the-handmaids-tale-season-2-finale-episode-13-recap-review. Accessed 16 December 2019.
Dvořák, Marta. "What is Real/Reel? Margaret Atwood's 'Rearrangement of Shapes on a Flat Surface,' or Narrative as Collage." *Margaret Atwood's* The Handmaid's Tale. *Modern Critical Interpretations*, edited by Harold Bloom, Chelsea House Publishers, 2001, pp. 141–53.
The Handmaid's Tale, created by Bruce Miller, MGM, Hulu 2017–.
Howells, Coral Ann. *Modern Novelists: Margaret Atwood*. St Martin's Press, 1995.
Kosin, Julie. "Elisabeth Moss Finally Finds Hope in *The Handmaid's Tale*." *Harper's Bazaar*, 12 June 2019, www.harpersbazaar.com/culture/film-tv/a27920141/elisabeth-moss-handmaids-tale-season-3-interview/. Accessed 16 December 2019.
Rigney, Barbara Hill. *Women Writers: Margaret Atwood*. Macmillan, 1987.
Sullivan, Rosemary. *The Red Shoes: Margaret Atwood Starting Out*. HarperCollins, 1998.
Wilson, Sharon Rose. *Margaret Atwood's Fairy-Tale Sexual Politics*. UP of Mississippi, 1993.

Shallow Focus Composition and the Poetics of Blur in *The Handmaid's Tale* (Hulu, 2017–)

David Roche

Resorting to the 1910s Hollywood strategy of adapting bestsellers and classics, in this case a Canadian novel famous for both its topicality and experimental writing, can probably not, in 2017, be put down to a socio-economic need to legitimize a medium or a form; the strategy's goal, here, is much more modest: launching a new streaming platform in a market dominated by Netflix and to a lesser extent Amazon. Released a few months after the 50th President of the United States took office, the first season no doubt benefited from its resonance with the context. Season 2 pursued this track by referencing the #MeToo movement in episode S2E9, when the Waterfords's visit to Canada leads to a protest with demonstrators wielding signs stating their names, Moira's reading, "I am Moira." But like other recent prestige drama series—*Mad Men* (AMC, 2007–2015), *Breaking Bad* (AMC, 2008–2013), *Sherlock* (BBC, 2010–), *Utopia*

D. Roche (✉)
Département Cinéma, Audiovisuel, Nouveaux Médias,
Université Paul Valéry Montpellier 3, Montpellier, France
e-mail: david.roche@univ-montp3.fr

© The Author(s), under exclusive license to Springer Nature
Switzerland AG 2021
S. Wells-Lassagne, F. McMahon (eds.), *Adapting Margaret Atwood*,
Palgrave Studies in Adaptation and Visual Culture,
https://doi.org/10.1007/978-3-030-73686-6_9

(Channel 4, 2013–2014), *Hannibal* (NBC, 2013–2015), *Top of the Lake* (UKTV/BBC, 2013–), *Big Little Lies* (HBO, 2017), and the incomparable *Twin Peaks: The Return* (Showtime, 2017)—the Hulu series also flaunts aesthetic ambitions, not just in terms of narration—most episodes resort to a flashback structure that has become fairly common in complex television storytelling since *Six Feet Under* (HBO, 2001–2005), *Veronica Mars* (CW, 2004–2007) and *LOST* (ABC, 2004–2010) (Mittel 11)—but also in terms of camerawork, editing, and sound design. On the surface, such ambitions seem to go against the notion that television is a writer's medium. And yet most of the time directors, cinematographers, editors, and production designers are allowed very little leeway.

A series is, in Jean-Pierre Esquenazi's words (91–95), a "story-making machine," with a formula that enables variation. Analyzing a series thus entails identifying its formula, which circumscribes the diegesis, narration and style or poetics. David Bordwell's definition of film poetics follows the classical Aristotelian definition: it is "the more general principles according to which the work is composed, and its functions, effects, and uses" (12). In the case of a series, these principles are established from the outset by the showrunner and her/his team as part of its formula; the director of the pilot, whether it be David Lynch for *Twin Peaks* (ABC, 1990–1991), J.J. Abrams for *LOST*, or David Fincher for the American version of *House of Cards* (Netflix, 2013–2018), is often in charge of setting the tone. *The Handmaid's Tale* (2017–) is no exception. Its poetics comprise reflexive devices such as looks to the camera; a self-conscious narrator addressing an unidentified addressee that might be us in voice-over; chiaroscuro and back lighting; profilmic surfaces such as curtains, mirrors, and windows; a color scheme in which red and to a lesser extent blue are set against monochrome backgrounds that are predominantly dark brown and occasionally bright white (the hospital, the supermarket) inside and pale gray (outside); Dutch angles; frame-within-the-frame compositions; off-center compositions; lens flares; blurring effects; and jump-cuts.

Many of these devices are meant to "adapt" the novel's aesthetics. Atwood's narrator mentions curtains[1] and mirrors,[2] and evokes optical

---

[1] "I lean forward, pulling the white curtain across my face, like a veil. It's semi-sheer, I can see through it" (Atwood 67).
[2] "In the curved hallway mirror I flit past, a red shape at the edge of my own field of vision, a wraith of red smoke" (Atwood 219).

effects such as the blur[3] and maybe even back lighting.[4] One paragraph in particular captured my attention while rereading the novel almost 19 years after studying it as a student.

> What I need is perspective. The illusion of depth, created by a frame, the arrangement of shapes on a flat surface. Perspective is necessary. Otherwise there are only two dimensions. Otherwise you live with your face squashed against a wall, everything a huge foreground, of details, close-ups, hair, the weave of the bedsheet, the molecules of the face. Your skin like a map, a diagram of futility, crisscrossed with tiny roads that lead nowhere. Otherwise you live in the moment. Which is not where I want to be. (Atwood 154)

With its mention of lack of depth, surfaces, framing, close-ups, and generally speaking of haptic aesthetics, this paragraph could very well be the blueprint for the Hulu series' poetics, and notably the cue for its reliance on shallow focus (i.e., the division of cinematic space into two layers, one focused, one blurry).

The repetition seriality entails actually makes the identification of the specific components of a series' poetics almost easier than for a feature film. Indeed, the majority of these devices have been noted by bloggers and journalists alike; writing about season 2, for instance, Heather Hendershot (2018) identifies "the shallow focus, extreme overhead shots, and tightly circumscribed color palette." The specific aspect I will be studying, shallow focus, has even been analyzed in a compelling video by Evan Puschak entitled "One Reason Why *The Handmaid's Tale* Won Emmys Best Drama."[5] Puschak explains that shallow focus has become a cliché—particularly in American indie cinema—often used just because it's "beautiful" and very "cinematic." The trend is confirmed by Martine Beugnet in her luminous study of the blur in cinema, when she explains that, though more common in avant-garde, expressionist, impressionist, underground, and experimental cinema, the aesthetics of blur have creeped into advertising, music video, and mainstream cinema and television (26). For Puschak (2017), however, there is nothing gratuitous about the use of shallow focus in *The Handmaid's Tale* where it is used "in a systematic way

---

[3] "Once in a while I think I can see myself, though blurrily, as he may see me" (Atwood 221).
[4] "I sit in my chair, the wreath on the ceiling floating above my head, like a frozen halo, a zero" (Atwood 210).
[5] https://www.youtube.com/watch?time_continue=19&v=cY4aCnfrqss   Viewed   on January 7, 2019.

as a motif of its visual language," that is always in relation to the story and characters. The technique, developed in the first episode by cinematographer turned director Reed Morano, is, according to Puschak, used in three ways:

1. to capture Offred/June's point of view with the use of close-ups; it "create[s] intense intimacy," "almost as if we're under a blanket with the character," but it also suggests that, in an authoritarian society, "your only agency is mental";
2. to help create the world of Gilead and underline how little the women know about it;
3. to connect two worlds, the past and the present, and ultimately to suggest that individuals in both worlds suffer from "limited perspective," one imposed by force in Gilead and one brought on by choice in the US.

Puschak demonstrates that the use of super shallow focus is by no means gratuitous, but is instrumental to both the storytelling and the political subtext, and is thus integral to the series' poetics. His basing his analysis entirely on episode S1E1 suggests that even the most knowledgeable viewers consider a series' pilot as the aesthetic blueprint for the rest of the series and subsequent episodes as mere variations.

So the question this chapter proposes to explore is not whether shallow focus is part of the Hulu series' formula; it is. Rather, I would like to assess how a poetics of blur is established and how dynamically it shapes the series' aesthetics. Is shallow focus utilized according to a consistent set of norms? Does it interact with other devices? Do specific scenes and episodes play on and even disrupt the formula? How does this poetics of blur contribute to the production of sensation and meaning? And does it have political implications? Finally, what does the series' use of shallow focus teach us about the poetics of a series and, more generally, about the status of the blur in an audiovisual medium? I hope to answer these questions following a typological analysis of the functions of shallow focus that will be organized from the most common to the less frequent, and that will be divided into four parts; these four parts, as we shall see, are actually three, devoted as they are to the construction of cinematic space, memory, and self.

An Intimate Cinematic Space

The prime function of shallow focus close shots is the creation of an intimate filmic space; this is achieved in combination with costume and lighting. Visually, the handmaids' robes, which do double duty as a sign of, and a veil for, the women's sinful bodies, mark the limit between the subjects' faces and their environment. This is heightened by the white bonnets they wear indoors, and even more so by the wings they add when going out. Both accessories resemble white halos cutting off their faces from their bodies and the blurry background; because of their breadth, the wings are often partly blurred themselves—season 3 (S3E2, S3E4, S3E9) adds POV shots framed by the blurry wings. Back lighting is sometimes utilized to heighten the contour of the human face against the background.

Such shots are primarily associated with two different situations. First, they evoke a character's inner life; they highlight the emotions the characters' faces express (June in every episode; Mrs. Waterford in practically every one, especially in season 2; Emily in S1E3, S2E2, and S2E12; Luke in S1E7; Moira in S2E7; Janine in S2E8) and frequently accompany June's voice-over. As Beugnet suggests, the blur expresses the character's "absorption," and thus that she has mentally abstracted herself from her surroundings (84). Shallow focus medium close-ups are also used when characters such as the handmaids or June and Nick converse in secret, occasionally conspire and increasingly, as the episodes go by, speak their minds in public spaces, such as streets and stores (at the end of S1E1 Emily tells June, "It was nice to finally meet you," while at the end of S2E7, the handmaids in the store tell each other their real names), and in season 3, they regularly conspire in such places (S3E2, S3E7, S3E10, S3E12). Thus, focus, as opposed to blur, comes to signify both the space the oppressive order has locked the subject in and the modest haven it fails to control. It is a virtual prison cell the handmaids carry with them—and that is the polar opposite of the intimate space created by free subjects, such as two expectant parents (June and Luke) cuddling under a blanket in S1E10, which finds its Gilead equivalent when June speaks to her baby in S2E5.

The series' poetics are thus adapted to the diegetic constraints imposed on the women's bodies and construct the face as a synecdoche of the subject, the mirror of the soul, a potential site of resistance to the order metonymized by the costume, and a topography our gazes explore. This becomes especially prominent in the use of extreme close-ups that single out specific parts of the face such as eyes (S1E8, S1E10, S2E5, S2E8, S2E10, S2E12), noses (S1E3, S1E6, S2E11), mouths (S1E2), ears (S2E5, S3E2) and even temples (S1E6), hair (S2E11), hands (S1E1, S1E4, S1E6, S1E7, S1E10, S2E1, S2E4–S2E9, S2E11, S2E13, S3E10, S3E11), fingers (S3E3, S3E8), and even objects like a blanket (S2E6), a record player (S2E8), candles (S3E3), or Eden's Bible (S2E13). Such shots that resort to a *bokeh* effect[6] create a visuality that is not just optical but haptic, as the increasing reliance on the motif of the hands suggest.

The haptic quality of the blur has also been noted by Beugnet in both experimental and art cinema (73–75). The blur becomes a sensual plastic material that washes over the face and encourages our gaze to likewise play over the surface of the screen. These haptic aesthetics can be reinforced by the kind of profilmic events identified by Laura U. Marks,[7] which draw attention to the surface of the image: transparent or semi-transparent surfaces such as curtains, windows, windshields (S3E11), and puddles (S3E10); lens flares provoked by sunlight or artificial light, a "technical veil" (Aumont 23) which reveals the image as a surface to be touched by our gaze just as the light plays over the lens/screen. The utilization of slow motion also contributes to the haptic aesthetics by attempting "to evoke the intensity of embodied experience" (Marks 216). I would thus add a nuance to Puschak's conclusion that "the shallow depth of field close-ups are an effective way to identify with Offred," which is mainly based on S1E1. Not only is filmic intimacy distributed among the main characters (Emily, Luke, Moira), but this space is simultaneously one of alienation (between the subject and the world) and one of connection (between two or more subjects, but also between the characters and the viewers). The use of shallow focus close shots indicates that subjectivity, in *The Handmaid's Tale*, should be understood as a corporeal and psychological state, as cognition, emotion, and sensation. It is this haptic visuality that operates, as in Laura Marks's thesis (191), as a mode of resistance to the optical visuality of the oppressive patriarchal world of Gilead, a place where subjects are under constant surveillance by the Eyes.

[6] "[I]n the 1990s it was recognised as an explicit technique, dubbed 'bokeh' after the Japanese word for blur, in which clarity and fuzziness are counterpoised in the same image (creating a distinction between 'good' and 'bad' bokeh, depending on whether or not the results are visually pleasing)" (Jay 92).

[7] Marks says: "The viewer's vision takes a tactile relation to the surface of the image, moving over the figures that merge in the image plane as though even faraway things are only an inch from one's body" (181).

An Oppressive Cinematic Space

As Kuschak points out, shallow focus also serves to construct the oppressive world of Gilead and the preconditions for its rise in the pre-Gilead US. It is combined with two classical horror movie strategies: the play on foreground/background and on onscreen/offscreen. The corollary to the intimate cinematic space created by the shallow focus close shots is that it reinforces the sense of beyondness of the blurry space by conflating the midground and the background in one homogeneous blur: everything that lies beyond the focused subject is a confused blur. This blur is just as expressive of the subject's subjectivity as the face.

Indeed, one of the series' key poetic devices is the alternation between shallow focus close shots and deep focus long shots with symmetrical compositions that have been described as Kubrickian (Buder 2017). Such long shots inscribe the women within a space that is objectively oppressive. In the close shots, however, Gilead is a fuzzy background inhabited by dark silhouettes. Mr. Waterford (S1E2, S1E4, S2E10), Commander Lawrence (S3E3), Guards (S1E10, S2E3, S2E9, S3E2, S3E10), Aunts (S1E1, S2E4, S3E1), the attorney representing the State (S1E3)—these characters materialize in the background as dark figures and sometimes even smudges that threaten to brutally invade the foreground to castigate, beat, rape, or kill the handmaids. This is also the case of Nick when he threatens Mr. Waterford (S2E13), and of Mrs. Waterford (S1E10) and even of the handmaids when they stone the alleged rapist (S1E1) or hang three traitors of Gilead (S3E7), though the color scheme (blue and red) makes the women more distinct. Coming into focus is thus synonymous with violation, whether it is an intervention in the foreground or just someone noticing the handmaids' transgression.

Shallow focus renders the presences in the background more spectral because the boundaries between the silhouette and the rest of the environment are less clear-cut. I would also suggest that, because of its indistinctness, the blur somewhat tempers the boundary between onscreen and offscreen space: that is to say, the offscreen is pictured in our minds as a vague continuation rather than as a sharply distinct world comprising streets, buildings, houses, trees, and so forth. It is thus the blurry background that is charged with a sense of permanent menace because the materialization of a dark presence seems both more likely and less noticeable than with deep focus composition. Viewers, like the characters, find themselves on their constant guard. The device becomes so systematic that its use is quite unexpected when a potential foe turns out to be a friend, such as the Mexican secretary who offers to help Offred (S1E6) or Nick (S2E2). In the pre-Gilead sequences, however, it draws attention to the fact that such threatening figures (the kidnapper in S1E2, a guard in S2E6) were already present; the flashback structure aims to make us aware of this and to realize that the characters were blind to the potential—just as we ourselves may be today.

Fallacy and Pregnancy of Memory

The flashbacks in the Hulu series are much more classical than the jarring analepses of a novel whose structure is based on fragmentation. Dennis Tredy notes that June's "flashbacks gradually disappear over time," making way for flashbacks from the perspective of other characters (212). In the series, the echoes between past and present are always based on obvious diegetic motifs, at least in retrospect. Episode S1E1 immediately sets the tone: June remembers Moira when walking past the Wall, her daughter Hannah at the aquarium when taking a bath, Janine's patched-up eye when thinking of punishment. Later episodes abide by this rule—in seasons 2 and 3, which features fewer flashbacks than season 1, episode S2E11 juxtaposes Hannah's and Holly/Nicole's births, episode S3E4 three communions—with only the episode (S1E7) relating Luke's escape being entirely unmediated.

The blur is a classical marker of dreams and memory (Beugnet 76–89). Often associated with, and even produced by, a dissolve,[8] and frequently combined with slow motion and sound bridges (Beugnet 80), it both highlights the distance between past and present and functions as a sort of visual bridge between the two. In the Hulu series, the use of shallow focus in the scenes of the past emphasizes the fragility of these memories. Again, episode S1E1 sets the tone: blurry images of June make way for images in which lens flare and blur are combined, when Hannah is taken away and when June drinks alcohol from a red cup, while the blurry background overwhelming the cinematic space of a lateral two-shot of June and Moira talking seems to foreshadow the forced separation of women in Gilead. In episode S1E8, June says of Nick in voice-over, "I want to know him, memorize him, so I can live on the image later. I should have done that with Luke because he's fading"—an image illustrated by the lateral close-

---

[8] Maureen Turim cites an example in *Humoresque* (Warner, Jean Negulesco, 1946) (121).

up of June and Luke kissing in S1E5, significantly in the episode where she makes love with Nick. And in season 2 (S2E10, S2E11), where both June and Emily express their concern that their children will have forgotten them, past images of Hannah are again blurry and often combined with lens flare (S2E11, S2E13)—such images can also be found in season 3 (S3E4, S3E13). The same combination of devices are associated with other characters: Serena when she remembers how passionate she and Fred used to be (S1E6), Luke when he thinks about Hannah and June (S1E7), Moira when she remembers her lover Odette (S2E7), Aunt Lydia whose past as a school teacher is revealed (S3E8). The series expresses in particular the ephemeral quality of joyful images: the figures cut against the blurry background evoking the emotional power they carry threaten to collapse into abstract shapes and color, for example, the memories of Hannah and Luke at the fair (S1E4) or the beach (S1E9). Significantly, this is not the case of the traumatic Red Center flashbacks (S1E1, S1E4, S1E10, S2E3), or of June and other women being herded into cages by brutal soldiers (S3E13), which, probably because they are so directly connected to the present state of the world (the handmaids are even sent back to the Red Center in S2E1), are thus cut off from the memories of better times.

Remembrance, as in Proust, requires an effort. But in *The Handmaid's Tale*, it is also an essential lifeline. For Offred, as for Emily in S2E2, losing touch with memory would mean losing touch with children, friends, and lovers. Pointedly, when Offred decides to subject herself to Gilead's order in episode S2E5, the flashbacks, along with June's voice-over, disappear. For the women of Gilead, oblivion is self-destruction. Remembrance can also be a coming to terms, as when June reflects on her relationship with her mother (S2E3), Serena gauges the difference between her former and current relationship with Fred (S1E6, S2E6), Nick realizes Commander Pryce was right to ask him to keep an eye on Waterford (S1E8), and, more dramatically still, Moira mourns the death of her lover (S2E7). The characters also have to come to terms with their responsibility in the new world order, whether they played an active role like Mrs. Waterford, Nick or Commander Lawrence, or a passive one like June and basically almost everybody else except people like her mother (in S2E3, June's study of articles from *The Boston Globe* leads her to remember her mother's activism). So the blur both expresses and symbolizes the vulnerability and resilience of the self.

Many flashbacks are framed by shallow focus close shots of the remembering subject. By affecting both the memories and the subject's face, the blur signifies the process of remembrance itself; it expresses a continuum—an overlap—between the subject and her memories, much like a soundbridge, a device that is often utilized in such scenes. The blur makes manifest the subject's cognitive and emotional experience of these memories; it colors the memory with bittersweet longing or sorrow. Often combined with slow motion, back lighting, and lens flares, the blurry images of the past equally resort to haptic aesthetics, suggesting that the subject's experience of them is not just mental but carnal. The images we are invited to touch with our gazes are images that touch June, Emily, Moira, Serena, Luke, and even Aunt Lydia, images that they can feel in their guts. The blur thus signifies both the cognitive fragility and emotional power of memory, the power to move, to hurt, to console.

Finally, it is the continuum created by the blur that may occasionally lead us to question the status of certain scenes. For instance, S1E3 opens with a close-up of Ofglen accompanied with June's voice-over saying, "I didn't even know her name". June's status as narrator, reinforced by the series' "Previously on"s (Gelly 2019), initially leads us to believe she is picturing Ofglen's fate, and it is only later on in the episode when the narration focalizes on Ofglen that we realize the narration had blended two separate realities (June's voice, Emily's image), thus breaching the initial terms of the narrative. Similarly, the second scene of S1E4, which is comprised of blurry images of June lying down in her closet, appears as a potential fantasy because it is enveloped in the same aesthetics as the flashbacks that frame it; it is only later in the episode that the reality of the scene is confirmed. The blur thus not only evokes the kinship between memory and fantasy; the visual homogeneity introduces a regime of uncertainty that generates tension and, aesthetically speaking, allows for potential variation.

Loss or Assertion of Identity

On occasion, the blur threatens to wash over the characters in the present as well. Such instances occur at moments when a character feels her identity or selfhood is threatened. Recalling the high school hallway scenes of *Elephant* (Gus Van Sant, 2003), in which horror and violence erupt against a soft background (Beugnet 106–7), the opening flashback of S1E10 presents entry into the Red Center as, dramatically, forced subjection and, visually, a dissolution of the Figure. The scene which opens the season 1 finale thus confirms what the gynecologist scene in S1E4 already suggested and that a similar scene in S2E6 merely drives in: the blur threatens to contaminate all, including those like the doctor and Mrs. Waterford, who are complicit with the system of oppression. In such scenes, the Figure that was cut against the blurry background fully merges with it, becoming a blotch of color—blue in the case of a Wife, gray in the case of the doctor. Because the blur is equated with loss of selfhood, stepping into focus logically becomes synonymous with empowerment or at least the struggle to maintain selfhood. This occurs as early as S1E2 when June is pacing her room, in S1E7 when Luke makes it to Canada, and at the end of S2E9 when June is reinvigorated by the discovery that Moira has escaped and looks at the camera and says: "I know I should accept the reality of you being born here. Make my peace. Well fuck that." The series' logic is to increase the number of instances of emerging from and fading into the blur as resistance gains momentum and the oppression accordingly acts to suppress it. A variation occurs in episode S3E7: a white blur threatens to erase Emily's face in close-up when she is questioned about the violent acts she committed in Gilead.

In such scenes, the image is momentarily flattened into a general blur. Utterly lacking any depth, it invites a haptic gaze more forcefully than in previous instances because the gaze is led to play over the surface in search of the fading Figure—this is all the more the case when the surface of the screen is redoubled by a profilmic surface such as a curtain or the lens flare's technical veil. Fascination for the mesmerizing blotches of moving light and color may even lead viewers to become momentarily sidetracked, as far as the narrative is concerned. Indeed, such moments are all the more jarring as the series largely abides by the conventions of classical narration (goal-oriented characters, cause-effect logic). Like the Bergman-influenced superimpositions of *Hannibal* (NBC, 2013–2015)—the image of Hannah in S1E1 touching the blurry aquarium recalls a shot from *Persona* (Ingmar Bergman, 1966) analyzed by Beugnet (87)—the moments of complete blur in which the characters threaten to dissolve become instances where plot threatens to disappear, and narrative cinema threatens to collapse into art or avant-garde cinema. This is not to say that they are utterly deprived of a narrative function—on the contrary, they express the character's loss of selfhood—but they do introduce a break in the narration that is more characteristic of art-cinema narration.

Quite paradoxically, given that the focus is a mechanical consequence of the optical apparatus, such blurry images are more pictorial than photographic, another paradox underlined by Beugnet in her book (90–104). They exhibit the dilemma Gilles Deleuze identified at the heart of painting: "Painting has neither a model to represent nor a story to narrate. It thus has two possible ways of escaping the figurative: toward pure form, through abstraction; or toward the purely figural, through extraction or isolation" (2). If shallow focus compositions evince a tension between the figurative and the figural, the instances of total blur evince a tension between the figural and perhaps not so much abstraction as "formlessness," if one follows Beugnet (103); in so doing, they seem to hesitate between the two paths much of painting has taken following the invention of photography and cinema. Such moments hark back to a pictorial ideal of cinema that was common in the early years of cinema when impressionist directors/film theorists such as Germaine Dullac, Jean Epstein, and Abel Gance and others were trying to defend the medium against the claim of merely reproducing reality. These moments adapt Atwood's aesthetics of fragmentation in a more radical fashion than the flashbacks, which remain, as we have seen, fairly classical in terms of narration and typical of complex television.

Conclusion

The poetics of blur are, no doubt, a means for the Hulu series to display its artistic credentials, inscribing itself in the noble lineage of Francis Bacon, Maya Deren, Ingmar Bergman, Stanley Kubrick, and Terrence Malick. But as Evan Puschak argues, it is also used to visualize the handmaids' intimate space and the threatening world that surrounds them, to suggest the fragile, dreamlike quality of memories and their power to touch in the present, and to manifest the danger of losing oneself and the resilience of maintaining oneself. The common denominator is that the blur is a marker of subjectivity. Shallow focus is used fairly consistently throughout series, more frequently depending on the narrative of a given episode. Variation is effected through expansion (to other characters), combination (with other devices), and occasionally inversion. Shallow focus thus participates in the organic cohesion of *The Handmaid's Tale* (2017–); though, like any device, it runs the risk of becoming hackneyed given the duration of a series, the specificity of blur—its fundamental vagueness—paradoxically produces an unstable homogeneity. Perhaps, the fault one could deplore is that Hulu's *The Handmaid's Tale* is so unremittingly unnerving.

Shallow focus is potentially dynamic in itself since it is based on a tension between focus and blur, and often between two layers. This dynamic potential is highlighted by the technique of rack focusing, that is, shifting the focus from foreground to background or vice versa, a technique which the Hulu series makes abundant use of. Rack focusing points to the instability of shallow focus: blur and focus can tip over into each other at any moment.[9] Far from being static, as might seem at first glance, shallow focus is charged with energy. Shallow focus is also productive as a site of multiple aesthetic modes. First, it is used both as a means to focus attention on key narrative elements and as mode of expression more typical of art and avant-garde cinema. Second, it is underpinned by the tension between optical and haptic visuality, a gaze that looks and a gaze that touches, the haptic involving attention to the details of the topography of the bodies captured as to the flat surface of the image. Third, its dynamics play on the tension between figurative and non-figurative on the one hand, and between figural and formlessness on the other.

These aesthetic tensions—notably between photographic and pictorial[10]—do more than express the tensions at stake on the narrative level—between an intimate and oppressive space, between past and present, between self and object. The paradox that blur can become focused and focused can become blur is an expression of the paradoxes at the heart of the series' politics: that the present is very much present in the past and that the past still resonates powerfully in the present; that an intimate space is paradoxically created by the oppressive space as a sort of surplus; and that subjection, as Judith Butler has argued, is also what produces both subjectivity and agency.[11] In *The Handmaid's Tale* (2017–), shallow focus expresses the transformative power of liminality: the idea that the political and the ethical will paradoxically be produced by the dominant

---

[9] So far, the series has not resorted to the possibility of reducing the aperture to shift from shallow to deep focus within a shot and produce a layered composition.

[10] Eileen Rositzka notes the influence of Edgar Degas's painting "Interior" also known as "The Rape" (1868–1869) on the design of the Waterfords's house's interior (200–1).

[11] "The paradox of subjectivation (*assujetissement*) is precisely that the subject who would resist such norms is itself enabled, if not produced, by such norms. Although this constitutive constraint does not foreclose the possibility of agency, it does locate agency as a reiterative or rearticulatory practice, immanent to power, and not a relation of external opposition to power" (Butler 15).

forces and materialized in their margins as a side effect. For in the end, June has become the activist daughter—and in season 3 the killer of bad men and the savior of children—her mother Holly wanted her to be: "Cause I ain't no hollaback girl/I ain't no hollaback girl."

Works Cited

Atwood, Margaret. *The Handmaid's Tale*. London: Vintage, 1996 [1985].
Aumont, Jacques. "The Veiled Image: The Luminous Formless." *Indefinite Visions: Cinema and the Attractions of Uncertainty*. Martine Beugnet, Allan Cameron and Arild Fetveit, eds. Edinburgh: Edinburgh UP, 2018, pp. 17–37.
Beugnet, Martine. *L'Attrait du flou*. Crisnée: Yellow Now, 2017.
Bordwell, David. *Narration in the Fiction Film*. Madison, WI: U of Wisconsin P, 1985.
———. *Poetics of Cinema*. New York and London: Routledge, 2007.
Buder, Emily. "'The Handmaid's Tale's: DP-Turned-Director Reed Morano on 'Disturbing, Kubrick-Inspired' Series." *Nofilmschool.com* (April 27, 2017). https://nofilmschool.com/2017/04/the-handmaids-tale-reed-morano-hulu. Viewed on May 12, 2020.
Butler, Judith. *Bodies That Matter: On the Discursive Limits of "Sex"*. New York and London: Routledge, 1993.
Cornillon, Claire. *Sérialité et transmédialité : infinis des fictions contemporaines*. Paris: Honoré Champion, 2018.
Deleuze, Gilles. *Francis Bacon: The Logic of Sensation*. London and New York: Continuum, 2003 [1981].
Esquenazi, Jean-Pierre. *Les Séries télévisées : L'avenir du cinéma ?* Paris: Armand Colin, 2014 [2010].
Gelly, Christophe. "Paratexte et idéologie dans le récit transmédiatique: le cas de *The Handmaid's Tale* (Hulu, 2017–)." "Péritexte et transmédialité: objects culturels en convergence." Keynote given at Université Téluq, Quebec, May 23–24, 2019.
The Handmaid's Tale. Creator: Bruce Miller. With Elisabeth Moss (June Osborne), Yvonne Strahovski (Serena Joy Waterford), Joseph Fiennes (Fred Waterford) Anne Dowd (Aunt Lydia Clements), Max Mignhella (Nick Blaine), Luke Bankole (T Fegbenle), Samira Wiley (Moira Strand) and Alexis Bledel (Emily Malek). Hulu, 2017–. 4 Seasons to date.
Hendershot, Heather. "The Handmaid's Tale as Ustopian Allegory: 'Stars and Stripes Forever, Baby.'" *Film Quarterly* 72.1 (Fall 2018). https://filmquarterly.org/2018/09/14/the-handmaids-tale-as-ustopian-allegory-stars-and-stripes-forever-baby/

Jay, Martin. "Genres of Blur." *Indefinite Visions: Cinema and the Attractions of Uncertainty*. Martine Beugnet, Allan Cameron and Arild Fetveit, eds. Edinburgh: Edinburgh UP, 2018, pp. 90–102.

Marks, Laura U. *The Skin of the Film: Intercultural Cinema, Embodiment, and the Senses*. Durham and London: Duke University Press, 2000.

Mittel, Jason. *Complex TV: The Poetics of Contemporary Television Storytelling*. New York and London: New York University Press, 2015.

Puschak, Evan. "One Reason Why *The Handmaid's Tale* Won Emmys Best Drama." *Nerdwriter1* (August 31, 2017). https://www.youtube.com/watch?time_continue=19&v=cY4aCnfrqss. Viewed on January 7, 2019.

Rositzka, Eileen. "No Light without Shadow: The Question of Realism in Volker Schlöndorgg's *The Handmaid's Tale* and Hulu's TV Series." The Handmaid's Tale: *Teaching Dystopia, Feminism, and Resistance across Disciplines and Borders*. Karen A. Rizenhoff and Janis L. Goldie (eds.). London: Lexington Books, 2019, pp. 195–205.

Tredy, Dennis. "Shifting Perspectives and Reaccentuation: Adapting *The Handmaid's Tale* as a Film in 1990 and as a Hulu TV Series in 2017/2018." The Handmaid's Tale: *Teaching Dystopia, Feminism, and Resistance across Disciplines and Borders*. Karen A. Rizenhoff and Janis L. Goldie (eds.). London: Lexington Books, 2019, pp. 207–21.

Turim, Maureen. *Flashbacks in Film: Memory & History*. Routledge, London and New York, 1989.

Wells-Lassagne, Shannon. *Television and Serial Adaptation*. New York: Routledge, 2017.

Feminism, Facts, and Fear: The Protean Reception of *The Handmaid's Tale* (Atwood 1985, Miller 2017–)

Elizabeth Mullen

When Margaret Atwood's visceral dystopia first appeared in 1985, Mary McCarthy of the *New York Times* criticized the book for its implausibility, unfavorably comparing it to the more convincing horrors of Aldous Huxley, George Orwell, and Anthony Burgess. McCarthy's main argument was that the "extreme feminism" of Atwood's tale posited a world so far removed from the realm of the possible that it could spark no real sense of fear in the reasonable reader in 1986 (McCarthy 1). Bruce Miller's 2017 television adaptation of Atwood's novel received no such censure. From the start, Miller's *Handmaid's Tale* has been lauded for its eerie resemblance to present-day America—to such an extent that protestors dressed in Handmaid costumes have demonstrated in front of the US Capitol, Donald Trump's Mar-a-Lago resort, and around the world (Hauser, *The New York Times*, 2017).

E. Mullen (✉)
Faculté des lettres et sciences humaines, Université de Bretagne Occidentale, Brest, France
e-mail: elizabeth.mullen@univ-brest.fr

© The Author(s), under exclusive license to Springer Nature Switzerland AG 2021
S. Wells-Lassagne, F. McMahon (eds.), *Adapting Margaret Atwood*, Palgrave Studies in Adaptation and Visual Culture,
https://doi.org/10.1007/978-3-030-73686-6_10

How do facts and fiction intertwine in Miller's adaptation and how has the series visibly impacted the American public? This analysis will focus on how the television adaptation of *The Handmaid's Tale* incorporates "real world" elements into its fictional realm, and how contemporary audiences have appropriated elements of Atwood's and Miller's fictional worlds to their own ends. The ramifications and significance of these various forms of appropriation in a post-factual world merit further exploration.

Fact and Speculative Fiction

Both Miller's series and Atwood's novel create their dystopian worlds by consciously blending contemporary factual and fictional elements. Atwood famously described *The Handmaid's Tale* as speculative fiction—that is to say, "a work that employs the means already to hand, such as DNA identification and credit cards, and that takes place on Planet Earth" (*The Guardian* 2005). In numerous interviews Atwood references Orwell's *1984* as a source of inspiration, as well her desire to create a dystopia narrated from a female perspective. The cultural and political climate of the 1980s fueled her tale, from increasingly repressive Republican policies under Ronald Reagan to the outlawing of contraception in Romania, as well as concern over the damage wrought by toxic waste and falling birth rates in North America. Then, as now, women's rights were under attack by vocal and media-savvy religious leaders increasingly associated with Republican conservatives in the United States.

This is the context of *The Handmaid's Tale*, a world in which the region formerly known as New England, home to the original Puritans, has been transformed into a rigid patriarchal theocracy. In this post-nuclear landscape, women have lost all agency and are sorted according to their biological worth: Wives (nominally above other women, but still forbidden to read, write, or travel independently), Handmaids (still-fertile women who serve as "walking wombs"), Aunts (female enforcers who train the Handmaids), Marthas (for housework and cooking), Econowives (multi-purpose females for the lower classes), and Unwomen (those of no physical use, banished to the Colonies to work in the toxic waste dumps). In this new Republic, renamed Gilead, women are stripped of all forms of agency and identity, forced to give up their former jobs, their former clothes, and their former names. In Gilead, they are defined solely in terms of men (be they Commanders, Eyes, or Econohusbands), color-coded by category in accordance to Biblical symbol and tradition: virginal blue for

Wives, military brown for Aunts, drab gray for Marthas (named for Christ's attendant who saw to His day-to-day needs and those of his followers) (Luke 10:38–42), and scarlet red for the Handmaids—a color reminiscent of bodies and sin, from Mary Magdalene to the Whore of Babylon to Hawthorne's *The Scarlet Letter*. Each Handmaid takes on the name of her Commander, further marking her loss of identity and her redefinition as property.

In her 1985 novel, Atwood's first-person narrator, Offred, creates a kind of textual flashback to compare her life before Gilead to her current situation, and in so doing draws on deeper cultural connotations. Recounting a walk through her former neighborhood, she reflects on changing codes surrounding women's behavior:

> I remember the rules, rules that were never spelled out but that every woman knew: don't open your door to a stranger, even if he says he's the police. Make him slide his ID under the door. Don't stop on the road to help a motorist pretending to be in trouble. Keep the locks on and keep going. If anyone whistles, don't turn to look. Don't go into a laundromat by yourself, at night.
>
> I think about laundromats. What I wore to them: shorts, jeans, jogging pants. What I put into them: my own clothes, my own soap, my own money, money I had earned myself. I think about having such control.
>
> Now we walk along the same street, in red pairs, and no man shouts obscenities at us, speaks to us, touches us. No one whistles.
>
> There is more than one kind of freedom, says Aunt Lydia. Freedom to and freedom from. In the days of anarchy, it was freedom to. Now you are being given freedom from. Don't underrate it. (34)

Released at the height of a wave of protests organized by Women Against Pornography—a movement that posited a link between pornography and violence against women (Bronstein)—the novel's readers would have been fully aware of the atmosphere of malaise that permeated North American society at the time, marked by the media frenzy around serial killers like John Wayne Gacy (The "Killer Clown") or Ted Bundy, who was known to impersonate figures of authority and the disabled in order to lure his victims. On a deeper level, the expression "freedom to" and "freedom from" hearkens back to Franklin Delano Roosevelt's Four Freedoms, revealingly organized around Freedom of Speech, Freedom of Religion (both gone in Gilead), Freedom from Fear, and Freedom from Want. Aunt Lydia underscores a particularly repressive and patriarchal interpretation of the last two Freedoms while simultaneously rooting Gilead within the context of American identity and history.

In the Hulu television series adapted from Atwood's novel, showrunner Bruce Miller takes a similar approach. He adapts the text's first-person narration through extensive use of Offred's voice in voiceover. Flashback scenes are filmed in such a way as to correspond to contemporary reality in a solidly blue state: (mostly white) liberal progressives getting coffee and carrying signs in protest marches; then, as the overthrow of the government takes hold, women being stripped of their bank accounts and their jobs before being rounded up and processed into groups within the new social order. These scenes draw their power from their intense realism: the viewer notes just how paralyzed by surprise, how completely unprepared the characters are for the swift, violent overthrow of their world.

We see an example of this reaction in a scene from Season 1, Episode 3. In flashback, Offred (June in the series) remembers a scene from her former life. June and her best friend Moira, a recently married lesbian woman of color, stop to get coffee at their regular spot after a run. The sun is shining as the two women joke and smile back and forth, paying little attention to the male barista taking their order despite his curt reply to June's question about the woman who usually works there. When June's card is declined "for insufficient funds," she reacts with surprise and asks him to renew his attempt ("Can you just run it again?"). His reply ("Can you come back when you have some money?) takes her aback; this feeling deepens into shock when he responds to Moira's admonition with vulgar hostility: "What's your problem? Fucking sluts—get the fuck out of here!" Dumbfounded, June remarks "Are you serious?" before herding a protesting Moira out the door (S1E3, 3:18–4:37).

The scene underscores the ease with which the women's agency and independence are overthrown. The increasingly violent remarks of the white male server provoke not shock and outrage but shock and dismay: faced with pointedly misogynistic abuse that seems to come out of nowhere, the women are left speechless. The shaky, rapid camera work in the scene mimics that of video footage shot on a mobile phone, yet the frame is constructed in a deliberate manner: as the young man behind the counter becomes more abusive, the back of his head and his upper body block out part of the frame, forcing the women to retreat through the back of the frame and creating a feeling of being trapped, cut off with no escape. A number of flashbacks throughout the series create similar effects.

Within the world of Gilead, the camera work is quite different, at times relying on drone shots and the use of a Steadicam to create a more dream-like quality, while at other times cutting sharply between shots. Color serves as a character here, the rich red of the Handmaids' uniforms contrasting with the sickly greenish blue of the Wives and the dull grays and browns of the Marthas and the Aunts. Miller draws on familiar scenes, then twists them slightly to create an atmosphere of malaise. For instance, in a series of supermarket scenes, it takes the viewer a moment to realize that there are no words on any of the products on the shelves, only pictures. Similarly, as subsequent seasons of the series move beyond Atwood's novel, violent images increasingly take the place of words, amping up the discomfort viewers feel while simultaneously drawing on the culture's collective visual and auditory memory by framing scenes in ways both familiar to contemporary audiences and reminiscent of the 1980s. For instance, in the opening scenes of Season 2, Episode 1, red-clad Handmaids are herded onto rows of gallows as Kate Bush's 1988 classic, "Woman's Work," a song about the pain and loss of childbirth, plays in the background (S2E1, 07:11–09:20). Similarly, in Season 2, Episode 6, (S2E6, 52:52–54:54) the tone and vocabulary of Commander Waterford's speech as he opens the new Rachel and Leah Red Center closely mimic those of current conservative politicians like Mike Pence.[1] Visually, the sequence also looks familiar. After the camera pans the room full of Commanders, with Handmaids clustered around the edges of the Center on the other side of the glass, one of them slowly breaks from the cluster of Handmaids; after turning her back to the Commander, she shows the detonator clasped in her hand to the group of Handmaids before running down the center aisle and blowing up the building. The pacing and camera movements of the scene follow those of Apple Computer's award-winning "1984" Superbowl commercial for the Macintosh computer (YouTube, *Apple 1984*). In it, an athletic woman runs down the middle of the aisle in a large auditorium filled with technocratic zombies. She flings a sledgehammer into the onscreen representation of old régime, causing the room to explode. By thus drawing on familiar cultural tropes, the series underscores both the familiarity and the immediacy of the narrative, incorporating facts (and artifacts) into fiction.

---

[1] See, for instance, Mike Pence's October 12, 2016, address at conservative Christian Liberty University, https://www.youtube.com/watch?time_continue=16&v=3drhHVKx1ys&feature=emb_logo. Accessed 22 May 2020.

Ordinary Horrors: *The Handmaid's Tale* and Contemporary Politics

Since the series début in 2017, the same year Donald Trump was inaugurated as the 45th President of the United States, numerous media outlets have remarked on the increasing permeability between the world represented in the series and the current cultural and political climate.[2] As Jessica Valenti of *The Guardian* puts it,

> That's part of what makes the show so terrifying—we don't have to be in full-Gilead to understand that we already live in a misogynist nightmare. American women may not be handmaids, but we are still living in a country where conservative politicians would mandate forced pregnancy. Where women are sentenced to decades in prison for ending their pregnancies. Where a man who believes 25% of the female population should be executed[3] is being hailed as a "singular talent" and "rigorous thinker."
>
> We don't have to imagine the worst, because women are already in deep, serious trouble. (Valenti)

Journalist Joe Berkowitz of *Fast Company* goes further, seeing distinct parallels between the fictional emergence of Gilead in Miller's adaptation and current political trends:

> *The Handmaid's Tale* doesn't happen overnight. *Nineteen Eighty-Four* doesn't happen overnight. Mao Zedong's Cultural Revolution didn't happen overnight. It's a slow, incremental slide, soundtracked by the people who guide and abet it denying what's happening. America's slide into fas-

---

[2] See, for instance, Joe Berkowitz, "America's Slow, Scary Transformation Into 'The Handmaid's Tale,'" *Fast Company*, 6-29-2018, www.fastcompany.com/90178409/maybe-it-is-okay-to-compare-2018-america-to-the-handmaids-tale. Accessed September 18, 2018. See also Jessica Valenti, "Why 'The Handmaid's Tale' is more relevant one year after the first season," *The Guardian*, 25 April 2018. www.theguardian.com/commentisfree/2018/apr/25/handmaids-tale-season-2-return-trump-america-2018. Accessed September 18, 2018. On the podcast, *Eyes on Gilead*, showrunner Bruce Miller discusses the show's increasing political relevance. www.sbs.com.au/guide/audiotrack/eyes-gilead-interview-handmaids-tale-showrunner-bruce-miller. Accessed October 5, 2019.

[3] Valenti refers here to conservative political commentator Kevin D. Williamson, who in a Twitter exchange and on a National Review podcast in 2014 claimed that abortion should be punished like any other criminal activity, up to and including hanging. See Michael M. Grymbaum, "*The Atlantic* Cuts Ties with Conservative Writer Kevin Williamson," *The New York Times*, April 5, 2018. https://www.nytimes.com/2018/04/05/business/media/kevin-williamson-atlantic.html. Accessed 29 May 2020.

cism may have begun before Trump got elected, but the descent ever since has been rapid. […]

It might seem alarmist, but in an America where women's bodily autonomy hangs in serious jeopardy, the president's fans embrace the concept of murdering the press, and dissent looks increasingly headed toward becoming illegal, being alarmist is merely a means of survival. (Berkowitz)

Atwood's 1985 text underlines a similar sentiment: "Ordinary, said Aunt Lydia, is what you are used to. This may not seem ordinary to you now, but after a time it will. It will become ordinary" (43). Clearly, the reception of Miller's and Atwood's texts points to a sense of urgency inspired by real-world parallels to those texts.

In an attempt to alert the general public to the dangers of this gradual slide toward Gilead, a number of protesters have embraced the visual symbolism in *The Handmaid's Tale* as a means of jumpstarting conversations around a number of issues, especially reproductive rights. Following the series's April 2017 release, scores of women dressed in red cloaks and white bonnets began turning up at rallies and protests around the country—at state capitols in Texas, Ohio, New Hampshire and Missouri, at Trump's Mar-a-Lago resort, and at national protest events everywhere from the Capitol building to the Supreme Court. Each protest focused on both individual threats to reproductive rights and a more generalized refusal to bow to patriarchal pressure. Signs bearing slogans like "Make Atwood Fiction Again," "Never Gilead," and "Nolite te Bastardes Carborandorum" specifically referenced ties between these real-life protests and the dystopian representation of patriarchal theocracy of the novel and the series. In the case of the Brett Kavanaugh Supreme Court hearings, the visual parallels between protesters in red cloaks lining the circular public gallery and the Rachel and Leah Center opening scene discussed earlier (a scene which aired after the hearings) further underscore both the adaptive power of the series and its uncanny relevance.

With all these elements clearly pointing to a climate of fear and to an increasingly thin line between fact and fiction, it is worth examining the impact and the real effects of the cultural "spreading" of *The Handmaid's Tale*. For all their visibility, the red capes and white caps do not seem to be effecting any real change in terms of policy: these scarlet-cloaked women are clearly being seen, but there is no evidence that they are being heard. A close examination of the adverse effects of the kinds of communicative abundance (Keane) demonstrated here may shed some light.

Communicative Abundance, Parody, and Commodification

In his essay on communicative abundance, Keane points out that, paradoxically, the widespread dissemination of information and content on an ever-growing scale can lead not to a more democratic shared understanding of reality but rather to the questioning of what, in fact, is real and what is not, depending on the source of the content and the range of its dissemination (21–23). The current phenomenon of "fake news" points to just such an interpretation. Along the same lines, parody in general, and recent parodies of *The Handmaid's Tale* in particular, bear closer scrutiny.

In her groundbreaking study, Linda Hutcheon points out that parody is by nature "a form of authorized transgression [...] an inscription of the past in the present" with both "potentially conservative" and "potentially revolutionary" elements (xii). A number of late-night comedy programs and comic websites have embraced this practice when it comes to *The Handmaid's Tale*. In his September 5, 2018, coverage of the Brett Kavanaugh hearings, *The Daily Show*'s Trevor Noah pictured Senate Majority Leader Mitch McConnell in a red robe and white bonnet, acting the role of a radical feminist (YouTube); in the same report, he revealed that the Senate had blocked the disclosure of hundreds of thousands of documents related to Kavanaugh's record as a judge.

Similarly, on two occasions, *Saturday Night Live* based sketches on the Hulu series. The week of May 7, 2018, shortly after the series premiere, a sketch featuring Chris Pine mimics the show's visual style and ominous soundtrack, juxtaposing the handmaids' terror with clueless remarks from "straight white bros" unable to comprehend the seriousness of the situation (SNL Handmaid Pine, YouTube). In a sketch the following week, entitled *Handmaids in the City* (May 13, 2018), comic Amy Schumer channels *Sex in the City*'s Carrie Bradshaw in voiceover as a group of red-cloaked women make grating jokes about their circumstances and laugh crazily along with a canned laugh track. The sketch ends with the tagline, "Handmaids in the city: if you're not traumatized, you're not watching television" (SNL City, YouTube). In both parodies, the comedic situation stems from the contrast between the actors' behavior and the appalling conditions portrayed.

Internet channel Funny or Die takes a different approach with their feature, *They Finally Made a Handmaid's Tale for Men*. In this version, in voiceover a male Handmaid mimics the opening lines of Miller's series as the camera intercuts between shots featuring men in red robes and images of recent protests:

> I was asleep before. When they didn't date us because of feminism, we didn't wake up. They ruined *Ghostbusters* [by making an all-female reboot] and we didn't wake up then, either. When they were being shrill bitches 24/7 [accompanied by images of Beyoncé and Elizabeth Warren], we didn't wake up. And now, we are Handmen. The feminazis own us. Like, more or less. My name is Manfred. I had another name—it was Fred. Before the war, I was a Senior VP. Now I'm a Senior VP with some female colleagues. (FOD)

Here the joke stems from the fact that the white male protagonists perceive gender equality as a form of oppression, organizing their resistance movement via Manosphere sites on Reddit and 4Chan. It is a particularly keen use of communicative abundance as it posits certain corners of the internet as safe havens for misogyny.

While pertinent (and hilarious), these parodies and others like them risk undermining the subversion they seek to create through their sheer multiplicity. As parodic references to *The Handmaid's Tale* become more common, they may begin to diminish the impact of the original, rendering such references more and more "ordinary." Witness for example a recent line on the network series *The Big Bang Theory* from Amy Farrah Fowler, a purportedly feminist-friendly character. When asked if she would be okay with her husband being a sperm donor, she cheerfully replies, "Oh absolutely not: I'm the only Handmaid in this tale!" (TBBT S12, Ep 12, 14:56). Referring to the exclusive nature of her marriage in such terms points to a serious reduction in the power of the handmaid signifier.

In a similar vein, we can point to the commercial commodification of *The Handmaid's Tale* in ways that diminish and at times contradict the violence of both the series adaptation and the adapted text. Recently, after a public outcry, costume retailer Yandy was forced to pull its "Sexy Handmaid" Halloween costume consisting of a thigh-length strapless red dress, long cape, and white bonnet (Elassar and Muaddi). Less offensive but equally commercial are the series-based brooches, key chains, wine glasses, T-shirts, mugs, stickers, phone cases, tote bags, cushions, crochet dolls, Christmas ornaments, and fridge magnets available on sites like Redbubble and Etsy. Many products feature sayings and slogans from the texts; among the most popular are feminist manifestos like "They should never have given us uniforms if they don't want us to be an army" and

"Nolite te bastardes carborandorum/Don't let the bastards grind you down." Others seem to take remarks out of context: cushions embroidered with "Praise Be" and fruit-emblazoned hand towels printed with "Blessed be the Fruit" seem to miss the initial significance of those words. Still others use puns to subvert the original message, as is the case with birthday cards which read "Praise be, bitch: here's your damn card" or "Blessed be birthdays: may the card open" (Redbubble.com, Etsy.com).

In the post-factual media landscape of the Trump era, what does the purchase of one of these products signify? Does it indicate a sense of belonging to a greater purpose, or does it take the place of activism altogether? Along similar lines, does the prism of parody help us better to comprehend the force of the parodied text, or does it diminish its power?

As the Hulu series enters its fourth season, global protesters around the world continue to claim the red uniform as their own. And yet, as Emma Grey Ellis points out in a 2019 article in *Wired*, the very universality of the red uniform prevents it from inspiring specific action:

> The costume's flexibility is part of its power, but also keeps handmaids from being real drivers of discourse. Women dressed as handmaids suggest connections between our world and Gilead, but while that's important to consider and the purpose of Atwood's work, it's hardly solution-oriented. Handmaids embody gendered pain and dread so vast it's hard to put into words: sexual violence, physical violence, governments taking control of bodies, bodies valued over beings, being reduced to a womb alone. All they really say is "No to all that," albeit in a highly concise and memorable way. So they win no hearts or minds (Ellis, *Wired* 2019)

Further evidence of the real-world limitations of the power of fiction can be found in the enthusiastic, yet uninspiring, reception of Atwood's 2019 sequel, *The Testaments*. Set 15 years after the events of *The Handmaid's Tale*, the sequel tracks the eventual downfall of the Gilead régime when Aunt Lydia, working as an undercover Resistance mole, manages to arrange for damning information about the Gilead régime to be leaked to the outside world, à la Edward Snowden. The resulting putsch overthrows the Gilead régime for good. The novel was widely praised, receiving numerous accolades, including the 2019 Booker Prize.

And yet, whereas *The Handmaid's Tale* came as a call to action, *The Testaments,* as Michelle Goldberg of the *New York Times* points out, serves more as an escapist fantasy:

Naturally, "The Testaments" is being mined for insights into our current predicament. That's the point of dystopias—to figure out where society might be going. But here's what's shocking about the book: rather than a warning, it reads, in 2019, like wish fulfillment. Instead of a new glimpse of hell, it's a riveting and deeply satisfying escapist fantasy. Gilead is far more barbarous than all but a few contemporary societies, but it's vulnerable in a way that modern populist autocracies are not, because even if women have little power in Gilead, truth does. (Goldberg)

In our current post-truth society, a combination of communicative abundance and the deliberate, weaponized spread of misinformation has led to a world where shocking revelations, no matter how truthful, have lost their power to shock—or to provoke action. In Goldberg's words, "Truth is less suppressed than drowned out."

Atwood's exercise in speculative fiction was written at a time when the United States was in the throes of a massive upsurge of the religious right, led by a former actor who prided himself on his savvy manipulation of the media. *Roe* versus *Wade* was facing challenges at the state level while the ever-escalating nuclear arms race and a wave of environmental disasters (Three Mile Island, Love Canal) left Americans shaken and unsure of the very ground under their feet. Miller's adaptation is being produced at a similar time in American history: religious fundamentalists have not held this much power in the United States since the Puritans first landed in New England (Gilead?) and the country is once again on the brink of nuclear and environmental disaster, led by a former reality TV star who also prides himself on his savvy manipulation of the media—media which, through a combination of communicative abundance and algorithmic polarization, has left its users increasingly unable to separate fact from fiction. Perhaps we can take our cue from Offred's own reasoning when faced with the surfeit of symbolism resulting from the reality of executed bodies hanging in the square, their faces covered and their supposed crimes surely fabrications:

> I look at the one red smile. The red of the smile is the same as the red of the tulips in Serena Joy's garden, towards the base of the flowers where they are beginning to heal. The red is the same, but there is no connection. The tulips are not tulips of blood, the red smiles are not flowers, neither thing makes a comment on the other. The tulip is not a reason for disbelief in the hanged man, or vice versa. Each thing is valid and really there. It is through a field of such valid objects that I must pick my way, every day and in every way. I put a lot of effort into such distinctions. I need to make them. I need to be clear, in my own mind. (43)

Works Cited

"Apple 1984 ad", YouTube. www.youtube.com/watch?v=axSnW-ygU5g. Accessed 20 September 2018.

Atwood, Margaret. *The Handmaid's Tale*. London: Vintage, 1996.

———. "Aliens Have Taken the Place of Angels". *The Guardian*, June 17, 2005. www.theguardian.com/film/2005/jun/17/sciencefictionfantasyandhorror.margaretatwood. Accessed 26 September 2018.

Berkowitz, Joe. "America's Slow, Scary Transformation Into 'The Handmaid's Tale'". *Fast Company*, 6-29-2018. www.fastcompany.com/90178409/maybe-it-is-okay-to-compare-2018-america-to-the-handmaids-tale. Accessed September 18, 2018

Bronstein, Carol. *Battling Pornography: The American Feminist Anti-Pornography Movement, 1976–1986*. Cambridge: Cambridge University Press, 2011.

Elassar, Alaa and Muaddi Nadeem. "Retailer Drops 'Sexy Handmaid's Tale' Costume Following Outcry". *CNN*, September 21, 2018. www.edition.cnn.com/2018/09/21/us/handmaids-tale-halloween-costume-trnd/index.html. Accessed September 26, 2018.

Ellis, Emma Grey, "*Handmaids Tale* Garb is the Viral Protest Uniform of 2019." *Wired*, June 5, 2019. https://www.wired.com/story/handmaids-tale-protest-garb/. Accessed 28 May 2020.

Etsy. "Popular Articles for 'The Handmaid's Tale'". www.etsy.com/market/the_handmaids_tale. Accessed January 28, 2020.

Goldberg, Michelle. "Margaret Atwood's Dystopia, and Ours", *The New York Times*, September 14, 2019. https://www.nytimes.com/2019/09/14/opinion/sunday/margaret-atwood-the-testaments-handmaids-tale.html?searchResultPosition=7. Accessed May 28, 2020.

The Handmaid's Tale. Bruce Miller, showrunner. Hulu, 2017–.

"The Handmaid's Tale". *Saturday Night Live*. May 7, 2018. www.youtube.com/watch?v=4ydHjbKaL5A. Accessed September 20, 2018.

"Handmaids in the City". *Saturday Night Live*. May 13, 2018. www.youtube.com/watch?v=RUCXD3_wW2w. Accessed September 20, 2018.

Hutcheon, Linda. *A Theory of Parody: The Teachings of Twentieth Century Art Forms*. Champaign, IL: University of Illinois Press, 1985 [2000].

Keane, John. *On Communicative Abundance*. London: University of Westminster Press, 1999. www.johnkeane.net/wp-content/uploads/1999/01/on_communicative_abundance.pdf. Accessed January 28, 2020.

McCarthy, Mary. "Untitled Review". *New York Times*. www.nytimes.com/1986/02/09/books/no-headline-423986.html?searchResultPosition=3. Accessed March 17, 2019.

Miller, Bruce. "Interview". *Eyes on Gilead* podcast. www.sbs.com.au/guide/audiotrack/eyes-gilead-interview-handmaids-tale-showrunner-bruce-miller. Accessed October 5, 2019.

Noah, Trevor. *The Daily Show*. September 5, 2018. www.youtube.com/watch?v=YH4VsNM6-Uc. Accessed September 28, 2018.

Redbubble. "Handmaid's Tale". https://www.redbubble.com/fr/shop/handmaids+tale. Accessed January 28, 2020.

"They Finally Made a Handmaid's Tale for Men". *Funny or Die*, June 14, 2017. www.youtube.com/watch?v=ciPszqk703k. Accessed September 20, 2018.

Valenti, Jessica. "Why 'The Handmaid's Tale' is more relevant one year after the first season". *The Guardian*, April 25, 2018. www.theguardian.com/commentisfree/2018/apr/25/handmaids-tale-season-2-return-trump-america-2018. Accessed September 18, 2018.

You Are Here: *The Handmaid's Tale* as Graphic Novel

Joyce Goggin

INTRODUCTION: HOW REAL IS FICTION?

Two events of 2016 continue to reshape and reform the USA, the UK, and ultimately the global economic and geopolitical landscape. The combined effect of a former reality TV star becoming president of the USA and the Brexit vote signaling the UK's exit from the EU has set in motion a wave of regressive political, economic, and cultural trends. As these trends harden into practice and their impact takes shape, a constant flow of neologisms enter into common parlance, such as "new reality" and "new normal", "fake news" and "alternative facts", to describe the "unprecedented" fallout from 2016. Importantly, at least for the purposes of my argument here, all of these newly coined terms point directly to our shifting relationship with reality.

Undeniably, much of what has happened since 2016 impacts women with particular, sustained, and mounting force, especially in the USA,

---

J. Goggin (✉)
Faculty of Humanities, Universiteit van Amsterdam,
Amsterdam, The Netherlands
e-mail: J.Goggin@uva.nl

© The Author(s), under exclusive license to Springer Nature
Switzerland AG 2021
S. Wells-Lassagne, F. McMahon (eds.), *Adapting Margaret Atwood*,
Palgrave Studies in Adaptation and Visual Culture,
https://doi.org/10.1007/978-3-030-73686-6_11

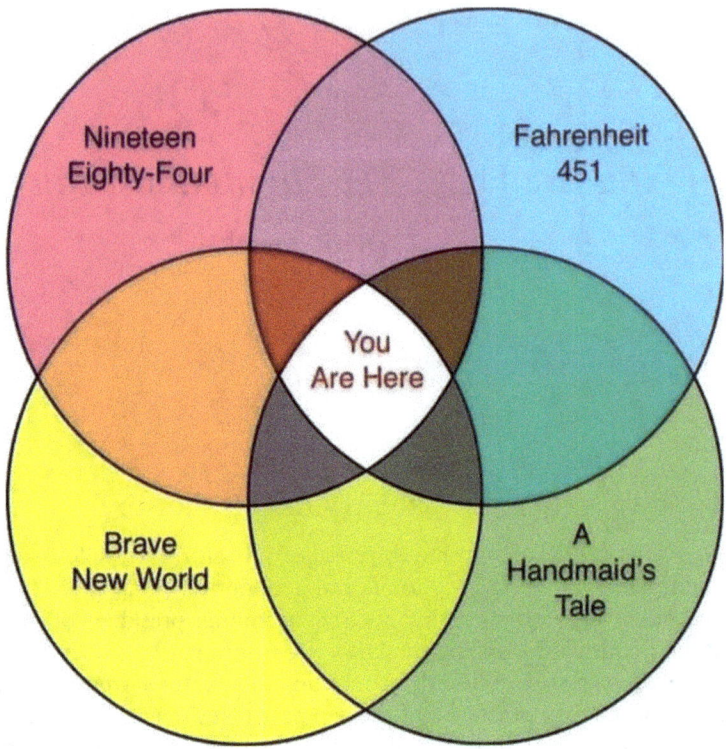

Fig. 1 How real is fiction?

where women's rights to reproductive freedom and sovereignty over their own bodies are being aggressively eroded under Trump's authoritarian presidency. Since he was "elected" to office, the now-impeached US president has consistently catered to his Evangelical base, whose members hold strong anti-gay and anti-abortion beliefs and engage in a transactional relationship with the president. This is to say that his supporters are able to overlook Trump's thoroughly un-Christian behavior in exchange for policies which, for example, have made abortion a punishable offense in many states, illegal in eleven new states as of May 2019, and punishable by life in prison in the states of Alabama and Georgia (Fig. 1).[1]

---

[1] American policy on abortion also threatens to impact on women in many other countries because "in 2017 President Trump reinstated and expanded a policy called the 'global gag rule' [… which] states that any overseas organization receiv[ing] US global health funding cannot even *mention* abortion as part of their counselling or education programs—even if the

In response to this cluster of draconian measures, protestors have begun wearing Margaret Atwood's unmistakable, now-famous, red Handmaid's uniforms at public demonstrations against laws intended to limit women's freedoms. Likewise, "You Are Here" memes such as the one pictured above, continue to proliferate, simultaneously making light of and warning against our dangerous proximity to the kinds of futuristic fictional worlds presented in novels like *The Handmaid's Tale, Nineteen Eighty-Four,* and *Brave New World*. Strikingly, while a quick internet search yields many such memes that sometimes include other titles such as Atwood's *Oryx & Crake*, or *Animal Farm*, all of these memes (at the time of writing), without exception, contain *The Handmaid's Tale* as part of the map of our present condition. Likewise, the sudden relevance and familiarity which has put Atwood's 1985 novel back on bestseller lists is intensified as the Trump election continues to inspire placards with slogans like "Make Atwood Fiction Again", carried by anti-abortion legislation protestors in red robes. And, oddly enough, when the First Lady decorated the White House for Christmas 2017, the decorations she chose—whether intentional or accidental—looked alarmingly like Atwoodian Handmaidens, and meme makers were quick to add the white bonnets to comic and chilling effect (Fig. 2).

The popularity and aptness of Margaret Atwood's terrifying tale of Gilead has, of course, not escaped the author's attention. In interviews Atwood has stated that she is "touched by the interest of young readers", due in part she opines, to the novel being taught in high schools as well as the enormous success of the Hulu TV series. More importantly, in accounting for the popularity and impact of her novel, Atwood goes on to explain that "[a]uthoritarianisms all have one thing in common: they roll back women's rights. So the possibilities in *The Handmaid's Tale* are *no longer seen as theoretical* by young readers, as they might have been in 1985" (my emphasis).[2] In other words, this tale of toxic events that culminate in a vast

money for these particular programs does not come from the US". https://www.amnesty.org/en/latest/news/2019/06/abortion-laws-in-the-us-10-things-you-need-to-know/.

[2] See: https://www.themarysue.com/exclusive-the-handmaids-tale-graphic-novel/. Lisa Jadwin has published a very detailed article on the context in which the novel was published the first time around which might have contributed to its success. See also Jadwin, 2009, passim.

Fig. 2 A photo-shopped image of Melania Trump surveying her Christmas decorations in 2018

wasteland and a cordoned-off, horrifyingly repressive society wherein women who have "sinned" by having children out of wedlock or by being second wives, and are still fertile, become handmaids for commanders' wives who themselves are no longer able to bear children. From the toxic spills to the strange literal interpretation of the Bible and the book of Genesis that informs Gileadian government and disciplinary culture, Atwood's narrative now seems to resemble various aspects of contemporary American society even more closely than it did in 1985. And while populism, nationalism, and the backlash against feminism continue to spread around the globe, the fictional world of *The Handmaid's Tale* increasingly coincides with the "real" world everywhere, so that "we are here" memes—stuck somewhere between Gilead, a brave new world, and Ray Bradbury's fictional America of 1999—compellingly evoke our current realities.

A good deal of the realism with which readers identify so strongly in *The Handmaid's Tale*—the strange and unsettling sense that we are reading actual documented history from the very near future—is attributable to its belonging to a category known as "speculative" fiction rather than science fiction, a point on which Atwood insists.[3] As the author explains in "What *The Handmaid's Tale* Means in the Age of Trump", when she began writing the novel back in the early 1980s, she decided that if she was going to create an imaginary garden [i.e. a fictional possible world], then she "wanted the toads in it to be *real*" (my emphasis, 2). To that end the author created rules, one of which dictated that she "would not put any events into the book that had not already happened in what James Joyce called the 'nightmare' of history, nor any technology not already available. No imaginary gizmos, no imaginary laws, no imaginary atrocities" (ibid.). In Atwood's *Other Worlds*, she further explains that her definition of "speculative fiction" would include "plots that descend from Jules Verne's books about submarines and balloon travel and such—things that really could happen, but just haven't completely happened yet" (*Other Worlds* 6). This she opposes to "science fiction" or "books that descend from H.G. Wells's *War of the Worlds*, which treats of an invasion by tentacled, blood-sucking Martians shot to earth in metal canisters—things that could not possibly happen" (ibid.). So, for this work of speculative fiction, Atwood included "group executions, sumptuary laws, book burnings, the *Lebensborn* program of the SS and the child-stealing of the Argentine generals, the history of slavery, the history of American polygamy" from the litany of real historical nightmares (Atwood "Age of Trump" 6).

Reality Effects and What Makes Fiction "Real"

In the preceding section I discussed how *The Handmaid's Tale* went from being received as realistic when it was first published, and how its "realness" has become increasingly palpable since the events of 2016. The remarkable coincidence of some of the occurrences in the narrative—or the very real-seeming possibility of their arrival—with current events, has given rise to heightened interest in Atwood's novel resulting, as noted

---

[3] In its English-language usage in arts and literature since the mid-twentieth century, "speculative fiction" as a genre term is often attributed to Robert A. Heinlein. He first used the term in an editorial in *The Saturday Evening Post*, February 8, 1947. Wikipedia.

above, in the successful and powerfully visual Hulu TV series and, more recently, in artist Renée Nault's graphic novel. Following from what I have been arguing concerning the gripping, possibly prophetic, realism of Atwood's novel, it is not without significance that the graphic adaptation is advertised as bringing "the terrifying reality of Gilead to vivid life like never before".[4] In this section then, I want to discuss realism and how its effects—the illusion of "vivid life"—are produced, in order to move on to a discussion of how adapting the text as a graphic novel might heighten the reality effect of *The Handmaids Tale* for contemporary readers.

So, what makes stories vivid, real, or realistic? This question has been an important concern since Aristotle's *Poetics* in which he discusses mimesis or imitation as the backbone of artistic production. This discussion is, in part, an answer to Plato's "Allegory of the Cave" from Book VII of *The Republic* in which the human perception of reality is likened to viewing shadows projected on the wall of a cave, so that what we take for reality is merely the shadows thereof, and these shadows are what mimesis mimics, hence the artist only "imitates what is already the simulation of an essence" (Barthes 145). Of course, much has been written on the topic of realism and imitation since, but Plato raises an important issue to which I will return, namely what appears to be real—what signals reality—and to whom? If artistic representations of external realities appear to be "real" or at least "realistic" even though the representation in question is a copy of a shadow of the real, to what kinds of subjects do such copies seem realistic?

In the twentieth century many scholars have discussed both realism and the real for various reasons, such as the "postmodern" breakdown of binaries including inside [the text]/outside [the text], reality/fiction, the real and the copy. Specifically, where the mimetic power of literature or narrative fiction to represent or even reproduce reality is concerned, Slattery explains that "realism is a reference that gives an illusion of exact correspondence with reality in its limited aspects" and does so by chronicling "the fragmented, flawed world of quotidian experience" or "flawedness simply as such", while "its occurrences are valued, [and] experienced as aesthetic" (55). Literary realism "is by its nature referential", which is to say that narrative realism seems to correspond to something outside of it, "with the mundane or at least with accessible things, familiar to us from our habituation to reality" (56). In other words, a realistic effect is achieved

---

[4] This is taken from the description on the back of the graphic novel; the same text is posted on amazon.com.

in fictional texts by representing the mundane, like the flies on Emma Bovary's glass, which then makes the story more real-seeming because it contains such insignificant, unpleasant, or even disgusting details that do little or nothing to advance the plot.[5]

Literary realism is also tied up with probability—that is, with probable outcomes from characters' actions and sequences of events: "if a plot has probability the effect is intensification of the tone and ultimately of the reference" and the degree to which readers suspend disbelief (Slattery 58). How and to what degree the outcome of the events that structure the plot accord with or reflect what readers at any given time will view as probable makes the story seem more or less realistic. This last point is also related to plausibility and ultimately to "internal consistency"—in other words, the narrative events have to lead up to a logical conclusion or resolution. When the plot has a realistic ending which is the "natural outcome of a whole plot development characterized by probability, the realism charms the reader"; or, perhaps better, in the case of the HMT, terrifies the reader with a narrative that contains both familiar mundane objects and a very plausible plot (Slattery 60).

In his 1969 essay on "The Reality Effect" Roland Barthes makes a number of similar points concerning how works of fiction like *The Handmaid's Tale* are made to feel real for readers. For example, he writes that authors of realistic fiction produce "notations which structural analysis, concerned with identifying and systematizing the major articulations of narrative, usually and heretofore [...] left out, either because its inventory omits all details that are 'superfluous' (in relation to structure) or because these same details are treated as 'filling' (catalyses), assigned an indirect functional value insofar as, cumulatively, they constitute some index of character or atmosphere and so can ultimately be recuperated by structure" (141). For Barthes, it is the compilation of what he calls fragmentary "useless details" that give fictional narratives the *feel* of reality, as opposed to history "which is supposed to report 'what really happened'" whereby nonfunctional details are of much less consequence or interest (146). The essence of his argument, then, is that futile details and detours in realist fiction signify nothing more than "*we are the real*" because it is "the category of 'the real' which is communicated, so that 'the very

---

[5] "Some flies on the table were crawling up the glasses that had been used, and buzzing as they drowned themselves in the dregs of the cider" (*Madame Bovary*, chapter 3).

absence of the signified [...] becomes the very signifier of realism'" (148). This, for Barthes, is how the *reality effect* is produced.

Quite obviously, *The Handmaid's Tale* is replete with these kinds seemingly insignificant details, from meticulous descriptions of uniforms worn by the Handmaids, the Wives and the Econowives, to the tokens used to buy supplies at shops with fitting names such as "All Flesh", "Lilies of the Field", and "Milk and Honey", to the décor of Offred's room, the Commander's office and club Jezebel, or the bloodied bodies of dissidents hanging on the wall as a public warning. The Aunts' names "derived from commercial products available to women in the immediate pre-Gilead period, and thus familiar" add a similar frisson of realness as a function of their very triviality; details which, as Slattery and Barthes explained, are the brush strokes of literary realism (Atwood, 1985, 321). Barthes refers to such superfluous details as "narrative *luxury*, lavish to the point of offering many 'futile details'" which comprise the "narrative fabric", of literary realism. To sustain the metaphor, *The Handmaid's Tale* offers a very plush narrative fabric; a sort of deep pile of details which combine to give weight and palpability to the claustrophobic world of Gilead. Indeed Atwood herself has referred to her novel as "a very visual book [...] awash in visual symbolism", which she offers as an explanation for its amenability to adaption.

But before leaving the topic of literary realism and the *Handmaid's Tale* there are at least two other aspects of the text that encourage the suspension of disbelief and our engagement with the reality effect of the text. In part this is generic. As Atwood explains, this is "the literature of witness" intended to be discovered "by someone who is free to understand it and share it [...] every recorded story implies a future reader" (Atwood, 2017: 6). Readers find themselves in the role of the one being witnessed to, and our direct interpolation—the direct addresses to the reader out of the text—heightens the reality effect. The story, moreover, acquires a yet thicker veneer of realism, attributable to the manner in which it was supposedly transmitted. This is, readers are told, the personal history of Offred, discovered long after she vanished, and we are made privy to her intimate musings recorded on some thirty tapes, each beginning "with two or three songs as camouflage no doubt" (Atwood, 1985: 314). The reality effect is further heightened with the inclusion of the titles of Offred's tapes: "Elvis Presley's Golden Years", "Folk Songs of Lithuania", "Boy George Takes It Off", and so on (ibid.). The cultural and historical referentiality established by way of these titles, the fictional injunction to believe that Offred's journals are "recordings", which are purportedly the analogue recordings of the voice of someone once present, all add to what is perceived as the realism of the text.

As the narrator of this section of the novel explains, there is also an Offred tape entitled "Twisted Sister at Carnegie Hall" and, he adds, "this is one of which I am particularly fond" (Atwood, 1985: 314). This is the voice of supposedly non-fictional Professor James Darcy Pieixoto, Director of Twentieth- and Twenty-First-Century Archives, Cambridge University, England, delivering a rather convincing keynote address on the events of the recordings and the history of Gilead. This narrative frame simulates conference proceedings including the speaker introduction, the mention of previous publications, and Dr. Pieixoto's lecture, which contains frequent references to the "authenticity" of the Offred tapes ("The labels on the cassettes were authentic period labels"), all presented as research undertaken by academics to whom we customarily attribute objectivity, which again serves to boost the text's realism or reality effect (Atwood, 1985, 314). The richness of detail—the assurance that tapes such as these are "very difficult to fake convincingly"; a machine reconstructed "capable of playing such tapes", the "painstaking work of transcription"; consultation with "voice-print experts"—lends the warp and weft of lived experience to the fabric of this text (Atwood, 1985, ibid.).

And, finally, there are striking moments of Offred's self-reflection and direct address to the reader on the status of her own narrative:

> I would like to believe this is a story I'm telling. I need to believe it. I must believe it. [...] It isn't a story I'm telling. It's also a story I'm telling. I wish this story were different [...] I wish it showed me in a better light, if not happier, then at least more active, less hesitant, *less distracted by trivia*. (Atwood 1985, 49, 279. My emphasis)

This address to Offred's projected listener-witnesses reading the transcript of her once-present voice, along with these moments in which she questions the nature of historical truth, and her own truth, quite strikingly, in a fictional text ("It isn't a story I'm telling. It's also a story I'm telling") coupled which moments of self-reflection ("I wish it showed me in a better light [...] *less distracted by trivia*") again considerably strengthen the reality effects of Atwood's novel. Oddly enough, it is almost as though Offred self-consciously chides herself here for recording precisely those kinds of details—*trivia*—that theoretically make realism feel real to the reader.

Graphic Realism: "The Question Is, What Corresponds with What?"[6]

The Handmaid's Tale has been adapted as a feature-length film, an opera, a full-cast radio production, a stage play, a TV series, and, more recently, Renée Nault's graphic novel, to which I now turn my attention. In this section I will ask why another adaptation is desirable or what perceived gap in the ecology of platforms for the dissemination of fictional narratives the graphic rendition can fill. What can a graphic novel do that a movie, an opera, and a TV show cannot? And perhaps most importantly, how can a graphic novel make a story that has spread across so many platforms, all presumably claiming to heighten the realness of a work of speculative fiction that already feels terrifyingly "real" and contains details about things that have really happened, make the experience of the text yet more vivid, more realistic? And, what corresponds with what in the real world that a graphic novel might make more realistic for readers?

In a detailed article on the cultural and historical context of *The Handmaid's Tale*, Lisa Jadwin pays particular attention to the rise of the "Moral Majority" and the Evangelical entanglement in government politics in the USA in the 1970s, their support of the Reagan presidency, and the link with anti-abortion politics. Along with the impact of the Thatcher years in the UK, these governments ushered in "neoliberalism", or a cluster of economic policies characterized by Naomi Klein as "the elimination of the public sphere, total liberation for corporations and skeletal social spending" (Klein 14–15). At the same time, repressive regimes in Romania and China focused on the reproductive rights of women, in the first case by forcing women to reproduce and in the second just the opposite (Jadwin 6). And, finally, the increasing toxicity of the planet led to a noted decrease in human fertility in some countries in the 1980s, which is of course, the central issue in *The Handmaid's Tale* and the core of much of the policy in place in Gilead. So it is from this context that readers of Atwood's novel, when it was first published, would have noticed correspondences between the real world and the fictional world of the text, including details such as those noted above that give the text its realistic feel.

By 2019 when the graphic novel was published, we had entered the supposed end of the neoliberal project and are currently dealing with the

---

[6] Slattery (56).

full force of deregulation, corporate welfare, the dissolution of the welfare state including planned parenthood in the USA, and, with all of this, the criminalization of abortion.[7] It is from within this context, some 35 years after the novel's publication, that the text now has even more points of correspondence with the real world; so much so that the appearance of protestors dressed as handmaids no longer surprises us. In other words, the realism of the text has entered directly into the reality of our day-to-day experience, which would suggest that, in order to heighten the reality effect of *The Handmaid's Tale*, a new strategy would be needed—and the graphic novel has stepped into that representational space in ways that perhaps even a TV series cannot.

One important factor influencing our notions and parameters of what constitutes markers of realism and how to represent reality in graphic narratives was significantly impacted by what Rik Spanjers has called "the *Maus* event". As Spanjers argues, the arrival of Spiegelman's *Maus*, its enthusiastic reception and enormous success "caused a shift in the perception of comics' ability for historical representation", whereby "drawn images and dialogue could make claims to realism that rival those made by photographs and historical discourse" (27). As Spanjers argues, what we take to be realistic changes along with formal conventions and the subject matter presented, so that any given mode of realism "is authenticated through its positioning in a broader network of modes of realism", which, in the case of *Maus*, was "dependent on a postmodern reconfiguration of the initial subjective connotation of the comics medium" (27, 28). In other words, contemporary subjects, like those reading Renée Nault's graphic adaption of *The Handmaid's Tale*, will recognize the multi-layered collage of first-person narration, drawings, dialogue, various fonts, and photographs that are characteristic of historic graphic novels—"comic's ability to combine different modes of realism in texts and images"—as being somehow at least as real, if not more so, than other discursive and/or representational modes (Spanjers 17). Or, as Atwood herself put it simply, "graphic novels have connected with a whole other readership", and one for which this adaptation will have particular resonance, with the

---

[7] "End of Neoliberalism: Project Syndicate". https://yaleglobal.yale.edu/content/end-neoliberalism-project-syndicate.

Maus event having paved the way to a new understanding of realism and new ways to represent it in graphic literature.[8]

So, to cite a few examples of the kind of deep, or at least currently recognized realism that graphic novels are able to communicate and how, I want to pause on key moments of Nault's graphic adaptation of *The Handmaid's Tale*. In a passage from chapter 28 of the text, Offred recalls working, "transferring books to computer discs", when "thousands of them [women] had jobs, millions", which in the "now" of her narrative of enslavement is "like remembering paper money, when they still had that" along with various other freedoms that formed the quiet and unnoticed background of her previous life (Chapter 28, Atwood, 1985, 134). In the graphic version of this passage from the novel, various objects that Offred's mother kept in a scrapbook, along with some paper money, are spilled across the background of the page on which blocks containing Atwood's text are printed. Notably, the photographs are rendered in a style that more closely simulates photographic realism than the drawing through which the central timeline is communicated, as are a one- and a five-dollar bill and two movie theater tickets.[9] Not only does the juxtaposition of styles suggest that Offred's past as a free, working woman is more real than her bizarre captive existence in Gilead, it also effectively sets off one mode of realism against another, namely subjective realism as opposed to the "realism of mechanical perception in the shape of photographs, films, or other kinds of records produced by machines" (Spanjers 39).

This reality effect, whereby one mode of realism is authenticated through its positioning next to other modes of realism, is repeated on the next page, where realistically drawn newspapers with headlines reading "Army Declares State of Emergency", and the familiar *New York Times* banner is visible along with half of a headline about terrorists. In a letter-box frame at the bottom of this page, part of a television screen is inserted into the collage of newspapers, with a drawing of a news anchorman, a "Channel 3" logo, and a "jagged contour balloon" in which we read "Keep calm. Everything is under control" (Forceville 63).[10] Notably, the

---

[8] Hale-Stern, Kaila. "Exclusive: Gaze Upon These Haunting Pages From *The Handmaid's Tale* Graphic Novel." *Mary Sue*, 25.03.19. https://www.themarysue.com/exclusive-the-handmaids-tale-graphic-novel/.

[9] The graphic novel has no page numbers, so these cannot be supplied in references to Nault's text.

[10] According to Charles Forceville in his work on "ballonics", jagged balloon contours that are angular and asymmetrical "have more negative connotations than roundness and sym-

text in this speech balloon is rendered in a standard, mechanically produced font, whereas the rest of the text in Offred's voice is reproduced in a font that simulates hand printing. So here again, the graphic novel produces layers of reality and strangeness through such visual clues and cues.

There is one more effect to which I would like to draw attention in the graphic adaptation of *The Handmaid's Tale*, indicative of how it is able to produce its reality effect at a glance through the visual embedding of the elements it contains and what Thierry Groensteen would call the taxonomy of the comics page. For Groensteen, comics are a system that necessitates focusing not only on units of meaning such as panels, or even sequences of panels in a strip, but rather on understanding the page and the spread as a system in which various spaces on the page interact with one another and produce effects unique to graphic literature, which in turn need to be "read" and understood through a visual logic rather than, or together with, textual logic.

So, one particularly good example of how graphics can add visual logic as well as a supplementary layer of meaning to text, while also conveying or collapsing temporality, is contained in two pages on which Offred's shopping trips with Ofglen are rendered. These panels each take up a full page in the form of an arch inserted into what looks like a street of Victorian houses, which arch contains four rows wherein the handmaids are depicted walking first in one direction and then back in a later, similar page arch. In the second such panel we read, "[n]ow and again we vary the route; there's nothing against it, as long as we stay within the barriers. A rat in a maze is free to go anywhere as long as it stays inside the maze." On the one hand, the inserted arch containing the promenading handmaids graphically communicates their confinement and the general claustrophobia of the text, these panels also manipulate "the relation between the visual and verbal means of conveying a sense of time", while Nault uses the affordances of graphic narratives, "the frame and the gutter, and the visual space of the page, in creating a sense of time" (Mikkonen 74). In other words, by embedding an image of the handmaids walking back and forth in the same space inserted into the page, we know these panels "carry more visual information, [and] propel the story forward more forcefully,

metry. Sharp, angular things are dangerous and potentially harmful, unlike rounded, smooth things. [...] The idea that asymmetry in balloon-contour connotes 'bad' things may therefore be rooted in embodied cognition" (Forceville 69). In this case, the reader is cued to understand the "bad thing" as the terrifying news blaring out of the television.

than others" while these key moments are visually emphasized through the use of different types of frames and, in this case, double frames that also provide a time signature (80) (Fig. 3).

And, finally, this passage: "Above on the white ceiling, a relief ornament in the shape of a wreath, and in the centre of it a blank space, plastered over, like the place in a face where an eye has been taken out" (Atwood, 1985: 17). This is, of course, the ceiling ornament from which a chandelier has been removed—"anything you could tie a rope to"—because Offred's predecessor hung herself from it. In the TV series, the suggestion that the wreathe resembles a face from which an eye has been removed is adapted, quite literally, as handmaid Janine's eye which is "plucked out" as that which offends.[11] Here however, the horror of Gilead is rendered by moving from one page on which the hanging bodies of supposed enemies of the state at the wall are pictured, followed by a black page titled "III Night" (which occurs in the novel just before chapter seven), with only a small detail of a ceiling ornament like the one described in the novel. These two pages are followed by an abrupt and vertiginous reversal of perspective on the following page, wherein we see Offred lying on a bed in her tiny room, pictured from far above, so that we view her from where the "eye" in the ceiling would be. While conveying a sense of the eye as constant and threatening surveillance, this sudden change in perspective startlingly reverses the focalization from the one seeing, to the one being seen; namely Offred.

This moment in the text and graphic novel is one of shock; a moment when the play in the text between reality effects created by the focalizer's self-soothing storytelling is shattered, and the sickening realization of the real breaks through. Such graphic shifts in the visual representation of Offred's story reverberate with or adapt such shifts in the original text as these:

> It isn't a story I'm telling.
> It is also a story I'm telling, in my head as I go along. […].
> But if it's a story, even in my head, I must be telling it to someone. […].
> A story is like a letter. *Dear You.* I'll say. Just you, without a name. Attaching a name attaches *you* to the world of fact, which is riskier, more hazardous: who knows what the chances are out there, of survival, yours? (Atwood, 1985, 49. Emphasis in original)

---

[11] This is also a reference to Mathew 5:29: "And if thy right eye offend thee, pluck it out".

Fig. 3 One of two full-page panels from Renée Nault's graphic novel that pictorially communicate the claustrophobia of the text

This passage holds perhaps, the key—or at least one of them—to the ongoing appeal of Atwood's novel: namely the terrifying play between reality effects, the real and the Real, in Lacan's terms, which has only become more forceful in the intervening years between 1985 and the present. This is to say that "the Lacanian real [sic.], 'pierces a hole' in the knowledge organizing the present, something which presents itself as an absolute singularity or anomaly by exposing a universal and indeed eternal, trans-historical content" (Besana, 214). The Real disrupts our sense of reality, "the Real [is] opposed to everyday social reality—the Real in its extreme violence [is] the price to be paid for peeling off the deceptive layers of reality" and reality effects (Zizek 6). In other words, those gut-wrenching moments in *The Handmaid's Tale* are glimpses of the Real that momentarily break through the reality effects created by the multitude of details that form the fabric of Atwood's narrative, and present us with frightening trans-historical content. That trans-historical content amounts to the various methods of oppressing and controlling women that Margaret Atwood's work of speculative fiction gathers into its narrative, as well as her vision thereof from the 1980s that seems evermore plausible and real today.

Conclusion: *Nolite te bastardes carborundorum*

According to Linda Hutcheon, part of the pleasure of adaptations "comes simply from repetition with variation, from the comfort of ritual combined with the piquancy of surprise" (4). While Atwood herself has commented that it was "simply intriguing to see what an expert visual/graphic artist such as Renée Nault would do" with her story, in this case, pleasure, piquancy, and surprise of adapting it are perhaps more accurately described as horror, terror, and abject fear.[12] And it is precisely this haptic aspect of Atwood's text, with its frighteningly detailed and realistic rendition of a near future, and our own present which is oddly past the future she predicted in 1985, arrested at the end-time to which the novel looks forward and in which we now find ourselves, that this graphic adaptation is particularly good at (re)producing. It is the bizarre dual temporality of Atwood's text and the reality effects that the author put into it in the form of meticu-

---

[12] Hale-Stern, Kaila. "Exclusive: Gaze Upon These Haunting Pages From *The Handmaid's Tale* Graphic Novel". *Mary Sue*, 25.03.19. https://www.themarysue.com/exclusive-the-handmaids-tale-graphic-novel/.

lous, richly imagined detail, that perhaps makes the text such a tempting narrative for adapters in film, TV, and Nault's graphic novel.

In his exploration of the graphic novel form, Adams describes the medium as having the potential to be "part of a radical practice of realism" which has been considered "appropriate for creating narratives that explore conditions of social crisis" (9). This general observation on the nature of graphic affordances for the representation of social crises most certainly applies to Nault's graphic adaptation of Atwood's novel. And if this form, as I argued above, is more apt for representing the reality effects of the novel to contemporary audiences, I want to suggest that the form might equally be more germane, at least since the "*Maus* event", to forcing us to take a peek at the Real—the inexpressible horror of a present-future too terrible to contemplate, and sublime violence best visualized, and processed by viewers and readers, in artistic media. Or, in Zizek's words our "'passion for the Real' [...] culminates in its apparent opposite, in a *theatrical spectacle*" (Zizek 9, emphasis in original).

There is a gag blog post about a video game called "The June Staring Simulator" which promises yet more visceral thrills than other media that adapt Atwood's tale, because it simulates the effect of "Elizabeth Moss staring into the camera [...] which is why a first-person game set in Gilead with June's glaring superpower will be so compelling for fans". Joke or no joke, the suggestion here is that fans of the story thrill to those moments of direct address to the contemporary player, just as Offred directly addresses her projected readers, thus letting flashes of the Real through the reality effects of the text for a petrifying second.

And this sensation of the Real piercing through all of our spectacular and narrativizing strategies for avoiding it is made flesh, as it were, in the current practice of having Atwood's mock Latin phrase—*Nolite te bastardes carborundorum*—tattooed on the body. A quick Google search produces countless photographs of body parts on which the bogus phrase is tattooed, pierced through the skin with needles so as to be made indelible and real, which ultimately turns Atwood's fictional faux-Latin phrase into startling reality. As Laura Bradley wrote in a *Vanity Fair* piece on the topic, "outside the world of the book, the phrase has taken on a life of its own, as a sort of feminist rallying cry for women" and Atwood has commented that "the weird thing about it" is that it was a joke from her Latin classes. "So this thing from my childhood is permanently on people's bodies." And while Zizek writes that the activity of cutters "represents a desperate strategy to return to the Real of the body [...] to ground the ego firmly in bodily reality against the unbearable anxiety of perceiving oneself as nonexistent" unlike the more superficial practice of "normal tattooed inscriptions on the body, which guarantee the subject's inclusion in the (virtual) symbolic order", I want to suggest that this is different (10). For just as Offred questions her own existence throughout the story as though Gilead had removed her own ontology by denying her personhood, and speaks to readers/listeners, willing us and believing us into existence, it is as though this particular act of tattooing Atwood's mock Latin phrase onto the body confirms the existence of the angst-ridden contemporary female subject.

There is sudden jolt that readers may experience with Offred when they learn that this subversive phrase, etched in her closet in the room to which she is confined, is really no resistance at all given that it came from the Commander, her oppressor. This shock is now multiplied along with the sudden uncanny appearance of handmaids in the crowds at a demonstration for women's rights. This is the shock of the text's reality effects becoming ever more real as the narrative moves from page, to screen, to small screen, to graphic novel, to videogame, to skin.

Are there any questions? (Atwood 1985: 324)

Works Cited

Adams, Jeff. *Documentary Graphic Novels and Social Realism*. Oxford, Bern, Berlin: Peter Lang, 2008.

Allardice, Lisa. "Interview with Margaret Atwood". *The Guardian*. 20.20.2018. https://www.theguardian.com/books/2018/jan/20/margaret-atwood-i-am-not-a-prophet-science-fiction-is-about-now.

Armstrong, Jennifer Keishin. n.d. "Why the *Handmaid's Tale* is so Relevant Today".

Atwood, Margaret. *The Handmaid's Tale*. London: Jonathan Cape Ltd, 1986.

Atwood, Margaret. "What *The Handmaid's Tale* Means in the Age of Trump". *The New York Times*, March 10, 2017.

———. *In Other Worlds: SF and the Human Imagination*. New York: Anchor Books, 2012.

Barthes, Roland. (1969). "The Reality Effect." *The Rustle of Language*. Trans. Richard Howard. Ed François Wahl. Berkeley: University of California Press, 1989, pp. 141–148.

Besana, Bruno. "Alain Badiou: The Problem of Subtractive Universalism". *The Scandal of Self-contradiction: Pasolini's Multistable Subjectivities, Geographies,*

Traditions. Ed. Luca di Blasi. Vienna and Berlin: Verlag Turia + Kant, 2012, pp. 209–237.

Bradley, Laura. *Handmaid's Tale*: The Strange History of "Nolite te Bastardes Carborundorum". *Vanity Fair*, May, 2017: https://www.vanityfair.com/hollywood/2017/05/handmaids-tale-nolite-te-bastardes-carborundorum-origin-margaret-atwood.

"End of Neoliberalism: Project Syndicate". n.d. https://yaleglobal.yale.edu/content/end-neoliberalism-project-syndicate.

Forceville, Charles, et al. n.d. "Balloonics: The Visuals of Balloons in Comics". In *The Rise and Reason of Comics and Graphic Literature: Critical Essays on the Form*, ed. Goggin, Joyce and Dan Hassler-Forest. Jefferson, NC: McFarland, pp. 56–74.

Groensteen, Thierry. *The System of Comics*. Trans. Bart Beaty and Anne Miller. University Press of Mississippi, 2007.

"Handmaid's Tale Video Game Revealed as June Staring Simulator". n.d. http://syn.org.au/handmaids-tale-video-game-revealed-june-staring-simulator-p1ng/.

Hale-Stern, Kaila. "Exclusive: Gaze Upon These Haunting Pages From *The Handmaid's Tale* Graphic Novel". *Mary Sue*, 25.03.2019. https://www.themarysue.com/exclusive-the-handmaids-tale-graphic-novel/.

Hutcheon, Linda. *A Theory of Adaptation*. New York and London: Routledge, 2006.

Jadwin, Lisa. "Margaret Atwood's *The Handmaid's Tale* (1985): Cultural and Historical Context". *Critical Insights*, 2008, pp. 21–41.

Klein, Naomi. *The Shock Doctrine: The Rise of Disaster Capitalism*. London: Picador, 2008.

Mancuso, Cecilia. "Speculative or Science Fiction: As Margaret Atwood shows, there isn't much difference." *The Guardian*. 10.08.2016. https://www.theguardian.com/books/2016/aug/10/speculative-or-science-fiction-as-margaret-atwood-shows-there-isnt-much-distinction.

Mikkonen, Kai. n.d. "Remediation and the Sense of Time in Graphic Narratives". *The Rise and Reason of Comics and Graphic Literature: Critical Essays on the Form*. Ed. Goggin, Joyce and Dan Hassler-Forest. Jefferson, NC: McFarland, pp. 74–87.

Nault, Renée. *Margaret Atwood's* The Handmaid's Tale. *The Graphic Novel*. New York: Random House, 2019.

Spanjers, Rik. *Comic Realism and the* Maus *Event: Comics and the Dynamics of World War II Remembrance*. Unpublished diss. University of Amsterdam, 2019.

Slattery, Mary F. "What is Literary Realism?" *The Journal of Aesthetics and Art Criticism*, Vol. 13:1, 1972, pp. 55–62.

Zizek, Slavoj. *Welcome to the Desert of the Real*. New York: Verso, 2002.

Offred at the Opera: Dimensions of Adaptation in Poul Ruders and Paul Bentley's *The Handmaid's Tale*

Helmut Reichenbächer

While adaptation studies often focus on a comparison between the new text and its source (Hutcheon 2012, 17), this study takes a different approach, identifying the several dimensions of adaptation. I deploy a directional approach (how did we arrive at the adaptation?) in order to analyze both source (a novel) and adaptation (an opera) as a system of signs to be decoded by their respective audiences.[1] This approach closely investigates the underlying three-step process: (1) the librettist condenses the novel's purely linguistic signals into a new genre, the libretto, ("A

---

[1] A socio-semiotic approach, for example, would consider "the socio-cultural context within which the meaning has been created" (Moghaddam 157). Such an approach might be of interest when looking at productions of the opera in the U.S., the setting of the novel. It would also recognize the considerable financial risk to an opera company existentially dependent on ticket sales and philanthropy, such as the Minnesota Opera which was unable to attract a corporate donor to its production (Peiken).

H. Reichenbächer (✉)
OCAD University, Toronto, ON, Canada
e-mail: hreichenbacher@faculty.ocadu.ca

© The Author(s), under exclusive license to Springer Nature Switzerland AG 2021
S. Wells-Lassagne, F. McMahon (eds.), *Adapting Margaret Atwood*, Palgrave Studies in Adaptation and Visual Culture,
https://doi.org/10.1007/978-3-030-73686-6_12

dramatic text to be sung and acted" [Balestrini 15]); (2) the composer develops a highly complex system that envelops linguistic signs in an acoustic sign system, the score, and (3) artistic and production teams work together to realize a performance, a text that encompasses a myriad of auditory and visual signals. (For fundamental insights into and a synopsis of thinking about adaptation in opera, see Linda Hutcheon and Michael Hutcheon's "Adaptation and Opera" [Leitch et al.]). Each of these three steps establishes its own specific dimensions for adaptation.

Feature film, television series, graphic novel, and dance drama[2] are among the various adaptations that Margaret Atwood's novel *The Handmaid's Tale* has undergone to date. Is opera the boldest adaptation of them all? Could a dystopian novel written in the first-person voice of a female protagonist victimized by a Christian fundamentalist regime be suitable for an opera? Even long-time opera fan Atwood had moments of doubt when she first learned that Danish composer Poul Ruders (1949–) planned to write an opera based on her 1985 novel: "I was surprised. Actually I thought: 'This person is mad.' I had a brief, nightmarish vision of a line of high-kicking Handmaids revealing their beige, utilitarian undergarments while singing some variation of The Anvil Chorus" (Atwood, "For God and Gilead").

Ruders felt compelled to choose Atwood's novel as the subject for his second opera.[3] In her inimitable, satirical voice, Atwood continues: "[He] was all a composer should be: fervent, wild-eyed, but with the single-minded focus of a dentist's drill." She goes on to write: "'As soon as I read this book, I saw it as an opera,' [Ruders] said. This was a great honour for him, and also a great chance, but he said that he wanted to do something he found relevant. He wanted to do *The Handmaid's Tale* and nothing but *The Handmaid's Tale* and if he couldn't do *The Handmaid's Tale* he wouldn't do any opera at all" (Atwood, "For God and Gilead").

While the contract for the commission of this adaptation took almost two years to negotiate (Bentley 36), actor and librettist Paul Bentley (1942–) jumped at the opportunity to participate in this challenging project. He sought out recordings of Ruders' work and was immediately

---

[2] Choreographer Lila York adapted the novel for the Royal Winnipeg Ballet in 2013. The same company performed a reworked version of the dance drama in 2018 (Harris).

[3] As Ruders explains in an interview before the North American premiere in St. Paul (MN): "You have illicit sex, perversion, betrayal, hope and love and such heartbreaking loss. But if audiences are going to be trapped for three hours, you have to grab and entertain them, and this does that quite well" (Peiken).

attracted to the Danish composer's music: "it was evident from the first that Poul was a supremely passionate, dramatic composer. As he said himself, he was no Puritan, he went for the jugular. The impact of the first movement of the Symphony was simply ferocious" (Bentley 16). Bentley was on board and started working on the libretto even before the agreement was signed.

The Royal Danish Opera premiered Poul Ruders and Paul Bentley's opera *The Handmaid's Tale* in Copenhagen in 2000 to critical acclaim ("a popular as well as a critical hit" [Littler]).[4] Since then, the opera has seen productions in London (English National Opera, 2003), Minneapolis (Minnesota Opera, 2003), Toronto (Canadian Opera Company, 2004), and more recently in Melbourne (Gertrude Opera, Yarra Valley Opera Festival, 2018) and Boston (Boston Lyric Opera, 2019). Following this latest production, *New York Times* critic David Allen called it "a brilliant, brutal opera, one that should be taken up widely" (Allen).[5] New productions were planned for 2020 for the Royal Danish Opera (Copenhagen) and the San Francisco Opera, but have yet to occur at time of publication as a result of the COVID-19 pandemic.

How did this ambitious project come about? It was Elaine Padmore, Artistic Director of the Danish Opera, who commissioned composer Poul Ruders to write an opera for Copenhagen, which hadn't seen the premiere of an original new Danish opera for over thirty years.[6] Padmore put Ruders in touch with Paul Bentley as a potential librettist. Bentley, a self-described "theatre animal, [...] who was nuts about opera and had written a couple of musicals," seemed a promising candidate, for he had spent "twenty-five [years] acting, singing, directing, and writing." Ruders' first opera *Tycho*[7] had been "anything but theatrical" (Bentley 11). In his recently published memoirs, Ruders admits:

> The discussion between the Danish astronomer Tycho Brahe and the German scientist Johannes Kepler about whether the Earth or the Sun is the center of the universe—is not the most obvious starting point for keeping an

---

[4] For an overview of critical responses to the opera's first four productions, see Laycock (115–132).
[5] Only the notoriously difficult London critics gave the opera "a critical shellacking" (Peiken).
[6] Ruders, *Man har* (89).
[7] Poul Ruders and Henrik Bjelke, *Tycho*. Opera in three acts. 3 vols. Copenhagen: Wilhelm Hansen, 1986. The Den Jyske Opera (Århus, Denmark), premiered *Tycho* in 1987.

audience in breathless excitement on the edge of their seats. And the libretto, written by the poet Henrik Bjelke, had the same dramatic clout as a versification of the telephone book.

However, this time, Ruders was instantly convinced that he had found the right match of a librettist for his new opera project: "Paul [Bentley] knew the theater from the inside. And that's what I needed. A professional theatre man."[8]

The two men quickly agreed on the type of adaptation for this opera: a fast-paced, narrative-driven work of music theater that would recreate *The Handmaid's Tale* plot, rather than a loose impressionist mosaic or an illustrated tone poem (Bentley 21). From the beginning, Bentley proposed a symmetrical plot outline which appealed to Ruders who thinks of "music [as] mathematics you can hear" and requested that "the structure should be as logical as mathematics" (Bentley 3, 11, 15). Bentley offered both musical and dramatic reasons for this approach:

> a symmetry of structure would surely be helpful musically. You could have an event major in Act One, its parallel minor in Act Two. A theme could be stated in One and inverted or reversed or developed or distorted or mirrored or minimorphosed or megamorphosed in Two. [...] However the Symmetries did not only have a musical use, they also had an architectural function. In constructing the libretto, my job had been a double balancing act, first embody the fragmented nature of Offred's memories and second, come up with a format which made the audience feel the story-telling was in good hands, that the narrative could be trusted not to meander confusingly. (17, 114)

Even Bentley's early synopsis outline from the spring 1994 showed his thinking in symmetries:

---

[8] "Diskussionen mellem den danske astronom Tycho Brahe og den tyske videnskabsmand Johannes Kepler om, hvorvidt Jorden eller Solen er universets centrum—er jo ikke det mest oplagte udgangspunkt for at holde et publikum i åndeløs spænding ude på kanten af stolene. Og librettoen, skrevet af digteren Henrik Bjelke, havde samme dramatiske slagkraft som en versificering af telefonbogen" (85). "Paul [Bentley] kendte teatret *indefra*. Og det var., hvad jeg havde brug for. En professional teatermand" (88). [My translation from the Danish] (Ruders, *Man Har*). For Poul Ruders and Paul Bentley's instant rapport, see Bentley (11).

Act One	Act Two
The wife	The commander
Ofglen	Ofglen
An Offer	An Offer
Forepray and impregnation	Foreplay and impregnation
Nick	Nick
Birth	Death
Unexpected danger	Unexpected danger
Release	Release (Bentley 18)

Composer and librettist's shared affinity for structural thinking sealed their agreement to work together on creating this opera.

ANALYZING TEXT TYPES: NOVEL VERSUS OPERA

Before moving into a closer analysis of the process of adaptation, observations are in order about the different nature of these two text types, novel versus opera. Among the theoretical aspects in the adaptation from novel to opera are the implications of translating one sign system (novel) into another (opera) and their effect on the decoding recipient. How are respective audiences accessing these texts?

Differences may be illustrated by the following thought experiment. Let us assume that we are overhearing the following conversation fragment: "I loved *The Handmaid's Tale*. I just couldn't put it down." Straightforward enough, we appear to have encountered a reader who enjoyed Atwood's 1985 novel. What is the object that elicited this statement? The enthusiastic reader made a statement about a book, written in individual lines of text, consumed through decoding a string of signs arranged in a linear sequence—a "single-track medium (words, to be read)" (Clark and Hutcheon 817)—a text that is potentially accessible to a wide range of literate populations. Furthermore, the book in question was composed by a single author, celebrated literary icon Margaret Atwood, who works in an "autographic" art form, a medium that is the direct product of the originating artist. While decoding such a text may lead readers into a myriad of directions that create meaning through the text's connotations and denotations, the process itself—reading—is immediate and accessible, and reproducible: the book remains an object that contains a stable, immutable text.[9]

In contrast to the experience of reading a novel, the genre of opera offers significant differences, illustrated by examining another anecdotal snippet of a fictional statement. "It's one of my favourite pieces, but I just hated last night's *Traviata*." Friends of opera will immediately understand that the first part of the statement ("one of my favourite pieces") refers to the 1853 opera written by composer Giuseppe Verdi and librettist Francesco Maria Piave. Not unlike the comment about Atwood's novel, it makes an overall statement about the work, based on a perceived unity of text and music in general arrived at by an unspecified number and kinds of previous encounters with the work. The statement's second part ("I just hated last night's *Traviata*") no longer refers to the work in general, but to a specific manifestation of the work. The audience member's assessment of this performance would have been influenced by numerous factors, such as the skills and interpretation of the singers, the conductor's impact, the caliber of the orchestral playing, the staging, as well as the spectator's state of mind.

Some critics of opera focus on the collaboration between librettist and composer, that is, opera in its abstract stage, as seen in the two dimensions of word and music combined in the score. Tina Hartmann, for example, adapts Wieland's metaphor for this double authorship ("doppelte Urheberschaft") and describes the genre of opera as well-developed twins who have two fathers or mothers (18). Armen Marsoobian underlines the close interconnectedness of words and music: "The interplay between the words <u>and</u> the formal structures of the music (its so-called syntax) articulates the meaning of the opera. Meaning here [...] is not asserted in the propositional content of the libretto, but exhibited in the interplay between words and music" (274).

A three-dimensional approach adds the analysis of scenic realization into the discussion. Opera is seen as a "multitrack medium" that offers "words plus aural and visual dimensions" (Clark and Hutcheon 817). This approach recognizes the process of producing opera, heard and seen, as a "translation, transformation, and transposition of language-and-music into the intersemiosic process of the dramatic genre of opera"

---

[9] While different editions of the novel will have variants, especially when it comes to paratexts (Genette), such as covers, cover art, and typography, among others, textual variants themselves would be rare for this particular text.

(Gorlée 587). Illie Balea describes opera as a text made audible and visible in order to depict the three parameters of music, linguistic textual, and the visual in terms of three overlapping circles which offer single, two-, or three-dimensional discussions of the genre, such as focusing on words and music (how are words set to music?), music and the visual (scenic realization of purely orchestral passages), visual and words (scenic realization of plot elements) (Balea 445). Live opera sits at the center of the graph (Fig. 1).

Arriving at the three-dimensional approach through adding scenic representation, we quickly realize that this parameter itself consists of a multitude of categories. Emphasizing the resulting semiotic complexity, Großmann offers two subsets: (1) static semiotic systems: performance space, set design, costume design, make-up, and hair/wigs, as well as physical appearance of the performers and (2) dynamic semiotic systems: props, lighting design, and kinesics (proximity, gesture, and facial expression).[10] Nelson Goodman's term "allographic" comes to mind: opera as an "artform requiring not a single artist but a phalanx of performers and producers to interpret and thus bring its two 'dramatic texts' to

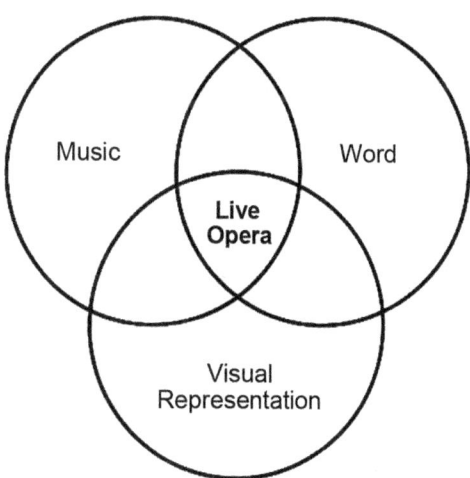

Fig. 1 Based on Balea 445

---

[10] "Statische Zeichensysteme: Bühnenraum, Bühnenbild/Dekoration, Kostüm, Maske/Frisur, Körperlichkeit" and "Bewegte Zeichensysteme: Requisiten, Licht, Kinesik (Proxemik, Gestik, Mimik)" (Großmann 124 ff. and 132ff.) [All translations from the German are mine].

musical and theatrical life on stage" (paraphrased in Hutcheon 2017). We've arrived at seeing opera as an n-dimensional universe.

For the sake of completeness, I will mention a phenomenon that Irene Morra describes: journalism that considers opera in a single dimension. Such writing dismisses the music in examples of contemporary opera as "deliberately inaccessible, self-consciously elitist, and challenging," while praising the libretto: "The 'theatre' of this opera resides in its plot, staging and libretto," as if the one can simply be lobbed off and considered separately from the other (Morra 121).

Already we can see how decoding opera involves dissecting dimensions at multiple levels of analysis and response. Decoding a fixed, stable text (such as the full score) that has been created by the collaboration between librettist and composer contrasts with a specific manifestation of this text (interpretations realized in a specific performance).[11]

Decoding Opera

In writing about the adaptation of Atwood's novel, it is important to be specific which text of the opera we are analyzing. Is it the fixed stable text encoded in print, that is, the full orchestral score (see below A1)? Or is it one of its increasingly adapted manifestations (A2 through C)? Here is a classification of the series of texts with increasing levels of adaptation and mediation:

A1. The full orchestral score contains encoded instructions for all musicians (orchestral players and singers) that indicate the music to be performed (including parameters such as tempi, pitch, rhythm, and dynamics) in addition to words to be sung or spoken as well as stage directions for the scenic realization of the work. Like the novel, this encoding is fixed in print. However, unlike the novel, it requires exceptionally specialized training to read a full score with the ability to hear mentally the music in the full spectrum of instrumental and vocal colors. In this instance, the reader must navigate an orchestral score notated on thirty-two staves for the orchestra, each indicating a different musical line, and

---

[11] Hartmann terms the individual performance as "transformation into a spatio-temporal event which is typically unrepeatable" [Transformation in ein raumzeitliches Ereignis, das tendenziell einzigartig und unwiederholbar ist] (Hartmann 7).

additional staves, as needed, for chorus and seventeen soloists.[12] See Appendix C, an excerpt from the orchestral score of the first "Worst Dream" sequence.

A2. The piano vocal score, a first adaptation, extracts from the full range of orchestral instruments the principal musical events playable with two hands on the piano, while reproducing the vocal lines and stage directions in full.[13] This adapted, simplified version is typically arranged for the use of rehearsal pianists, vocalists studying their parts, and theater professionals involved in preparing an opera's production. While the piano vocal score of the classical repertoire might be "readable" to the lay person interested in recreating the opera's music on their pianos at home, the more difficult examples of twentieth- and twenty-first-century repertoire, such as Poul Ruders' score, that may create sound clusters, bitonality, or even polytonality in complicated rhythmic patterns, and complex orchestrations, are accessible only to a small number of specialist "readers" who can translate its simpler musical notation into sounds in their heads. While this piano vocal score adaptation makes the work more accessible, it also flattens the wealth of orchestral voices and colors from the 32+ staves of Ruders' orchestral score to only two (or sometimes four) staves to be played solely on the piano. This flattening of sound may be compared to watching a film shot in Technicolor on a black-and-white television screen.

B. Given the complexities involved and specific expertise required for hearing vocal and orchestral scores, many score readers rely on the support of an auditory realization. At the most basic level, such readers would use a machine-made translation which converts digitized musical notation into sound, such as the MIDI that Poul Ruders shared with his impatient librettist: "Weeks went by without my knowing how the score sounded. Very frustrating" (Bentley 68). While MIDIs can reproduce digitized

---

[12] For the Toronto production, COC General Director Richard Bradshaw conducted an "orchestra augmented by 18 players for a total of 74. While the strings remain at normal strength, the score calls for a doubling of brass and woodwind. Five percussionists will handle the many unusual instrumental demands, and digital keyboards also supplement the orchestral forces. The chorus will also expand beyond the usual 20 male and 20 female voices with the addition of eight women" (Domville 2004, 9). For the Boston production, Ruders reduced the orchestration to make the work more accessible for performances by smaller companies (Barone).

[13] Notwithstanding the habit of some composers to develop a smaller orchestral version either in short score (with a reduced number of instruments indicated) or for piano first, typically, the ideal goal is to publish a full orchestral score as the definitive text from which to create a fully staged production.

scores, their sound quality is far from ideal. Much more attractive are the fully realized recordings now accessible to critics and amateurs, such as the live recording of the Copenhagen world premiere in March 2000 published on the Danish Dacapo Records label. This recording, the opera's only recording to date, reflects a specific interpretation determined by the conductor's choices for tempi, dynamic, shaping of orchestral and vocal colors, the choice of singers, the quality of the instrumentalists involved, and, particularly in a live recording, the spirit of the moment, as well as ultimately the interpretative decisions of the recording team. Given that this CD relies on recordings from four performances, recording producer Hennik Sleibork and sound engineer Peter Bo Nielsen were instrumental in producing an edited recording that intends to reflect the composer's vision.

C. From an audience's perspective, a staged production—a fully realized text—remains the most easily read. Music, scene, and words become more easily decodable visual and auditory stimuli. The staged, live performance is arguably the epitome of the visceral opera experience. However, as we can see in the staged productions of the opera to date, such realizations inevitably include the numerous interpretative decisions made by stage directors (Phyllida Lloyd, Eric Simonson, Linda Thompson, or Anne Bogart), conductors (Michael Schønwandt, Elgar Howarth, Antony Walker, Richard Bradshaw, Patrick Burns, or David Angus), and stage designers (Peter McKintosh, Robert Israel, Joseph Noonan, or James Schuette) to name but three leaders of artistic and creative teams of decision makers (Appendix A). What do the protagonist's appearance and vocal qualities contribute? Mezzo-sopranos Marianne Rørholm, Stephanie Marshall, Elizabeth Bishop, Sarah Heltzel, and Jennifer Johnson Cano have all tackled the exceedingly challenging role of the handmaid Offred. And what about performing spaces? The world premiere performances were staged in Copenhagen's Royal Danish Theatre, a nineteenth-century building, now called the Old Stage, with four rows of gilded balconies, whereas the Boston Lyric Opera performances were staged in Harvard's basketball arena, the gymnasium alluded to in the novel. Which *genius loci* might have lurked in the corners of this most recent set of performances?

In this sequence of adaptations, we can observe the transition from a stable fixed text—the published score—to a series of interventions: selecting what constitutes the most important musical detail for the piano vocal score, to interpretations that lead toward full visual, scenic realization of a staged production that involves adaptive processes going well beyond the initial creators of the opera, the librettist and composer.

To illustrate the significance of which version of the opera any analysis is based on, let us review two passages derived from the novel from full and piano vocal scores (texts A1 and A2) which are no longer present in either the recording or staged world premiere production (texts B and C). While the difference consists of only the excision of a dozen or so bars each (1001ff. and 1697ff.), this simple change affects our interpretation of the work. Without these two passages, audiences encounter a meeker and more subservient version of the protagonist.

In the first passage Offred purposely drops her pass at a checkpoint so that one of the Guards picks it up to hand it to her. Her subversive thoughts in the score ("speaks to herself: I hope he gets a hard-on. Much good may it do him" 1001ff) are not found on the recording. Director Phyllida Loyd eliminated this passage from the world premiere performance on which the recording is based. Apparently, she felt that "this came too early in the action; the punters would suppose that was how Handmaids acted all the time" (Bentley 96).

Likewise, when Offred is the first to arrive in Serena Joy's sitting room the night of the Ceremony, in text A, the subversive thought "I would like to steal something from this room" (1697) occurs to her. While stealing an innocuous object, such as an ashtray or a silver pill box, may seem a senseless act of revolt, the score has Offred justify this thought for herself with the line: "ev'ry once in a while [I would] take it out and look at it and try to believe that I have the power to defy their power" (1718ff.). Again this passage of subversion is excised in texts B and C. Losing these two passages of Offred's modicum of self-initiated subversiveness against the regime arguably presents us in texts B and C with a more conformist version of the protagonist than initially devised by librettist and composer in the score (text A).

This is why critics need to decide what is the object of their study of opera: score (road map, instructional manual, recipe) or performance (embodied interpretation, dished up meal), with the latter specific to that occasion, and therefore unique. While I, as a critic, benefited from attending performances of Ruders/Bentley's *The Handmaid's Tale* in Toronto and Minneapolis (versions of text C), this study focuses on the score (texts A1 and A2), as a more stable, fixed text, read with the assistance of the acoustic realization of the world premiere recording (text B). Furthermore, to engage in a full analysis of opera, the ideal critic would combine expertise in at least three distinct academic disciplines: musicology, literary and theater studies.[14] As Balestrini advocates: "Analysis should ideally provide sufficient depth to satisfy the requirements of each of the involved disciplines. At the same time, the desire to address readers of various backgrounds demands accessibility" (16).

The Process of Adaptation

"What do you read, my lord?"
"Words, words, words".
(*Hamlet*, Act 2, Scene 2)

In the beginning was the Word. (John 1:1)

Adapting a novel to an opera involves a three-step process: (1) writing the libretto or "verbal resemiotisation" from novel to libretto, (2) composing the music or "musical and theatrical resemiotisation," and (3) preparing the performance, a "performative resemiotisation" (Sindoni and Rossi 387).[15]

Atwood herself has described the libretto as a genre in unflattering terms as "a coat-hanger for the composer to make the rest of the thing hang on. If it's a bad coat-hanger, that will be unfortunate, but if it's a good coat-hanger, nobody will notice it" (quoted in Everett-Green 20). The context for Atwood's belittling statement is her own work as librettist. The late Richard Bradshaw, former General Director of the Canadian Opera Company, had commissioned, in collaboration with composer Randolph Peters, an opera tentatively entitled *Innana's Journey*, a project that never came to fruition.

Not surprisingly, the librettist's task is more complex than Atwood allows. A primary function is to condense the linguistic and dramatic material of the source text into its essence, reducing its complexities while maintaining the major plot outline. For example, the librettist will reduce the number of subplots and characters: only one professor in the "Historical Notes" frame, only one female servant in the Commander's household

---

[14] See Gier 28 and Hartmann 2 for the demands on research in the field of opera as genuinely comparative ["genuin komparatistische Forschung"].
[15] See also "transcodifications" (Moghaddam 355).

rather than the novel's two. The librettist also relies on monologue and dialogue, the spoken and sung words of a character, while retaining a high potential for dramatic staging. Bentley, an experienced theater professional, understood the practical needs of the stage and how to achieve effective staging.[16]

In mere quantitative terms, Bentley's libretto needed to reduce Atwood's text from a novel that takes an entire day to read out loud,[17] to a much shorter text which could be set to music for a theatrical evening of no more than two and a half hours. In addition, as Bentley was much aware, music is a "retarding agent" (Rosmarin 49); a sung text takes much longer to perform than simply to speak:

> I remembered performing in a production of the full text of Wagner's *Götterdämmerung* back in 1972, which we did as a play with percussion. *Götterdämmerung*, the opera, lasts about five hours. Our play lasted 45 minutes. (Friedelind Wagner, the composer's grand-daughter, loved it, by the way. And it did work as a play, as Wagner predicted it would. We know because we asked the audience afterwards.) (Bentley 39)

So Bentley was fully aware of the challenge he faced as Ruders' librettist.

For an effective dramatic experience, the libretto will also need to externalize the world of the novel's text, created through descriptions, into spoken and sung text for characters (monologues and dialogues) with other types of characterizations relegated to stage action, design, and musical expression. Narrator figures who might offer such background are rare in opera; Stravinsky's *Oedipus Rex* or Britten's *Rape of Lucretia* offer rare examples of opera employing narrators. While Wagner's characters notoriously re-tell events from their past (*Walküre*, Act I) rather than showing them to the audience, theater audiences are more engaged when witnessing a plot unfold in front of their eyes rather than being told about (and having to imagine) off-stage events. As Linda Hutcheon and Michael Hutcheon summarize, the task of the librettist is "to render what they select from the adapted text into equivalences within opera's various sign

---

[16] In addition to his extensive acting and singing career in drama and musical theater, Bentley wrote the lyrics for *Shylock*, a musical based on *The Merchant of Venice*, and spent three years in Munich to become an opera director (Bentley 6).

[17] The audio book read by Claire Danes consists of twelve hours of audio (Atwood, *The Handmaid's Tale. Narrated by Claire Danes.*).

systems in order to show rather than tell, and to do so concisely and with maximal dramatic impact" (Leitch et al.). Andrew Blake summarizes the issue: the librettist's principal tasks will include condensation, dramatization, and preparing a singable text (192).[18]

While the librettist's work focuses on reduction and condensation, the composer creates a score that matches the librettist's words with vocal lines and envelopes them with orchestral music, resulting in a rich auditory complexity. The composer transforms the condensed, purely linguistic dramatic text into an entirely new set of dimensions, the multi-spectral universe of music. This process yields the fixed, stable text that combines libretto, written stage directions, and music to be published as the full orchestral score.

The third step that brings an opera to life results in additional dimensions of complexity as the opera is produced: the creative and productive responsibilities of conductor and stage director. They will develop the production's overarching concepts and vision. Singers and possible understudies will be contracted, determining the auditory sound palette available to the conductor who will control the musical expression of *The Handmaid's Tale*'s nineteen singing roles, chorus, and an orchestra consisting of over sixty musicians. The stage director in turn will collaborate with costume, set, and lighting designers in developing the production's visual aesthetics in the three dimensions of the performance space. These teams will jointly develop their creative approach in order to produce an auditory and visual experience that will distinguish it from any other production of the same opera.

THE WORK OF THE LIBRETTIST

Which of the novel's elements lend themselves to adaptation as a dramatically satisfying opera? The novel's plot offers the opportunity for dramatic shifts between introspection, the protagonist's interior monologue of intimate thoughts (memories of earlier life with her partner and their child) to explosive drama (failed escape, public execution, doctrinal ritual, and institutionalized rape).

---

[18] Albert Gier summarizes the essential characteristics of the libretto genre as: "(1) Kürze; (2) diskontinuierliche Zeitstruktur; (3) Selbständigkeit der Teile; (4) Konstraststruktur; (5) Primat des Wahrnehmbaren [(1) brevity, (2) discontinuous time structure, (3) independence of parts, (4) contrastive structure, and (5) primacy of the perceptible]" (1998, 33).

The Opera's Opening Frame

The novel closes with "Historical Notes," from an academic symposium of Gileadean studies, held far in the future, after the fall of the regime. Ruders, however, requested from the very beginning that this historicizing frame open the opera. Rather than offering traditional signposting for operatic beginnings, such as the dimming of the house lights, the conductor's downbeat for the orchestra, and the raising of the curtain, Bentley's scenario immerses the audience into the opera's fictional world the moment people wander into the auditorium. Audience members are taken by surprise when they enter the house and encounter a proscenium-arch-filling video conference screen (as indicated in the score's stage directions) that displays slides announcing the "Twelfth Symposium on the Republic of Gilead," followed by an on-screen countdown "as the house lights fade" and "the Symposium transmission commences" (Ruders xiv).

The opera itself starts with a visual and auditory shockwave: "a minute or so of fast-moving Surreal Montage of images (still and moving) and headlines from the period which led up to the establishment of the Republic of Gilead, accompanied by a soundtrack of sound effects (jet engines, gun shots, explosions) and music" (Ruders xviii). This assault on the senses is followed by the calm speech of the professor at the conference. Bentley consciously constructed these alternations between dramatic intensity and relative calm.[19]

This dramatic device has been described as a dramatic and effective metatheatrical surprise for the visitor (Reichenbächer), yet moving the novel's closing frame to the opera's beginning serves yet another practical purpose. The first few minutes of the opera cleverly manage to convey a plethora of information about the sociopolitical context of the protagonist's first appearance on stage: The audience learns the background to Offred's world in both a concise and a dramatic manner.

---

[19] Bentley describes the alternating tension and relative relaxation in The Prologue and the Red Centre scenes of the opera's beginning:

> wham!—the short, fast and furious Surreal Montage,
>
> the civilised calm of the two professors,
> Offred's opening monologue, quiet and reflective,
> wham!—Offred's "Worst Dream", the Wall, and the Red Centre onslaught. (Bentley 55)

The opening offers yet another metatheatrical effect in the transition from symposium to introducing Offred, highlighting how Offred's tale is mediated to the opera audience. Professor Pieixoto, who had explained that their source text for this historical document, *The Handmaid's Tale*, consists of a set of audio cassette tapes with the recorded voice, presses the button of a tape recorder as if causing the orchestra's first chord and the physical presence of the singer Offred to appear on stage as she begins to intone her first words. The Toronto production's transition darkened the pre-curtain symposium scene, reducing visibility with a single spotlight narrowing its focus on the elevated tape recorder. As the curtain opens and the figure of Offred emerges from the dark, a visual/auditory cross-fade occurs from the disembodied voice on the cassette tape to the physically materialized historical figure of this story on stage.

Narrative Structure: From Sequential to Simultaneous Flashbacks

One of the novel's prime characteristics is its non-linear narrative structure, a "seething mass of flashbacks" (Bentley 9). The novel frequently moves between Offred's experience while in the Commander's Household (Time Now), her indoctrination at the Red Centre (Time Between) and her previous life with Luke and their daughter (Time Before). While acknowledging that dramatizing continual flashback is not easy, because "it's very easy for [theater] audiences to get confused" (Bentley 22), Bentley seized this challenge head on: "Trying to work out how best to do it is a lot of fun" (Bentley 21). He thus offered Ruders several possible solutions for the integration of flashbacks:

1. Offred in the Time Now would freeze and tell us about the events in her past. However, Bentley dismissed this option right away: "[it] would be clumsy and unsatisfactory. […] it's much easier for an audience to clock an event if they actually see it happening, rather than being told about it" (22). Showing action is more dramatically satisfying than simply telling.
2. The different times could be spatially distributed on stage: "If you had a separate part of the stage for each of the three time zones you could have the three Times serially interwoven (i.e. freeze in one stage area, lights up in another), or played simultaneously, (or both)" (23).

3. While the singer of Offred could change costume and appear in another time zone, Bentley proposed another solution, the idea of splitting the role of Offred into two. One singer portrays Offred of the Time Now and another Offred in the flashback episodes. Bentley's thinking was that this approach "would double the wages but halve the presumably huge amount of singing Offred has to do" (23).

This strategy of a simultaneous past and present while working with a double, raised during the first year of their collaboration, found its way into the final score. Costume design offers the audience a clear visual clue as to the difference between the Time Now "everyone in uniform—red or blue or black" versus the Time Before "all in Eighties or Nineties civvies" (34).

Bentley, the theater professional, had sent Ruders to see two Stephen Sondheim musicals, *Company* and *Passion* in 1996. Ruders said "that it was cunning of [Bentley] to invite him to those two shows, because they had indeed taught him a good deal about the staging of flashbacks" (Bentley 68). The opera makes use of consecutive flashbacks, such as Offred's taking shopping instructions from the servant Rita moving to Offred's Double talking to Moira about having an affair with a married man, Luke. This time shift is cued and easily understood by a change of lighting and by the characters' different costumes. This conventional approach to staging flashback is later expanded to a highly complex strategy that involves not only the visual cues of lighting and costume design, but also the juxtaposition of musical styles and tonalities in the "Amazing Grace" scenes discussed below.[20]

Ruders' Musical Language

Among the many musical choices faced by opera composers is aligning their singing characters with existing voice types and conventions, while controlling for preferred vocal characteristics, such as dramatic or light, high or low, agile or weighty. These *a priori* decisions are important for casting in

---

[20] While Paul Bentley wrote the libretto in English, composer Poul Ruders translated Bentley's text into Danish for the world premiere in Copenhagen. The published score includes both languages.

preparation for actual performances. Each voice category, or "Fach" (Steane), comes with certain expectations and a wealth of historical precedents.

Characterization Through Voice Types

While Bentley has provided the opera's characters with words, Ruders' task is to give a voice to the character. Ruders clearly operates within the genre's long-established conventions and traditions, and his placing of the characters within certain vocal types in and of itself offers insights into the characterization of these roles.

Aunt Lydia, "dragon of the Red Centre" (Bentley 33), a middle-aged, authoritarian, and merciless defender of the regime's ideology, for example, is introduced spouting formulaic doctrines and catechisms. The regime's perversion of the Ten Commandments now includes "Thou shalt not commit abortion" and "Thou shalt not commit gender treachery." Ruders reinforces the Red Centre's classroom indoctrination through mindless repetition by composing an appropriate vocal style of antiphonal singing, short phrases sung alternately between two groups; the Aunt's formulas are echoed by the handmaids-in-training. As Aunt Lydia's teachings become ever more insistent, her vocal range (*tessitura*), already sitting unnaturally high, rises even further. Ruders has her increasingly agitated exclamations shoot up into stratospheric vocal heights. Phrases thrown at the Handmaids, such as "a volunteer to testify" (140–141)[21] or "who led them on" (153–4), swoop up into the highest register (*"fortissimo* scream") without specifying the pitch. Tension increases throughout the Red Centre Prelude with a vocal climax composed for Aunt Lydia on the line "to be seen, is to be penetrated" (361ff.), a phrase indicated in the score to end on a "hysterical," extremely loud phrase (*fortissimo*) sung on four piercing high Cs (C_6) that stretch over two bars (Fig. 2).

While the score marks Aunt Lydia's role as a dramatic soprano, roles such as the Queen of the Night in Mozart/Schikaneder's *Magic Flute* come to mind, for the Queen is a hysterical, authoritarian mother figure whose vocal lines also resort to the highest vocal register. Vocal

---

[21] Numbers reference the specific bar in the score.

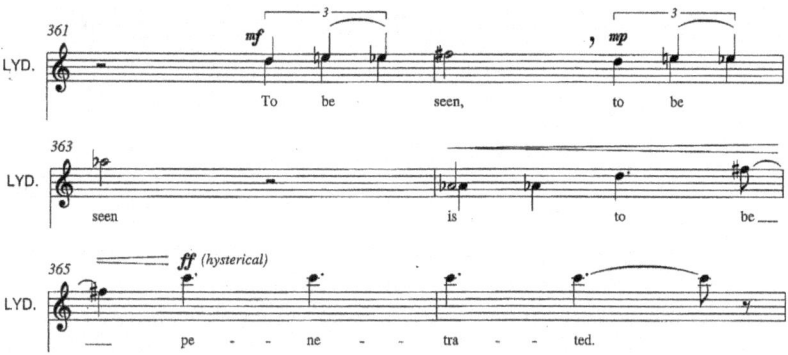

Fig. 2 AUNT LYDIA

Fig. 3 OFFRED

expectations for the role of Aunt Lydia include dramatic heft in a high register in order to be heard over a large orchestra and the choir of the assembled handmaids.

Developing a character's vocal characteristics, such as the swooping up of line endings, serves as a non-verbal means to demonstrate how Offred's indoctrination in the Red Centre is successful. After Moira's failed escape from the Red Centre, Offred reprimands her friend for attempting to flee ("I told you not to try it" 332ff.), a passage that ends with the same vocal line, imitating Aunt Lydia's hysteria, to less extreme heights, a mere F sharp ($F\#_5$), but with a similar upward swoop on the syllable "again" in her appeal to Moira, but followed with a softening "please" (243ff.) (Fig. 3).

The Commander's wife Serena Joy, an authority figure to be sure, remains willing to work around the regime's strictures. For example, she procures the consent of the chauffeur Nick in order to impregnate Offred. A mellower character than Aunt Lydia, Serena Joy's role is designated as an alto, as she plumbs the lowest female vocal range. However, even in this extremely low register, her voice clearly contains threatening elements. The passage "take her to her room" (660ff.) descends to a preternatural

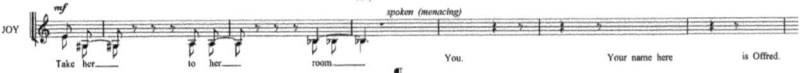

Fig. 4 JOY

low G sharp (G#$_3$), followed by a "spoken (menacing): 'You. Your name here is Offred'" (665ff) (Fig. 4).

Rounding out the group of secondary characters are three men cast as tenors. In usual practice, the tenor remains the conventional voice type in opera for romantic or love interests. Nick, Luke, and the Doctor are tenor roles who either have or desire to have sexual encounters with Offred.

The Commander, a bass, has the deep voice and vocal heft of an authority figure. The world premiere's Aage Haugland frequently sang the role of Hunding, another menacing authoritarian in Richard Wagner's *Walküre*. Basses in opera conventionally have more success with state authority and political power than in matters of love.

This leads us to the title character. Where is Offred's voice cast? As a mezzo-soprano, she is positioned in the moderate middle between the extreme heights of Aunt Lydia and the dark and low voice of Serena Joy. Few opera heroines are cast as mezzos. If they are, they might be extravagant, like Bizet/Meilhac/Halévy's seductive Carmen or Dalila in Saint-Saëns/Lemaire's *Samson et Dalila*. However, more often mezzo-sopranos are cast as secondary figures, a confidante or maid, such as Suzuki, in Puccini/Illica/Giacosa's *Madama Butterfly*. Rather than typecasting Offred as a dramatic heroine, Ruders' vocal choice for Offred consciously placed her into the category of an average person:

> Before I set "pen to paper", I had decided that Offred should be sung by a *mezzo-soprano*, that is, a woman's voice in the middle between soprano and alto. Offred is not a heroic coloratura soprano, but an ordinary human being, a little introverted, yet with the courage of her opinions.

Ruders already had in mind a notable Danish mezzo-soprano for the premiere of his opera:

It can only be one, I thought. Marianne Rørholm. Marianne, apart from her splendid voice, *resembled* the version of *Offred* that I imagined, both during the reading of the book—and later during the composition work.[22]

At least one critic sees Offred's vocal typecasting in a negative light: "the vocal range of Offred, pointedly a mezzo-soprano and not a soprano to emphasize that she is a slave and not a heroine, is narrow and introverted, allowed to soar only in her most private moments" (Barone). At the same time, literary critic Alan Weiss found substantiating evidence for Atwood's vision of her character that parallels that of Poul Ruders' intuition. Atwood herself described Offred as "an ordinary, more-or-less cowardly woman (rather than a heroine)."[23] Typecasting her as a mezzo-soprano within the operatic tradition underlines her as an ordinary person's experience within the confines of such a religious dictatorship.

Orchestral Language and Compositional Techniques

Ruders' orchestral language is complex: for large musical forces, rhythmically energetic, and full of dystopian dissonant sound clusters. The composer does not shrink from constructing aggressive sound waves in passages of violence, such as when the protagonist's relives her failed attempt to escape Gilead. Offred watches armed Guards drag Luke off stage in one direction, her daughter in the other, and her former self standing alone in the midst of this violent abduction. Deploying it as a recurring motif, Ruders creates an initial loud sonic cluster (*forte*) emerging from the depth of double basses, brass, and a percussive piano chord rushing upward, accompanied by pounding eighth notes and an atonal whir of wind instruments and strings that mutate and crescendo into a very loud (*forte*

---

[22] "Inden jeg satte 'pen til papir', havde jeg besluttet mig til, at Tilfred skulle synges af en *mezzosopran*, altså en kvindestemme midt mellem sopran og alt. *Tilfred* er ingen heroisk koloratursoprantype, men et almindeligt menneske, lidt indadvendt, men alligevel med sine meningers mod. Der kan kun være tale om én, tænkte jeg. Marianne Rørholm. Marianne, bortset fra hendes pragtfulde stemme, *lignede* den udgave af *Tilfred*, som Jeg forestillede mig hende, både under læsningen af bogen—og senere under kompositionsarbejdet" (Ruders, *Man Har* 88–89).

[23] Alan Weiss quotes this line from the manuscript version of Atwood's article "If You Can't Say Something Nice, Don't Say Anything at All" (Atwood's papers at the University of Toronto, MS 200 Box 147, page 18).; and furthermore notes: "[But it] was omitted from the published version, which appeared in Libby Scheier et al., eds. *Language in Her Eye*" (Weiss, 138, endnote 2).

Fig. 5 Introspective, descending harp motif

fortissimo) atonal chord that is punctuated by the sound of gunshots. It eventually thins down to an ominous quiet low bass note (55ff.).[24]

This passage ("Worst Dream") recurs with variations several times in the opera. While some might criticize this repetition, the subjectivity of reliving such trauma appears psychologically realistic. Bentley points out, "the repetition would be useful and would underline the idea that we were watching Offred's memories, not just a chronological, naturalistic, sequence of events" (43). Critics agree: it is the heroine's *ideé fixe* and the reiterations' "cumulative effect increases rather than decreases the impact" (Domville 2006, 876).

Other elements of his orchestral sound world include a quiet, descending droplet motif in the harp, replete with dissonant intervals (tritones) which accompany the mournful, contemplative passages, such as Offred's first lines of the opera ("I'm sorry my story is in fragments"), which repeats this motif four times (Fig. 5). "Like a *leitmotif*," this musical gesture is repeated "each time [Offred] sings such introspective statements" (Fairbrother Canton 130).

The Example of "Amazing Grace"

Appropriate for a dystopian setting, the opera's sound world is predominantly dissonant and atonal. Therefore, this musical style makes passages where tonal elements and recognizable melodies occur all the more conspicuous. For that purpose Bentley and Ruders pick up on one of the few references to music

---

[24] Even more dramatic versions of the "Worst Dream" occur in Act One, after Offred's aria about longing for a child "Ev'ry moon I watch for blood" (1438). The nightmarish passage starts (1569) with awkward staccato intervals on the oboe, continues with increasingly threatening short notes, trombones spit out their descending chromatic line that crescendos into a chaotic triple forte swirl of notes punctuated with shots and a pounding rhythm in the timpani. The passage ends in an eerie, open chord (octaves and fifths only) that is held over several bars. The nightmare recurs in Act Two (2809) and (2864).

from the novel, the imminently recognizable gospel hymn "Amazing Grace" and insert it no less than four times into key scenes of the opera, symmetrically distributed between Act One and Act Two and musically expressing spiritual love, while placing the hymn into parodic counterpoint to sexual love or even rape. (See symmetries 3 and 11, Appendix C.)

In Act One, Offred recognizes the commander's wife as the former television gospel singer Serena Joy from the Time Before (713–893). This connection is underlined acoustically through the "phenomenal"[25] presence of the hymn tune. In the Time Now, Serena plays a video tape of her former gospel singing self. Overhearing this acoustical signal triggers Offred's memory of her hotel room assignation with Luke, who was still married at that time. Bentley implements his concept of the simultaneity of past and presence so that the audience sees Offred's double from the Time Before switching on the television. The audience now sees and hears the relevance of "Amazing Grace": Serena and Offred are both remembering their former selves. The double physical presence makes it clear that Offred's earlier self is really a staging of Offred's memory, underlining the subjectivity of the narrative's perspective.

Ruders expresses the simultaneity of past and present through the clash of two different tonalities. "Amazing Grace" is drawn out in slow motion and given "the full Hollywood treatment" (Bentley 113) with three verses and a fourth one hummed over eighty bars sung in Serena Joy's sonorous alto voice. Serena's hymn is supported by a full women's chorus and electronic organ in D major. Against this, Offred and Luke's dialogue, on the other hand, is written in short, speech-like phrases accompanied with a bouncy and vivacious eighth-note pattern oscillating in the tonalities of A flat, E flat, and B flat major, which create grating, dissonant half-tones against Serena Joy's drawn out religious hymn.

More grotesque parodies appear in the second and third occurrences of the hymn when its allusions to sacred and spiritual love occur in Act One and Act Two during the impregnation ceremonies, the institutionalized rape prescribed by the regime (1876ff. and 2377ff.). The hymn tune recurs one last time in an emotionally charged scene in Act Two (3305ff.) at the illicit night club, Jezebel's. Offred has just said her final farewell to her best and only friend Moira while the Commander sits on the bed waiting for an assignation with her. Ruders has the chorale sound very quietly (*piano pianissimo*) as if from a distance (*espressivo lontano*) just before

---

[25] In the sense described by Carolyn Abbate; instances in which characters within opera perceive another character's singing specifically as music or song (Abbate 119ff).

Offred enters the room. This time the hymn tune appears with dignity and restraint, purely instrumental (in the strings), written in D flat major without the dissonant clashes composed in Act One.[26]

"Amazing Grace" as a hymn offers a multitude of connotations for the audience. Written by John Newton, an eighteenth-century slave trader–turned-Anglican priest, the lyrics address the question of forgiveness of sins, thereby overcoming spiritual and material challenges. The current melody has come to be associated with a wide range of social movements, particularly in the U.S., ranging from populist, evangelical religion to injustice committed against Indigenous populations (sung on the 1830s Cherokee's Trail of Tears) and the civil rights and anti-war movements (Turner 195ff.). Turner has counted over 1000 currently available albums featuring versions of the hymn (172). In the U.S., it has been called "Our Spiritual National Anthem," as the subtitle of Rourke's monograph indicates. Ruders cleverly draws on this eminently recognizable tune and shapes it into a *leitmotif* that recurs, as we have seen, several times during the opera. *BBC Music Magazine* critic Stephen Johnson considers Ruders' usage "splendid, gruesome variations" (quoted in Bentley 132).[27] The composer has picked up on one of the novel's few references to music or song: "such songs are not sung any more in public, especially the ones that use words like *free*" (Atwood's italics, *The Handmaid's Tale* 64). In the context of the novel, however, the hymn is sung by Offred silently in her head. She enjoys the "lugubrious, mournful, presbyterian" aspects of the song. Since this song has been outlawed in Gilead, the novel offers here also another instance of Offred's quiet insubordination.[28] In the novel, Serena Joy is not specifically associated with

---

[26] Keen ears and eyes will even pick up a brief fifth "Amazing Grace" reference. At Jezebel's, the Commander tells Offred "I will meet you. In Room 121" (3249) as she goes to meet Moira in the washroom. Underneath the party scene music, the trombone reiterates the hymn as *leitmotif* (3251ff.), foreshadowing, the Commander's sexual intentions.

[27] Christian fundamentalists in the U.S., on the other hand, were particularly offended by the opera's parodic use of "Amazing Grace": "To have your religion distorted and ridiculed and then to have one of your culture's most deeply treasured expressions purposely profaned—well, it's not very pleasant ... Some would go on further to call the opera—and not without justification—an example of 'hate speech'" (Michael Linton, "The Bigot's Opera" from *First Things: A Monthly Journal of Religion and Public Life*, quoted in Laycock 127).

[28] The other song, Atwood references in her novel is Elvis Presley's "Heartbreak Hotel" from which Offred only half-remembers the lyrics, "I feel so lonely, baby,/ I feel so lonely I could die" (64), which clearly echo Offred's situation in the Time Now and resonate with the hotel room scenes elsewhere. Presley's lyrics run: "I'll be so lonely baby/ Well, I'm so lonely/ I'll be so lonely, I could die" ("Songfacts"). Atwood slyly points here to another issue raised by the novel, the status of the narrative as a subjective first-person reconstruction of events from memory. However, Presley's 1956 song is still under copyright, less iconic

"Amazing Grace." Offred reports hearing "the thin sounds of Serena's voice, from a disc made long ago and played now with the volume low, so she won't be caught listening as she sits there … remembering her own former and now amputated glory: *Hallelujah*" (64). Through the hymn's association with adultery and illicit sex in the opera, critics see the parodic use of it as "more suitably titled 'Amazing Disgrace'" and the hymn itself as "debased through the various kinds of hypocrisy—religious, social, and sexual—practiced in Gilead" (Domville 2006, 878). As Fairbrother Canton remarks, tonal elements, such as the recitations of dogma in open intervals of fourths and fifths, as well as the tonal melodies of "Amazing Grace" belong to the sound world of the regime. In contrast, Offred's world is represented through anxiety and dissonance.[29]

Conclusion

In the adaption from novel to opera, the inherent qualities of one genre—such as the single-author, single lines of the novel's linguistic sign system—is transformed through a collaboration of librettist and composer, who condense the source's linguistic elements to expand and envelop them with music and stage directions into a new, more complex sign system captured in a stable format in the shape of an orchestral score that encapsulates linguistic, auditory, and visual information, an entire set of dimensions not present in a novel.

As we have seen, building an actual production of the opera necessitates a complex process of decoding the score that involves multiple layers of transformation and adaptation. Artistic and creative production teams decipher and interpret the stable orchestral score either directly or with the aid of simplifications—the piano vocal score perhaps supported by digital or live recordings—in order to prepare a spatially and temporally envisioned text—the production—to be turned into a realized text, the performance. This process necessitates decisions concerning visual and auditory matters that add significant and additional layers of meaning to the composer/librettist text.

---

than "Amazing Grace," and would be far more difficult to integrate into the sonic universe of Poul Ruders' opera.

[29] Harry Somers and Rod Anderson's opera *Mario and the Magician* (1992) similarly uses the hymn of the Italian Fascist Party "Giovinezza" which also stands out for its conformity in simple tonality in the context of Somers' contemporary musical idiom.

In the case of the opera *The Handmaid's Tale*, librettist Paul Bentley applied his insights as an experienced theater professional to his collaboration with composer Poul Ruders. Their teamwork went beyond conventional thinking in the two dimensions of melded words and music. From the very beginning, they addressed dramatic strategies in their thinking. Together they created a fully fledged concept for staging that is captured in the opera's stable source text, the orchestral score. This complex sign system, the score, transforms the novel's first-person subjective point of view through word and music in conjunction with innovative staging solutions: Offred's autobiographical voice emerges from a tape recorder at the opera's beginning as her story's "source text." It creates psychological realism by repeating the protagonist's trauma painted in expressive orchestral colors. It externalizes the protagonist's memories through simultaneous presentation of past and present. Based on their professional experience, Bentley and Ruders faithfully translated Offred's story into word, music, and the visual, from one to three dimensions.

From the start, their teamwork operated in the multidimensional universe of opera that includes creative staging solutions to deliver a text (full score) that offers theatrical effect and drama. Poul Ruders fully embraced the collaboration with Bentley, engaged with and integrated his librettist's dramatic suggestions and, in turn, invented highly expressive sound patterns to enhance the story's emotional weight. Ruders adds layers of meaning through his choice of the color palettes in orchestration and provides musical contrasts (introverted Offred versus explosive moments), often connected through repeating *leitfmotifs*. It is this multidimensional approach of the libretto/composer team that makes the product of this collaboration so particularly successful that opera companies in Denmark and the U.S. planned to collaborate on fully staged productions in 2020.[30]

The task of the multidimensional critic of opera, then, ideally plumbs the genre's essence—the interaction of performance, music, and words—to develop a multi-disciplinary analysis that combines elements of musicology, literary, and theater studies, in order to communicate a rich and productive experience of this highly complex text, called opera.

---

[30] Opera companies working towards new productions include the Royal Danish Opera, Copenhagen, originally set to open in May 2020, in a co-production with the San Francisco Opera that was to open in October 2020. Neither opening was realized due to ongoing COVID-19 restrictions.

Appendix A: Performances to Date

	Copenhagen 2000	London 2003	Minneapolis 2003	Toronto 2004	Melbourne 2018	Boston 2019	Copenhagen (originally planned for 2020)	San Francisco (originally planned for 2020)
Company	Royal Danish Opera	English National Opera	Minnesota Opera	Canadian Opera Company	Gertrude Opera, Yarra Valley Opera Festival	Boston Lyric Opera	Royal Danish Opera	San Francisco Opera
Conductor	Michael Schønwandt	Elgar Howarth	Antony Walker	Richard Bradshaw	Patrick Burns	David Angus	Giedre Šlekyte	Thomas Søndergård
Director	Phyllida Lloyd	Phyllida Lloyd	Eric Simonson	Phyllida Lloyd	Linda Thompson	Anne Bogart	John Fulljames	John Fulljames
Stage design	Peter McKintosh	Peter McKintosh	Robert Israel	Peter McKintosh	Joseph Noonan	James Schuette	Chloe Lamford	Chloe Lamford
Offred	Marianne Rørholm	Stephanie Marshall	Elizabeth Bishop	Stephanie Marshall	Sarah Heltzel	Jennifer Johnson Cano	Rachel Kelly	Sasha Cooke
Sung in	Danish	English	English	English	English	English	Danish	English
Performance space	1600-seat Royal Danish Theatre (1874)	2359-seat Coliseum Theatre (1904)	1700-seat Music Theater, Ordway Center for the Performing Arts (1985)	3200-seat O'Keefe Centre (1960)	200-seat circus tent	2200-seat Lavietes basketball pavilion	1700-seat New Royal Opera House "Operaen" (2005)	3145-seat War Memorial Opera House (1932)

Originally planned for performances in 2020, the Royal Danish Opera and San Francisco Opera's postponed their co-production of The Handmaid's Tale, due to COVID-19 restrictions.

Appendix B: A Summary of Symmetries

Act One	Act Two
1. THE WALL—DEATH BY HANGING Offred looks at a dead body	1. NEXT MORNING "DEATH BY HANGING" Offred's body looks dead
2. THE HOUSE IN THE DAY—HER Offred and Serena joy talk in her sitting room	2. THE HOUSE AT NIGHT—HIM Offred and the commander talk in his study
3. OFFRED'S ROOM—ALONE Offred is alone Memories of Luke making love to her	3. JOY'S ROOM—WITH HER AND HIM Offred is with Serena joy and the commander He starts "making love" to her
4. SHOPPING—MILK AND HONEY The Martha and Nick and Ofglen Shopping for food Pregnant Janine, model handmaid	4. SHOPPING—SOUL SCROLLS The Martha and Nick and Ofglen Shopping for prayers Offred and Ofglen, rebel handmaids
5. THE WALL—SAFETY Ofglen says "may day" Offred does not understand Ignorance is safety	5. THE WALL—DANGER Ofglen explains "may day" Eyes seize a man Knowledge is danger
6. THE HOUSE IN THE DAY The commander in Offred's room She is tense—*No lite te bastardes carborundorum*	6. THE HOUSE AT NIGHT Offred in the Commander's room She is relaxed—Nolite te bastardes carborundorum
7. THE WALL—PRESCRIBED TALK With Ofglen	7. THE WALL—PROSCRIBED TALK With Ofglen
8. THE DOCTOR'S OFFER To make Offred pregnant Bribe—no colonies	8. THE WIFE'S OFFER To get Nick to make her pregnant Bribe—a photo of Offred's daughter
9. OFFRED ALONE She thinks	9. OFFRED ALONE She prays
10. JOY'S SITTING ROOM—FOREPRAY a godly gathering of men and women prior to sex	10. JEZEBEL'S—FOREPLAY Ungodly gathering of men and women prior to sex
11. LICIT SEX An official impregnation— Offred and commander and Wife	11. ILLICIT SEX An unofficial impregnation— Offred and commander (and Luke)
12. THE HOUSE AT NIGHT- DANGER Unlawfully, Offred tries to steal a keepsake from joy Nick comes to her—they kiss once Danger—they do not take chances	12. THE HOUSE AT NIGHT—DANGER Unlawfully, joy shows Offred a photo of her daughter She goes to Nick to make love often Danger—they take chances
13. THE BIRTH DAY Women celebrate life— They help Janine have a baby	13. THE DEATH DAY Women celebrate death— They help kill criminals
14. THE UNEXPECTED Unlawfully, Offred meets the commander Who wants to break the rules— Joy knows nothing	14. THE UNEXPECTED Lawfully, Offred meets a new Ofglen Who wants to keep the rules— Joy knows all
15. RELEASE Offred's tension is released by laughter	15. RELEASE Offred's tension is released by escape

Bentley (20)

Appendix C: Full Orchestral Score Sample
(Bars 54ff)

This section is scored for: 3 flutes, 3 oboes, 3 clarinets, 3 bassoons, 4 French horns in F, 3 trumpets, 3 trombones, 4 percussionists, digital piano, vocal soloists, chorus, first and second violins, violas, violoncellos, and double basses with all strings playing double or triple stops (two or three notes simultaneously) (Fig. 6).

Fig. 6 Full orchestral score

Works Cited

Abbate, Carolyn. *Unsung Voices: Opera and Musical Narrative in the Nineteenth Century*. Princeton University Press, 1991.
Allen, David. "'The Handmaid's Tale' Is a Brutal Triumph as Opera." *New York Times*, 11 May 2019, p. 2.
Atwood, Margaret. "For God and Gilead." *The Guardian*, 22 Mar. 2003, p. 18.
———. *The Handmaid's Tale*. McClelland & Stewart, 1985.
———. *The Handmaid's Tale*. Narrated by Claire Danes et al. Audible, 2017.
Balea, Ilie. "Vers une sémiologie de l'opéra: Systèmes-Structures-Interférences Sémiologiques." *Etudes littéraires*, vol. 13, no. 3, 1980, pp. 437–59.
Balestrini, Nassim Winnie. *From Fiction to Libretto: Irving, Hawthorne, and James as Opera*. Peter Lang, 2005.
Barone, Joshua. "'The Handmaid's Tale' Comes Home to Boston. As an Opera." *New York Times*, 3 May 2019. Web. 4 May 2019.
Bentley, Paul. *A Handmaid's Diary*. Wilhelm Hansen, 2004.
Blake, Andrew. "'Wort Oder Ton'?: Reading the Libretto in Contemporary Opera." *Contemporary Music Review*, vol. 28, no. 2, 2010, pp. 187–99.
Clark, Caryl Leslie, and Linda Hutcheon. "Adapting a Canonical Canadian Novel for the Operatic Stage: A Dystopia for Our Times." *University of Toronto Quarterly*, vol. 75, no. 3, 2006, pp. 815–20.
Domville, Eric. "New Productions/New Roles: The Canadian Opera Company Presents the Canadian Premiere of The Handmaid's Tale by Poul Ruders and Paul Bentley." *Opera Canada*, vol. 45, no. 3, 2004, pp. 9–10.
Domville, Eric. "The Handmaid's Detail: Notes on the Novel and Opera." *University of Toronto Quarterly*, vol. 75, no. 3, 2006, pp. 869–82.
Everett-Green, Robert. "Canadian Opera Company Unveils New Season." *Globe and Mail*, 17 January 2007. https://www.theglobeandmail.com/arts/canadian-opera-company-unveils-new-season/article20391898/. Accessed June 1, 2020.
Fairbrother Canton, Kimberly. n.d. "'I'm Sorry My Story Is in Fragments': Offred's Operatic Counter-Memory." *English Studies in Canada*, vol. 33, no. 3, pp. 124–44.
Genette, Gérard. *Paratexts: Thresholds of Interpretation*. Cambridge University Press, 1997.
Goodman, Nelson. *Languages of Art: An Approach to a Theory of Symbols*. 2nd ed. fourth printing 1981, Hackett, 1976.
Gorlée, Dinda L. "Intersemioticity and Intertextuality: Picaresque and Romance in Opera." *Sign System Studies*, vol. 44, no. 4, 2016, pp. 587–622.
Großmann, Stephanie. *Inszenierungsanalyse von Opern*. Königshausen & Neumann, 2013.

Harris, Holly. "Don't Be Afraid of the Dark." *Winnipeg Free Press*, 12 October 2018. Factiva. Accessed 26 May 2020.

Hartmann, Tina. *Grundlegung einer Librettologie: Musik- und Lesetext am Beispiel der "Alceste"-Opern vom Barock bis zu C.M. Wieland*. De Gruyter, 2017.

Hutcheon, Linda. *A Theory of Adaptation*. Routledge, 2012.

Hutcheon, Linda and Michael Hutcheon. "Adaptation and Opera." *Oxford Handbook of Adaptation Studies*. Ed. Thomas Leitch, Oxford University Press, 2017. Oxford Handbooks Online. Accessed 21 Jan. 2020.

Laycock, F. C. *Contemporary Opera as Relevant and Effective Socio-Political Critique: Two Case Studies*. North-West University, 2007.

Marsoobian, Armen T. "Saying, Singing, or Semiotics: 'Prima la Musica e poi le Parole' Revisited." *Journal of Aesthetics and Art Criticism*, vol. 54, no. 3, 1996, pp. 269–77.

Moghaddam, Nita M. "From Page to Virtual Stage: A Socio-Semiotic Reading of Stage Directions." *Social Semiotics*, vol. 26, no. 4, 2016, pp. 351–65.

Morra, Irene. "Outstaring the Sun: Contemporary Opera and the Literary Librettist." *Contemporary Music Review*, vol. 29, no. 2, 2010, pp. 121–35.

Peiken, Matt. "X-Treme Opera: Profanity? Illicit Sex? Perversion? Grisly Deaths? The Minnesota Opera Throws Caution to Prevailing Winds and Presents the North American Premiere of the Controversial *Handmaid's Tale*." *Saint Paul Pioneer Press*, 9 May 2003. Web. Accessed 24 January 2020.

Reichenbächer, Helmut. "Offred Reframed: The Adaptation from Novel to Opera." *University of Toronto Quarterly*, vol. 75, no. 3, 2006, pp. 835–49.

Rosmarin, Leonard. *When Literature Becomes Opera: Study of a Transformational Process*. Rodopi, 1999.

Rourke, Mary, 1949. *Amazing Grace in America: Our Spiritual National Anthem*. Angel City Press, 1996.

Ruders, Poul. *Har Man Hørt Så Galt: Et Tilbageblik*. Kahrius, 2019.

Scheier, Libby, et al., eds. *Language in Her Eye: Views on Writing and Gender by Canadian Women Writing in English*. Coach House Press, 1990.

Sindoni, Maria Grazia, and Fabio Rossi. "'Un Nodo Avviluppato': Rossini's *La Cenerentola* as a Prototype of Multimodal Resemiotisation." *Social Semiotics*, vol. 26, no. 4, 2016.

"Songfacts." *Heartbreak Hotel Lyrics*, https://www.songfacts.com/lyrics/elvispresley/heartbreak-hotel. Accessed 20 Jan. 2020.

Steane, J. B. "Fach." *The New Grove Dictionary of Opera*. 4 vols. Ed. Stanley Sadie. Oxford University Press, 1992. Vol. 2, pp. 102-103.

Turner, Steve. 1949. *Amazing Grace: The Story of America's Most Beloved Song*. Ecco, 2002.

Weiss, Allan. "Offred's Complicity and the Dystopian Tradition in Margaret Atwood's 'The Handmaid's Tale'." *Studies in Canadian Literature*, vol. 34, no. 1, 2009, pp. 120–41.

Recording

Ruders, Poul. *Tjenerindens Fortælling/The Handmaid's Tale/Der Bericht der Magd*. Performance by Michael Schønwandt, conductor, Royal Danish Opera Chorus and Royal Danish Orchestra. dacapo, 2001. 8.224165-66. 2 CDs. Recorded live at the Royal Danish Theatre on 6, 8, 9, and 11 March 2000.

Orchestral Score

Ruders, Poul. *Tjenerindens Fortælling/The Handmaid's Tale/Der Bericht der Magd*. Wilhelm Hansen, 2000. Music Online: Classical Scores Library, Volume III Database. Web. http://go.utlib.ca/cat/12121299.

PART III

Atwood in the World: Atwood Adaptation Practitioners

Staging *The Penelopiad*

Penny Farfan
With contrib. by Kelly Thornton and Vanessa Porteous

Margaret Atwood's only play, *The Penelopiad* (2007), was adapted from her novella *The Penelopiad* (2005), which revisits the myth of Odysseus from the perspectives of his wife Penelope and her twelve maids. The script was developed in collaboration with the Royal Shakespeare Company and premiered at the Swan Theatre in Stratford-upon-Avon in July 2007 in a co-production with the National Arts Centre in Ottawa, where it had its Canadian premiere in September 2007. The play subsequently went on to receive acclaimed productions by leading theatre companies across Canada, including Nightwood Theatre in Toronto, Alberta Theatre Projects in Calgary, and Arts Club Theatre Company in Vancouver. In the interviews that follow, directors Kelly Thornton and Vanessa Porteous reflect on the challenges and opportunities *The Penelopiad* presented as a stage adaptation of a non-dramatic text and on their productions as adaptations in their own right—further echoes in the reverberating chain embedded in

---

P. Farfan (✉)
School of Creative and Performing Arts, Faculty of Arts, University of Calgary, Calgary, AB, Canada
e-mail: farfan@ucalgary.ca

Atwood's adaptation of a myth that has been adapted repeatedly over time, taking on new resonances in traversing millennia.[1]

"EVERY NIGHT IS A NEW ECHO": KELLY THORNTON'S *PENELOPIAD*

Kelly Thornton directed *The Penelopiad* for Nightwood Theatre, where she was Artistic Director from 2001 to 2019. Thornton's production premiered in January 2012 and was remounted the following year with a few changes to the cast.

Penny Farfan: What drew you to *The Penelopiad* and how did you come to direct it?

Kelly Thornton: I knew about *The Penelopiad* from the Royal Shakespeare Company and National Arts Centre co-production in 2007. In 2009, I organized an event called 4x4: A Festival of Female Directors. We premiered four mainstage shows by four different female directors and we also had an industry series and masterclasses. One of the masterclasses was for emerging directors from across the country, and I broke *The Penelopiad* into ten parts and gave each director a piece of it. I partnered with the Shaw Festival, so half of the actors were Shaw actors and the rest were in our Emerging Actors program. We had two Penelopes. The company would go from room to room rehearsing scenes, and the Penelopes divvied up half the scenes each in order to do it within the schedule that we had—I think we did it in one week. We put the whole thing together, teched it, and threw it on the stage. It was super-interesting to see all the visions of each of the directors, but somehow also it all held together. After doing that, I fell in love with the material and was itching to direct it myself. A couple of years later, it came to fruition in Nightwood's 2011/2012 season.

PF: The play is an adaptation of Atwood's novella *The Penelopiad*. As a stage adaptation of a non-dramatic work, did it pose particular challenges to you as a director?

KT: The biggest challenge of all is that Penelope's monologues—and there are plenty—are right off the page of the novella, so we had to find

---

[1] My interview with Kelly Thornton was conducted by telephone in November 2019. My interview with Vanessa Porteous took place in Calgary in December 2019. Both interviews have been condensed and edited for publication. Thanks to Brittany Pack for her assistance with the interview transcriptions.

the dramatic action of these passages that had been lifted off of a page. I worked with Megan Follows as Penelope to find her arc inside of this journey.[2] Why are we telling this story, and what makes it urgent? What is the act of telling this story now? What is it doing to her by telling the story out loud? She has come back to tell this story to this particular audience as a witness. So, making the monologues dramatic was the biggest challenge. The rest of the play is kind of a director's playground because Atwood doesn't give you a score—she doesn't tell you in the script what to do with the maids. You can compose it however you want and that obviously has a relationship to how you want to choreograph it, how you want to move the story around on the stage. That was super-fun—that was great!—so the biggest challenge was making the monologues dramatic and engaging, lifting them off the page.

PF: In Atwood's published script, the rape of the maids takes up around four lines on the page and is followed by a page-long ballad to be sung by the maids. Your staging of this scene was remarkable in its theatrical power and emotional impact, and it seemed to be the center or core of your production. Could you talk about your work on this scene—your thinking about it as the artistic director of a feminist theatre company, your process of figuring out how to put it on stage, the style of the scene and how it coalesced in terms of the use of double-casting and transformation, the costumes, performances, choreography, soundscape, and musical style?

KT: The first and foremost thing is that I wanted to represent the brutality of the scene—the realism—but I needed to stylize it, so we put it into slow motion so you could see the gruesome details, but also you're once-removed from people flying across the stage in real time. I worked a lot with the choreographer, Monica Dottor, on how to create these stage pictures, and also with the sound designer, Suba Sankaran. We worked very hard to create a kind of epic moment within the play because it's really a turning point. The play is very much about class, and these maids sacrificed everything for Penelope. I needed to represent how violent and real that injustice was for the women who were the front line for her. The Nightwood production was in the days before intimacy directors,[3] and it was not easy for the cast. I think it was pretty brutal for the ones playing

---

[2] Follows herself directed a production of *The Penelopiad* at the Grand Theatre in London, Ontario in 2019.
[3] On the recently established field of intimacy directing, see, for example, Derr.

the suitors to stage it—to live the brutality. In terms of the design, I was very influenced by Alexander McQueen, and costume designer Denyse Karn and I were really excited to go into that world of quite fantastical costuming—McQueen's use of bones and horns and furs—and to make very overt theatrical choices. The maids themselves are playing the suitors. They're still wearing their maids' dresses, but as soon as they put on those shoulder pads with the horns coming out of them, it became a much more base, animalistic representation, which is how we saw the suitors.

PF: It was fascinating to see the suitors then transform back into the victimized maids.

KT: Yes, because it happened to all of them. The way the story is told is the maids have come back to tell their story and they play all the characters. I think the really impactful thing about that scene was them playing both sides.

PF: Could you say a bit more about the portrayal of the male characters in the enactment of the past scenes from the lives of Penelope and the maids? A number of reviewers of the Nightwood production commented on the remarkable portrayal of Odysseus by Kelli Fox,[4] and I wondered if you could talk about what challenges and opportunities the cross-gender casting presented to you as a director and how you worked with the actresses on finding those male characters, including performing the sex scene on the wedding night of Penelope and Odysseus. How did this casting convention inform your approach to particular characters and scenes, and how did you think that convention would impact the audience's perception of the material?

KT: Well, the script calls for it, ultimately. The conceit in the story is that these are the maids. There's a reckoning that Penelope is having with the maids, and the maids take on all of the characters to retell the story. Penelope is engaging in what happened and they recreate it. Some university productions have cast men and women, but I don't think it works as effectively because ultimately it's between Penelope and her maids: she is looking for forgiveness and is not necessarily released. So, I think the actual storytelling calls for the maids to play everybody. The theatricality and the opportunity to go cross-gender with this is great, and Kelli Fox is a champion. She's an amazing actor with a lot of appetite and curiosity and really there—always present in a rehearsal hall to roll up her sleeves and dig in and play and see how she could embody these characters. Kelli and

[4] See, for example, Nestruck.

Megan Follows developed a great relationship working together. And there's a lot of comedy, but also the brutal truth that he has taken Penelope away from her family and what that experience was like for her. But ultimately I think it was the trust of those two actors that really brought that sense of play to the portrayal of their relationship. Kelli as an actor is a shapeshifter, and I think Odysseus is one of the greatest characters she has ever played. She got so much attention and had such a fun time because he's a rascal! He's a fun character and really dynamic to play, and Kelli nailed it. In both iterations, I had a great company of actors to work with, all very diverse in terms of their talents. They all had a lot of skill, and between singing, dancing, and playing multiple characters, they had a blast doing it and it was a great acting opportunity. It was a great directing opportunity for me because there was so much to play with in terms of the text, and a great opportunity for the actors to really bond as an ensemble. They won a Dora Award for Outstanding Ensemble that year.[5] Everything obviously spirals around those Penelope monologues, but they acted as an ensemble. Megan is an amazing actor and such a team player. It was always about making sure we were telling the story. How are we communicating this story? Are we getting everything across?

PF: Atwood has sometimes been resistant to having her work categorized as feminist. How did you understand her intervention as an adapter of a canonical male-authored and male-centered heroic epic, and how did you see your own approach as the director of her play, in terms of both your choice to direct it and your interpretation and staging of it?

KT: Well, I think Atwood's work is all feminist. I think she is very deeply engaged in the status of women inside of storytelling. She was asked to write the novella for the Canongate Myth Series, and I think from the moment she went into *The Odyssey* and saw that there was so little representation—just a couple of lines—to kill twelve women who had protected Penelope.... It's inherently feminist work. She's investigating the lost or buried stories of women that are not represented in literature. Within the novella, that's what she did, but I also think she's exploring a really interesting question around feminism or feminisms, which is the question of class, the question of race and privilege. Feminism has been criticized as a white women's movement that doesn't take into account privilege and the fact that not everybody is lucky enough to be liberated. It's a question of accountability, I think. Penelope takes this sleepy drink

---

[5] The Dora Awards recognize outstanding theatre in Toronto.

and goes to sleep while her twelve maids are executed, and even while they're alive, she turns a blind eye to how brutal the front line was to stave off the suitors. Penelope isolated herself more and more as the palace became overrun with suitors—she kind of abdicated from protecting the maids. She turned a blind eye to protect herself; it became self-interest. So there's an interesting thing that Atwood is unpacking within the question of feminism, which is around class and privilege. When I was running Nightwood Theatre, I wasn't always interested in just telling a heroic journey of a feminist, but in really looking at women—giving a 360-degree look at our struggles as women. I think Atwood provided that in *The Penelopiad* because certainly Penelope does not come off as a hero. She's conflicted and she's left struggling with what happened and having to confront what she has done. It's inherently feminist because Atwood is unearthing this story that was misrepresented or just ignored altogether in terms of the role of the maids and the death of the maids. That we can dispose of twelve lives in four lines is problematic.

PF: In her introduction to the published play, Atwood states, "The play you hold in your hand is an echo of an echo of an echo of an echo of an echo of an echo" (v). She's referring to layers of adaptation over time from ancient myths and legends about the Trojan War and its aftermath, to Homer's *Odyssey*, to subsequent echoes in other classic and modern texts like James Joyce's *Ulysses*, to her own novella *The Penelopiad*, to a staged reading of the novella that she herself performed in, to the dramatization of the novella that is the published text. Do you see theatrical production as another form or layer of adaptation, another step in the echoing process that Atwood describes, and if so, how did your particular production for Nightwood Theatre in Toronto, Canada in 2012 add a new layer to this echoing process of adaptation, revision, transformation?

KT: The act of theatre is ritualistic by its very nature, so I think it *is* another layer of the echoing because when we all agree to sit together in the dark and breathe together and our heart rate starts to sync up and we witness this story all together, something happens that is different than any other iteration, than when you're reading the book. All the different layers of that storytelling and the history of that story finally arrive onto a stage. In the storytelling, you can see the layers all the way back to the myth, but you pull that thread through to the here and now where you're sitting in the audience, witnessing with Penelope. Every night, the act of telling it is about the need to tell it tonight in front of this audience, to use them as witnesses.

PF: Linda Hutcheon theorizes adaptation as both interpretation and creation, "second without being secondary" (9), "repetition without replication" (7), so an adaptation is not simply an interpretation of a prior text, it's a creation of a new artwork.

KT: Absolutely. It takes its own form. To me, every night is a new echo in a way. It always has to live immediately. Every night the struggle has to begin anew for Penelope to tell that story and to confront herself.

PF: There's a huge amount of interest in Atwood right now, in part due to the recent television series of *The Handmaid's Tale*, which is going into its fourth season, but which has been controversial in part due to its relentless depiction of violence against women. There are some resonances between *The Handmaid's Tale* and *The Penelopiad*—the sexual violence in both, and there's a threat of mass hanging in *The Handmaid's Tale*. How do you understand the unique potential of theatre as a medium distinct from mass media forms such as television and film, and how does that understanding connect to *The Penelopiad* and your work on it?

KT: We hosted a teachers' night at the Manitoba Theatre Centre recently, and I commended all the teachers who bring their students for understanding the value of theatre and getting kids off their screens to experience the liveness. I go all the way back to the birthplace of Western theatre in Greece, where going to the theatre was an obligation. As a citizen, you had to go to the theatre and you went there to confront and unpack the critical issues of the day—it was about being a good citizen to show up and experience these things. And the nature of theatre goes all the way back to storytelling, sitting around a campfire and listening to one story being told, hearing a hero's journey. The very nature of telling a story live and having the interchange between the actor and the audience—that exchange is palpable. Theatre doesn't live unless it has an audience. Watching a film or reading a book is a wonderful experience, but there's not the same immediacy. I value all the other ways of telling stories, but there's something very impactful for audiences to experience something that's living. And the construction of *The Penelopiad* is all about *meeting* the audience. Penelope is coming back. I staged it so that she was coming out of the antechamber in Hades and talking to the audience (Fig. 1). She was trying to confront herself, and she had to do it by coming out and exposing herself.

PF: Thinking back to your earlier discussion of particular scenes in your production, do you see transformation as part of theatre's distinctiveness?

Fig. 1 Megan Follows as Penelope in *The Penelopiad*, Nightwood Theatre, 2012; photo by Robert Popkin

KT: The script calls for a director to make theatrical choices. Atwood doesn't provide a roadmap, there are no stage directions, and there are no composed songs. You see the ballad on the page, but how do you want to do that? How are you going to inject living, breathing characters into these constructs within the play? So, I think the construction of the piece as we're going to go back into the story, we're going to tell the story as we remember it, calls for a kind of an overt theatrical staging. Also, even when I'm staging realism, I don't like to waste opportunities to remind people that we're in a theatre because theatre is magic. Theatre should be arresting and exciting and collective. The most fundamental thing about it is that it's a collective experience for the actors and audience together. And I want to reiterate that the creative team around me on *The Penelopiad* was incredible. There were so many important people in the production and design teams and in the cast that were all deeply engaged in representing the story, in memory of all the women that are thrown away—all of the narratives that are lost or deemed unimportant. At Nightwood Theatre, we were very, very, very mindful to be telling the stories of the invisible women because that's the most important story to tell.

"EACH PRODUCTION IS ANOTHER STEP IN THE ECHOING PROCESS": VANESSA PORTEOUS'S *PENELOPIAD*

Vanessa Porteous was Artistic Director of Alberta Theatre Projects in Calgary from 2009 to 2018. Her production of *The Penelopiad* premiered at ATP in September 2010 and was presented by the Arts Club Theatre Company in Vancouver the following year with some changes to the cast.

Penny Farfan: Your production of *The Penelopiad* in 2010 was the first production of your first season as the first woman artistic director of Alberta Theatre Projects. What drew you to the play, and how did you come to choose it as your first production as Artistic Director of ATP?

Vanessa Porteous: I went to a conference for women theatre-makers organized by Kelly Thornton at Nightwood Theatre in Toronto in the spring of 2009 when I was starting at ATP in the role of Artistic Director.[6] As part of the conference, they did a staged reading of *The Penelopiad* and I had a brainstorm that I should direct it at ATP. I called my team and said, "I know this is insane. There's a million people in this show, but I think we can try to put together a budget. We could use all local artists and designers, with Meg Roe as Penelope; we could do it on a thrust stage, which would be cheaper than doing it on the proscenium; and we could have a fundraising campaign where women in Calgary could support it and we could launch a new relationship with the donor community." It felt like we had stumbled upon a kind of rebranding product, but it arose from a very genuine response to the material.

PF: The play is an adaptation of Atwood's 2005 novella of the same title. As a stage adaptation of a non-dramatic work, did it pose particular challenges for you as director?

VP: Yes, it did. Working with actress Meg Roe as Penelope, an insight came to us early in rehearsals in Calgary that we needed to let Atwood be Atwood. The texture of Atwood's writing—her linguistic metaphor and imagery, the fact that the meanings are in the language, tone, and narrative point of view—are the strengths of the piece. We wanted to make our production an evening of theatre that celebrated, highlighted, and lived in that world and worry less about the dramaturgy of the scenes that are written like dialogue, like those about Telemachus and Penelope. The other material that is more like poetry—song, monologue, even narrative, like

---

[6] On Nightwood's 4x4 Festival, see Thornton in this chapter.

when Penelope is filling in the story—is stronger from a writerly perspective than the dialogue scenes. We saw the piece more as a story told in theatre than as a play—a brilliantly beautiful and complicated piece of theatre.

Another example is that in the novella version of *The Penelopiad*, the passages with the suitors that kick off Act 2 in the play are written sort of comedy-style—there are these jokes. In rehearsal, I initially tried to get the actors to make these jokes funny, but the scenes about rape were not going to be funny on stage. It may be possible in the book because there's a distanciation in the prose on the page, and there's also that Atwood wryness, dark irony, and bitter humor, but when you bring characters like the maid Melantho into being on stage, you've invited the audience to really invest in her and her relationship with Penelope. You've built it on stage, and then she gets raped and there are jokes, but in the theatre, those are not funny jokes.

PF: The play moves between Penelope's direct address to the audience, the choral odes, and the re-enactment scenes. How did you understand the relationship between those elements?

VP: What pulls it all together is the question of why Penelope is telling the story and why the maids are telling the story, because there's a dual narrative. In the theatre, at least in our tradition, the intention of the storyteller is the key to the whole experience because they build a relationship with the audience and that's the main relationship in the play. We needed to figure out why Penelope is telling the story, and also figure out what the maids want, and that is actually the central conflict of the play. We decided that Penelope is retelling the story hoping to change the outcome. If she can get in there at the point where she feels like she made her big mistake, maybe she can change the outcome. Meanwhile, the maids are trying to get her to see the impact of her actions on them. So both sides are motivated to re-enact the story, but never are any of the events actually happening—they're all happening in Hades, and that's why there can be a folk song, a poem, a movement piece, or a scene. That premise affected everything, even our lighting cue session when we realized we had to make some changes because of this rule about it always being in Hades. We ended up with these very fundamental principles that organized everything.

PF: The work of the chorus in your production was striking, especially the first choral ode, with all the echoes and repetitions of lines of the text and the choreography with the neck and foot movements that suggested the hanging scene and the hints of the geese from Penelope's dream. How did you develop that staging?

VP: Denise Clarke, who was playing Helen, was the choreographer for the production, and she came up with the idea of making the choral odes rhythmical. She took what Atwood had put on the page and moved it from poetic rhythm into physicality rhythm. We had already established a movement vocabulary that included the geese, cleaning, and other maid things referenced by Atwood in the text. Denise used that vocabulary to build the dance piece for the opening choral ode and then she coached all of those movements into the rest of the show, because, again, we're always in Hades—they're always ghosts of the maids. The maids got hanged, so they're shades revisiting their past, demanding that Penelope not ignore what she did. According to interviews I've read, that was Atwood's impulse: to take that little quatrain from *The Odyssey* and ask who those maids were, to bring into the historical record the experience of the female working class in the story, and to name them. One major moment in the play is the naming of all the maids, which is when they get a big part of what they want out of the evening. In our production, they got named and then stepped forward and looked around at the audience because their goal as characters is to not be forgotten. There are supposed to be twelve maids, but we did it with ten plus Meg, so there were eleven people in the show. At the moment when the maids were named, two didn't step forward, but as far as I know, nobody noticed.

PF: You couldn't get the budget for the twelve maids?

VP: Twelve was just too rich for our blood.

PF: Did you feel you had to achieve a balance between Penelope and the maids?

VP: I made a decision casting-wise that I wanted the maids to be a range of individuals. The point of the show is that these were real women, so I needed them to have different body types and ages and a cultural range, and to never use them as a singular choreographic element because that repulsed me politically. They needed to have their own individual reactions. So in terms of a balance with Penelope, it wasn't a group of ten versus one. It wasn't a two-person show, one of which is ten people. It was an eleven-person show.

The other casting issue that arose for me was the question of how old Penelope should be when she's telling this story. I wanted her to be the age she was when the events involving the maids occurred, not the age she got to be when Odysseus came home and they had a life together. She's in her psychic age for the story. She should be the young wife.

PF: In Atwood's script, the rape scene is around four lines of text and is followed by a ballad. In your production, the actresses playing the suitors transformed into the victimized maids and then more came on stage. There was a violinist playing live, standing within an upstage cluster of dangling ropes.

VP: And in Vancouver, Penelope came with a bowl and washed Melantho's feet. The music was by Allison Lynch, a composer and singer who was part of the cast. There was an emotional toll on the cast as we worked on those scenes. Staging physical violence is a very technical experience. It's a lot like, "what if you lifted your left leg and you lowered yours," and everyone's like, "yes, sure, I could do that," or, "I can't because of my sore wrist." But after working it for a bit, people were upset—they were feeling it. Anyway, we got it staged and then the ballad was them in the attic where they live after it's over, trying to comfort each other. Penelope's complicity was a big question. Her presence for the end of that song made it clear that she was not unaware.

The notion of the rapists turning into the victims of rape was a move that characterized our production. We saw it in innocent form on the day when Odysseus runs the race and suddenly we meet the men, who are played by the women taking their dresses down and tying them around their waist. Where it pays off, from a motif point of view, is when the maids play the suitors getting shot, transform back into the maids wiping up the blood of their rapists, and then step into the line-up to be hanged. The maids' cleaning gesture all the time in Hades is their trauma gesture, wiping up the blood of their rapists while hearing that they're about to get hanged. That's the injustice Atwood is on about—historic and ancient and universal. So turning into their own rapist was the first round of that. And that's what theatre can do, and that's what's so exciting about doing a piece like *The Penelopiad*. Atwood does it in the writing and then we do it in our physicality, and those are different modes of expression.

PF: How did you approach the cross-gender role-playing by the maids, including the wedding night scene with Penelope and Odysseus?

VP: The dramaturgical premise of the piece is that the maids come into the world of the play to tell their version of the story, so they embody all the characters in the play except Penelope. Eurycleia isn't really Eurycleia, she's one of the twelve named maids. Never is it really Odysseus. All the actresses in the production are playing women, and then those women undertake the roles of the men they feel like talking about. For that reason, we didn't really get fussy about it. The challenge in the wedding night scene was that the bed was on a swing that was kind of narrow, about the size of a twin bed and a half. So the sex scene was actually about those beautiful poses that they did while Meg Roe as Penelope narrated. In the audience's imagination, they witnessed the sex, but what they were really witnessing was actress Jamie Konchak as Odysseus trying to hold the bed steady while they moved through four or five poses that we had carefully worked out and Meg delivered Penelope's monologue. It ended up being beautiful, but it was quite a technical exercise.

Toward the end of the play, there's a little scene between Odysseus and Penelope where they say, we're older now, we really love each other, but we don't understand or know each other. That scene in our production had Odysseus roll off the back of the bed, walk upstage shedding the rope harness that showed the world that that was Odysseus, and join the line-up of maids.

PF: And the maids were present on stage for the entire scene, so Odysseus leaving again had a visual and emotional sense that is maybe not as clear in the text on the page.

VP: We also decided in our production that the maids would never look at Penelope except when they're playing roles in the re-enactment scenes, and that meant partly that her longing to reconnect with the maids was motivating the enactments. One of our cues for this decision that they would not otherwise look at her was the passage at the end of the play when Penelope says, "They never talk to me, down here. They never stay. I hold out my arms to them, my doves, my loveliest ones. But they only run away" (82).

PF: And Penelope has to live with what she did ever after.

VP: That's it. It's that simple.

PF: Atwood describes the published script of *The Penelopiad* as "an echo of an echo of an echo of an echo of an echo of an echo" (v), referring to the layers of adaptation over time that are embedded in the text. How does theatrical production fit in that echoing process? Is it another form of adaptation?

VP: For us, Atwood was much more present than Homer, but the piece live is not the same as the published text, nor is one production the same as the next, so yes, absolutely, each production is another step in the echoing process. In the introduction to her new translation of *The Odyssey*, Emily Wilson talks about the question of solo authorship or whether *The*

Odyssey is a transcription of bardic material. There's also the old idea that nothing brilliant could be written by committee that has been debunked with the Bible, the Book of Common Prayer, and the *Oxford English Dictionary*, and possibly that's the case for the Homeric material. In a similar way in the theatre, a production can't ever be credited to just one person, and certainly not in the case of *The Penelopiad*, which was immensely collaborative in both Calgary and Vancouver. My work as director was in part a gathering of artistic forces and gut impulses. For example, the idea of the set being all ropes was set designer Terry Gunvordahl's, and then I realized that ropes could also be used for Odysseus's bow and arrow and for the loom (Fig. 2). The texture of the soundscape was all Allison Lynch. Much of the conceptual rigor of the production came from Meg Roe. The beautiful staging was Denise Clarke. Costume designer Deitra Kalyn was interested in Greek echoes in the costumes, I had an idea that the maids should wear work dresses like the ones

Fig. 2 *The Penelopiad*, Alberta Theatre Projects, 2010. From left to right: Kathi Kerbes, Esther Purves-Smith, Vanessa Sabourin, Jamie Konchak, Elinor Holt, Meg Roe, Adrienne Smook, Janelle Cooper, Lindsay Mullan, Allison Lynch, Denise Clarke; photo by Trudie Lee

sold at the Kensington Market in Toronto, and Meg had a dress and thought it would be great if Penelope's dress was exactly like it except in blue. I'm not trying to erase myself here, but it's important that the names of these people be in the record, kind of like the maids' names need to be. All these ideas felt harmonious to me, and the production was extremely unified in all of its choices, which actually came from many different sources.

PF: So the theatrical process in a sense echoes the writing process of both Homer and Atwood, and each production of *The Penelopiad* adds its own echo to the long chain of echoes that Atwood describes as embedded in the published script.

VP: Yes.

PF: There's a lot of interest in Atwood right now, in part due to the recent television series of *The Handmaid's Tale*, which is about to go into its fourth season and has certain resonances with *The Penelopiad*—the sexual violence, the mass execution by hanging. What do you see as the unique potential of theatre as a medium distinct from mass media forms, particularly television but also film, and how did that inform your work on *The Penelopiad*?

VP: There are things theatre can do that other media and forms of storytelling can't, and there are things those other forms of storytelling are very good at that theatre can't do. What's great and maybe unique about theatre is that there needs to be a hole in it—there needs to be a space for the audience to contribute their imaginative energy. It's often in the visual field, but it can be anything. So, there needs to be gaps, or cracks, where we show you one part of it—the metonymic nature of theatre is maybe its unique feature. In other media, like in television, they have to wrestle with some other challenge around a full screen—there are no gaps. We show you a coil of rope on the shoulder of an actress, and that is the military uniform of Odysseus, one of the great heroes of our cultural tradition. We put the actresses playing the maids in work dresses, and everyone in the audience will immediately understand who they are. That metaphor, symbol, icon, or ideograph (as director Julie Taymor calls it)— that one thing stands in for a whole universe of knowledge and meaning, and then that makes the audience excited because they see it and are doing the *mise en scène* with you in their own minds. I think maybe that's the strength of theatre, and if you can kind of nestle into a groove when you're making theatre that acknowledges or is aware of that power of theatre, then you might make something good.

PF: Atwood is somewhat resistant to having her work categorized as feminist. How do you understand her intervention as an adapter of a canonical male-authored, male-centered heroic epic, and how did you understand your own approach as a director of *The Penelopiad* in terms of both your choice to direct the play and your interpretation and staging of it?

VP: Atwood ushered in an era of Canadian literary feminism that defines my entire life, so whatever she feels like calling it, I certainly call it feminism. The story is about female voicelessness and competitive voicelessness—Penelope feels powerless and the maids feel powerless. I also feel like *The Penelopiad* is a piece of the puzzle in the story of *The Odyssey* that comes right out of the sources. It's not a superficial vaudeville on *The Odyssey*; I kind of take it literally. I didn't have to say "feminist" in my director's note in the program. To me, the show was talking about injustice and inequality through time and continuing today.

Works Cited

Atwood, Margaret. *The Penelopiad: The Play*. Faber and Faber, 2007.

Derr, Holly L. "The Art and Craft of Intimacy Direction." *HowlRound Theatre Commons*, 30 Jan. 2020, https://howlround.com/art-and-craft-intimacy-direction.

Hutcheon, Linda, with Siobhan Flynn. *A Theory of Adaptation*. 2nd ed., Routledge, 2013.

Nestruck, J. Kelly. "Fine female cast makes for a magical Penelopiad." *Globe and Mail*, 13 Jan. 2012, https://www.theglobeandmail.com/arts/theatre-and-performance/fine-female-cast-makes-for-a-magical-penelopiad/article630458/.

Wilson, Emily, trans. *The Odyssey*, by Homer. W. W. Norton, 2017.

Filming *Alias Grace*

Fiona McMahon

On October 23, 2019, Brendan Steacy was interviewed by Fiona McMahon about his work on the Hulu adaptation of Atwood's Alias Grace (2017), addressing on that occasion both the efforts to depict the historical setting realistically and the complex nature of the narration. Steacy is a celebrated cinematographer, well-known for his work both in television (Titans, Alias Grace) and in film (Backstabbing for Beginners, Stockholm, Lucky Day). Writer, actor and director Sarah Polley wrote the screenplay and Mary Harron directed the miniseries.

Alias Grace, Margaret Atwood's 1996 novel, is captivating for many reasons. It is a tale of mystery whose intrigue unfolds in a Victorian setting that readily incorporates the décor and the darkly troubled psychology redolent of the gothic tradition. The shades of horror and inscrutability that seep into the novel are interwoven with the acute attention devoted to the portrayal of the everyday life of Grace Marks, a convicted murderer, in mid-nineteenth-century Upper Canada, formerly a British colony in what is the present-day province of Ontario. While the novel exhibits

---

F. McMahon (✉)
Université Paul Valéry Montpellier 3, Montpellier, France
e-mail: fiona.mcmahon@univ-montp3.fr

© The Author(s), under exclusive license to Springer Nature Switzerland AG 2021
S. Wells-Lassagne, F. McMahon (eds.), *Adapting Margaret Atwood*,
Palgrave Studies in Adaptation and Visual Culture,
https://doi.org/10.1007/978-3-030-73686-6_14

features of the neo-gothic strain that has shaped Canadian postmodernism and is lauded in a more specific regional sense as an example of the Southern Ontario Gothic style, it is equally indebted to historiographical fiction, another mode prominent in contemporary Canadian fiction. The plot is mirrored after an actual double homicide whose circumstances Atwood learned from the documentary research of the trial proceedings and from Susanna Moodie's account of her meeting with Grace Marks at the Kingston Penitentiary, as told in her chronicle of pioneer life, *Life in the Clearings Versus the Bush* (1853).

The manner in which Atwood combines the relevance of memory, its multiple pathways explored in historical fiction and the disturbing presence of the uncanny and the monstrous is noteworthy. A densely layered narrative is brought into focus, whose doubleness and distortions of reality only heighten the tension surrounding the circumstances of the protagonist, a young penniless emigrant woman who is serving a life sentence after being convicted as an accessory to the murder of her employer and her employer's housekeeper.

The audiovisual adaptation of the novel finds itself faced with the ephemerality underwriting this narrative. What fascinates viewers of the miniseries is how it seeks to channel the slow reveal of a complex character whose psychological portrait offers up both presumed perpetrator and disarming victim Grace Marks.

In our discussion with Brendan Steacy, the cinematographer lays bare the processes by which the visual language of the miniseries was developed for the Hulu television adaptation. Steacy reflects upon how cinematic techniques take their cue from the screenplay and build an aesthetic in response to the narrative dynamic that is carried over from the novel. As Steacy explains, a composite photographic vocabulary evolves from first-person retrospective narration, interior monologue, dreams, dialogue, Doctor Jordan's correspondence and flashback. When the camera is paired with the confessional, autobiographical mode of the screenplay, the paradox of Grace Mark's narrative voice becomes an integral component of cinematographic design. The discussion that follows on Steacy's photography gives a sense of the challenges faced when keeping pace with the degrees of narrative control and unreliability afforded to Grace Marks, whose part is played by actress Sarah Gadon. For the cinematographer, photography investigates the duality of voice, the disquiet and the variability of experience, as conveyed through the screenplay and the performance of the actors.

The following transcript has been edited for content and clarity.

Fiona McMahon: Could you relate how you approach cinematography when working on a film adaptation from a work of literature? What changes for you? In the case of *Alias Grace*, was your source material restricted to Sarah Polley's screenplay? Or did your research involve your reading Atwood's novel as well?

Brendan Steacy: In the case of *Alias Grace*, I took most of my cues from the screenplay, as Sarah Polley wrote it so specifically, and since it's not exactly the same as the book, I chose not to reread the book, but to make the version of the story that Sarah had written. That said, it was important to still do research around the story—the actual historical unfolding of events, for instance, that Atwood based the book on, and also the period in general.

FM: Could you describe the research that you did in order to build a visual canvas that reflected the Victorian backdrop to the story of Grace Marks?

BS: I gave careful consideration to how we might recreate the visual environment and the perceptual experience of the mid-nineteenth century. The way people saw the world, and each other, had to be translated somehow through our photography. Lighting in that period, for instance, could come only from the sun, or fire (primarily candles), and that not only leads to a very specific look, but also determines the way one lives somewhat. The challenge, however, is to try to represent the way a candlelit room feels as opposed to how it actually looks on camera. In some instances (like where Grace walks through a house, carrying a single candle), I did actually use only candlelight, but most of the time this simply doesn't work. My sense of how a room lit by many candles feels is soft and warm, but in reality it can be very contrasted, and the light from candles is quite hard, so in scenes like the Christmas figgy pudding party, for instance, I used a combination of real candles and a large amount of LED lighting to soften and broaden the reach of the real candles. The LEDs were usually on a very subtle candle (flicker) effect that kept their levels fluctuating so as to maintain the inconsistency of candlelight (Fig. 1).

FM: Can you elaborate as to how light performs as a structuring device in reference to diegesis, as an indication of timeline, tone and character? For instance, can you tell us about the use of bright light when Grace is in court as a witness? Is the emphasis on light and, conversely, the retreat of shadows ironic in any way?

BS: To be honest, the courtroom lighting was somewhat dictated by the restrictions of the location, and I did not have as much control there

Fig. 1 Christmas figgy pudding party—augmenting candlelight with LEDs. (Photo courtesy of Brendan Steacy)

as I had hoped for. We did make a conscious effort lighting Grace in certain scenes to seem saintly and ethereal when speaking with Dr. Jordan in an attempt to emulate how he may see her, but I was also very much concerned with the motivation of light and keeping it within the world of naturalism (with the exception of the scenes that are specifically scripted to be outside of that, like the stylized light the first time we meet Nancy, or the "impossibly bright moonlight" Grace encounters when she finds the tree full of angels).

FM: How important was the alternating play between light and shadow, and what role did it play with respect to the narrative? Metaphorically, how do the techniques you employ expose the tension between truth and untruth in the miniseries?

BS: Conventionally cinematographers have always used shadow to conceal details—either physically or metaphorically, and we did do a certain amount of that in *Alias Grace* as well, but there are many notable exceptions. Sarah Gadon had such exceptional insight into her character and was great at maintaining the moral ambiguity of Grace Marks, but she also does beautifully subtle things with her face that I believe are good clues as to where she was at with Grace at any given moment. She wouldn't really discuss her opinion on Grace's guilt/innocence while we were shooting, so I clung to those subtle expressions, and even when I thought she was hinting to us that she was concealing something, I tried to leave enough light on her to allow viewers the joy of studying her face and trying to decipher her take for themselves.

FM: Are there any camera techniques that help establish the theme of otherworldliness and the occult (hypnosis scene, black veil)? Are there angles or types of lighting used that are prevalent in the horror genre?

BS: The darkness in the interior parlor scene was particularly interesting to stage. Once all the curtains were drawn, there were a host of technical problems to solve with respect to photography. That's an historic property that doesn't allow very much equipment inside. We weren't allowed to use any atmosphere, or do any rigging from above, but I needed to be able to see the whole room at once, so I also couldn't do much lighting from the floor. I actually lobbied to leave the curtains open a crack, so that there was at least some motivation for light in the room and I could have a nice natural base to start from (Fig. 2).

FM: In your adaptation of the novel's first-person narration, the camera is anything but a neutral observer. Can you explain how the use of photography in the series sought to approach the problem of narration? How do you translate the subjectivity of the protagonist's experience? How does the camera and lighting reinforce the narrator's unreliability?

BS: Because *Alias Grace* is partially about subjectivity vs. objectivity, and explores different versions of the same narrative, as well as jumping around in time, all through the voice of an unreliable narrator, we actually had to be careful to not make it altogether too disjointed. We did have a few subtle techniques (we hinted, for instance, whose POV—even in objective-seeming shots—we might be watching by the height of the

Fig. 2 The occult séance. (Photo courtesy of Brendan Steacy)

camera), and to try to hint at reality vs. fantasy, but ultimately it all had to work seamlessly together enough that the ambiguity is maintained and the viewer isn't forced too firmly into the thesis of the filmmakers (even if that's ultimately inevitable).

We maintained a very shallow focus through most of the production for a couple of reasons. Early on, Mary [Harron] had showed me some old large format photographs that she loved the character of. Because the negatives are so huge in these images, the depth of field was extremely shallow, which we tried to emulate by shooting on really fast prime lenses close to wide open. Because we're dealing with fallibility of memory as well as deceit, this soft focus falloff seemed like an appropriate choice as a visual representation of details being lost in their recall (Fig. 3).

FM: How is outdoor light used as a framing device, as compared with indoor lighting? Could you relate the techniques used to stage the lighting with respect to the arrival scene from the boat in Toronto?

BS: The tone of the arrival in Toronto was very specific in the screenplay and that whole sequence was one that Sarah Polley fought very hard to preserve as she felt it was really important to create the context for Grace's arrival in Toronto, and how she came to be in the situation she found herself in. It was probably the most complicated sequence of the show from a production standpoint. The boat scenes were shot both

Fig. 3 The emigrant ship. (Photo courtesy of Brendan Steacy)

under sail on a real ship in Lake Ontario for anything above the deck and then on a gimbaled set on a stage for anything below deck. Once you're below deck on a ship, there are no windows, and daylight can make it in only through two small doors in the deck, so to keep it feeling believable and to get viewers into the headspace of how terrible that environment might have been, I just smashed as much light as I could through those two tiny holes and then augmented that feeling from inside the ship with small sources. Once they arrive in the port, and she walks through Toronto streets for the first time, we needed to maintain the feeling of a gloomy, muddy city shortly after a rain fall. That meant that I had to cancel out the sun, which was an enormous undertaking, utilizing multiple construction cranes and telehandlers. The effect, however, was really important in conveying the mood of those scenes in the way they're written (Figs. 4 and 5).

FM: We're presented with an ambiguous multi-layered narrative in *Alias Grace*. How important was it to layer references to different media? Is painting an aesthetic model for your camera? Does your camera entertain a strong relationship to the lighting one finds in painting? There is the suggestion that the film aims to build upon different canvases which it borrows from other forms of representation. Not only the formal elements but also the themes. Did the visual cues come from Sarah Polley or Mary Harron?

Fig. 4 Lighting the two openings in the ship's hold. (Photo courtesy of Brendan Steacy)

BS: It's one thing to turn off lights in a room and study how it looks, but I was really interested in understanding how the people perceived light working in a pre-electricity/pre-photography world. Historically, I'm not sure if anyone has mastered window light like the Dutch masters, so that was an obvious starting place, but I looked at lots of references of how people painted their subjects in light from a nearby window, and as much as possible tried to coax blockings into similar relative positions, which is actually quite natural, because without electricity, people wanting to see what they're doing are intuitively going to gravitate toward windows (Figs. 6 and 7).

FM: Does your photography borrow from the pastoral model and the larger Romantic tradition? How does the camera build a sense of the seasons in these flashbacks, from one season to the next (winter at the Parkinson's to spring at Kinnear's; Nancy leaning over flowers)?

FILMING *ALIAS GRACE* 237

Fig. 5 Cancelling out the sun for the arrival in Toronto. (Photo courtesy of Brendan Steacy)

Fig. 6 Window. (Photo courtesy of Brendan Steacy)

Fig. 7 Window-arrival in Toronto. (Photo courtesy of Brendan Steacy)

BS: My aim in the photography wasn't specifically to borrow from any pastoral art work, but the idea is definitely there in Sarah Polley's writing. From my perspective, my responsibility in the photographic representation of the seasons was primarily to put the viewer in the headspace of what that would be like. The degree to which weather could affect everything in that era helps contextualize the significance of the seasons during which any certain event takes place. There was an enormous dependence on nature, and I just wanted to show that as much as possible.

FM: How does photography convey the choice of breaking the fourth wall at the end of the first episode, solidifying the parallel with the viewer, when Grace Marks seeks out an audience?

BS: Through most of the show Grace is ostensibly speaking with Dr. Jordan, but this is clearly a narrative device to allow her to speak to the viewer. By having her break that wall and turn to the camera, it reminds us of the artifice both of film making and of her story, and is at once both an invitation to empathize with her and a warning that she can't be trusted. We also played with eyelines throughout the project in other ways (varying between wider and extremely tight), but generally kept it really tight with Grace—sometimes almost like the POV of the other person in the frame—which allows us another opportunity to study her face for clues, but also to live in that contradiction of questionable honesty.

Filming *The Handmaid's Tale*

Shannon Wells-Lassagne

Hulu's The Handmaid's Tale *(2017–) has been a breakout success, receiving Golden Globes, BAFTAs, a Peabody award, and eight Emmy awards (including "Outstanding Drama Series") in its freshman season alone. Among those Emmys is Colin Watkinson's for Outstanding Cinematography for a Single-Camera Series. His work on the series has been crucial in creating the visual aesthetic that several of our chapters discuss in detail, and he spoke with Shannon Wells-Lassagne on November 15, 2019, to discuss this adaptation.*

Colin Watkinson has shot music videos for some of music's best known performers (Pink, Korn, Avril Lavigne, Katy Perry) and was the cinematographer for Tarsem Singh's surreal The Fall *(2006); he has also been prolific on the small screen (*Emerald City, Entourage, Monday Mornings, Truth Be Told*), and has recently added an American Society of Cinematographers award to his collection for his work on* The Handmaid's Tale. *In this interview, he discusses many of the hallmark techniques that are used to great effect*

S. Wells-Lassagne (✉)
University of Burgundy, Dijon, France
e-mail: Shannon.Wells-Lassagne@u-bourgogne.fr

© The Author(s), under exclusive license to Springer Nature
Switzerland AG 2021
S. Wells-Lassagne, F. McMahon (eds.), *Adapting Margaret Atwood*,
Palgrave Studies in Adaptation and Visual Culture,
https://doi.org/10.1007/978-3-030-73686-6_15

in the story, as well as examining how the series relates to both Atwood's texts and her intentions, and the specificity of television storytelling. This transcript has been edited for content and clarity.

Shannon Wells-Lassagne: I was wondering if you could talk, first of all, about your job. What exactly does it mean to be director of photography? And does that change depending on whether you're working in TV or in film?

Colin Watkinson: To me, it doesn't. I don't think there's any difference. I feel as if my job is—it sounds very cliché, but—I'm a storyteller. And when you tell a story, you have to make it the best it can be for people to sit up, and watch, and listen. And I think today, with the amount of content or stories that are out there, you have to work a little bit harder to get people to listen to your stories or watch your stories. I take it very seriously. I've always loved visual storytelling, from the people I've worked with growing up, but it still has to be poignant. It can't be visual for visual's sake. It has to mean something. That's always my aim, to try and make it something visually—pleasing is the wrong word, but—visually arresting or visually poignant to the story that you tell at the time.

SWL: I was wondering if you could talk a little bit about how you decided on the aesthetics that are so specific to the series—shallow focus, overhead shots, extreme close ups—can you talk a little bit about the decision making process that went into that?

CW: It was [director] Reed Morano, she was instrumental to what *The Handmaid's Tale* is in a visual sense. She came to me. [...] I read the book in 1989, I think it was, [...] and it blew my mind. I love dystopian films (or I did at the time), and I couldn't wait to see it big screen. But I went to see [the 1990 adaptation], and I was terribly disappointed. So when Reed [Morano] started talking about it, the first things we talked about was color. What was wrong with the film was that the color felt wrong. I couldn't describe it at the time. I didn't know why it was wrong, but it was wrong. So color is the first thing that got us excited. Then when I got to Toronto, the question was "what am I really doing here?" Because Reed is an ASC [American Society of Cinematographers] cinematographer in her own right. And she'd already run off on various things, so I wasn't sure where I fit in with this whole concept. And she said it would present itself. Don't worry. We both liked atmosphere, [what we called] "volumetric lighting"; we knew we were going to do that. I put in my pitch that there had to be frames that had to hold on their own accord for a long period of time. They had to be beautiful. We wanted to create beauty in Gilead, even though it's really the worst place on the planet, and she want to tie that in with sort of Kubrick-esque symmetrical shots. And then she wanted this ethereal, handheld sort of [aesthetic], thinking that it suggested that this world existed, that this world could exist. And then the aerial shots—I knew she wanted an overhead shot. (It was the matriculation in Episode 1.) Once we did that and we realized the strength of the imagery behind that, it became a show signature. She described it as entrapment. Looking down on this character, [the viewer knows] that she was trapped in this world. The title itself, *The Handmaid's Tale*, meant that it was a point of view show, and that we would have to concentrate heavily on where the camera had to be to tell that story. It had to be—as much as we can—from June's perspective. So the overhead shot is not her perspective, but it's her perspective of her perspective. Does that makes sense?

SWL: Yes!

CW: It still makes sense to me. But I think it can get overused, and it did get overused in season three, [where there were] too many high shots. It devalues what that actually means. We chose a particular lens for anything that was introspective with June—with Offred, at the time—what June was thinking, we would use that lens. We didn't use it anywhere else in the series: that would be her lens. And again, in season two, they started breaking those rules and using it incorrectly. It's like, "no. You can't do that." It was very particular and it really worked in season one, to separate [that perspective] out. [...] That closeness gave a slightly warped perspective on [star and executive producer] Lizzie's [Elizabeth Moss's] face, which made you think that it was all about how she was internalizing what was going on. The close focus again was an entrapment in this world. What else what else do we have? The symmetry of Gilead [contrasted with] the reality of the real world, the handheld, ethereal nature of the real world. Most of our work centered around all of those ideals.

SWL: I find what you said really interesting because one of the most difficult things, of course, to translate onto the screen is the narrator; the idea of having a specific lens to add interiority for Offred is fascinating. I also liked this idea of being Kubrickian in the overhead shots, and offering a real geometry of space. There is this real geometry of space that you're constantly setting up, not just Offred's vision of the world, but the world as a whole. And we see that expanding as the series goes on.

CW: The more you go into that structured world—Gilead was very structured—the difference to the real world with this very shaky camera was vast. That's the thing: it doesn't take much for your world to change completely. A lot of the story is saying, "people, get off of your phone and look up what's going on around you!" If you don't pay attention, your world may change beyond your comprehension. That was the idea. That was a real stretch. And then we have to find a default, to try to tie the world together, so they feel like the same again. We would go handheld in the Gilead world; we would go symmetrical in the world of the past. And then the flares would tie the two together as well, using flares in both worlds, so all of a sudden they're vastly different, but connected. That was what we were trying to do.

SWL: Oh, thank you for bringing that up. The lens flares are very interesting. The natural lighting, especially in that in the first season, is very interesting. And I was wondering—Atwood said that she was inspired for the Handmaid's outfits, by the old "Dutch cleanser" packaging from the 1940s. And in the series, it looks very typical of the clothing of figures in the works of Dutch Masters to me: the wings and the bonnet and so on. And I was wondering if you were trying to evoke that same kind of influence of Dutch painting in your world.

CW: For me, it was a strong influence. Well, there was no connection to that [Atwood comment], but we wanted a painterly feeling more based around why we chose it to be Kubrickian: the frame has to be able to hold its own for a longer period of time than it usually would. And the way to make that happen is to look back at old paintings, because you can stare at a painting for a long time, where nothing happens, but in your head, so much goes on. And that's what we were trying to create. If you look into how those old masters' paintings were built up, they were layers and layers of paint, and the artists would go over and over it again. So the question is, how do you do that with cinematography? We rationalized it with volumetric light creating layers, with a volumetric light in front of the subject, and/or behind it. And then, you have depth of light. That was my version of the Dutch Masters. We just happened to choose the lenses we chose. For me, it was definitely more the softness to them than anything else. The natural feeling that you get with all of these pictures of the same space with that one natural light. Reed is from the independent film world, and when she walks into a location, she literally gravitates to a window. She can feel a pull, because she knows that's where the most beautiful position is going to be. And so that all made sense as well. When we started working together in scouting, I knew I was going to be lucky, that there would not be fighting as there sometimes is with other directors. With Reed, I knew I was always going to be in the right place because that's how she thinks.

SWL: But of course, when you're working in television, you're working with several other directors.

CW: Yes, Reed, then Mike Barker, then Floria [Sigismondi], Kate Dennis and Kari Skagland did the first season.

SWL: So did you become kind of the "keeper of the flame" for the aesthetics of the series from one episode to the next?

CW: The demonic keeper of the flame, yes. [Laughs] I think I kept what the show did well, because if not I don't think they would have asked me back, but I did become slightly obsessed by it. When I saw what Reed did, it felt like a duty to maintain it. And Lizzie was seriously involved as well.

We would battle to keep the style of the show, and that carried on in season two; directors would come in with their ideas and say, "We usually-" "Well, we don't do usual." They'd look at you like they want to poke you in the eye, but well, I'm sorry. That's the way it is. Mike Barker was fantastic at just running with it; he said he took all these notes and then he saw the pilot and we said, oh, what are you bringing to the table? And he replied, I just tore all my notes up and started again. I love watching him turn into the most amazing filmmaker. Again, the show sort of energized filmmakers to really think about how to work, how to tell a story, with all the rules that we had—and that came directly from Margaret's book. And it's been harder as you go through seasons one, two and three with all the different stories, how to keep hold of that sort of feeling. I remember, we argued about a POV shot on the set. It was messing with our brains, because we can't shift POV from June's; it can only be the one. We can show intensity of emotion—[for instance] Serena's journey was a big journey last season. Yvonne [Strahovski] is one of the most amazing actresses I've ever worked for.

SWL: Yes, she's incredible in the series.

CW: Yeah. I mean, we have so many good actors. Yes.

SWL: When you spoke of switching point of view shots, I was also thinking about the colonies. You were saying that all of this comes directly from Atwood's book. But how are you adapting your series when you move to season two, or when you move outside of the frame that Atwood has set up—with little America in Canada, or Washington, DC, or the colonies—how does that work? Do you feel like you're still adapting?

CW: Trying to keep a handle on it is tricky. Again, you try and look at the story, for example with Emily/Ofglen. I think we managed to tell the story, maintain the show's visual integrity, and just pull back, just enough, so Emily's character wasn't given the introspective moments that Offred or June was. There is certainly a separation—and it's important for the star of the show to maintain that, you know, that star level—even in story. The show has to maintain its infrastructure.

SWL: So it's still the handmaid's tale.

CW: Yes, it's still the handmaid's tale. I think we rode it really close, but I think we just managed to keep it. Even with Yvonne's backstory in seasons one and two, we managed to get this very strong emotional storytelling without crossing the line to [mirroring] what we shoot with Lizzy. She holds the mantle for the interior stuff.

SWL: It's a difficult balance, I imagine, the fact that in the end a novel can be a first-person novel, but a TV series is often expansive. So you have to have a choral aspect to a TV series over a duration. In a shorter TV series it might be possible to limit storytelling to one character. But in the end, you're adapting TV as much as you are adapting Atwood. I don't know if that's accurate to say that or not.

CW: When people watch television, they're after human interaction with other humans and stories that happen to humans. It's not about the bigger picture. That's why TV has a lot more closeups than, say, cinema. The format dictates that. Luckily for this, [given the] design of the show, it has that in droves. It's like it's all about human connection. And what are the things that are happening to humans—like that new Star Wars show *The Mandalorian*: how can a show with a guy who wears a helmet for 10 episodes ever work? This is where you need great actors. Because what goes on onscreen doesn't stop with their face. I remember watching and thinking, "How'd you do that?" It's just his neck moving—it's amazing. It's been fascinating watching actors do not a lot, but have it be everything. Ryan Gosling does it amazingly, where he's not moving a lot, but you can't take your eyes off him. And Lizzie's the same.

SWL: So how interactive is that process then for you as a director of photography? Do you follow their lead or do you discuss it ahead of time?

CW: If you were going to do a shot that would be very intimate, I'm following the story. I can sometimes guide the story back into the frame where I need it to be, but only if I feel like it's slipping, I could ask them to come back round. So there is communication—and again, I don't know how often this will be possible going forward in my career, because I think if you talk to some actors in the middle of their acting, they say, what the fuck are you doing? But Lizzie can take that, and she wants it. She can focus. [...] She can literally click in and out of insanely emotional scenes and take direction in the middle of a scene. Again, there's a huge amount of respect and it's not barking; it's just if she needs to be guided back [...]. We can do that together, which makes the shots that we can do, as simple as they are, feel very connected, and the viewer feels like they're right there.

SWL: So it's expansive and immersive at the same time, I guess.

CW: It's like a dance, yeah.

SWL: We see that again in this constant back and forth, between the extreme close ups and the long shots. Do you have a say in the editing process to create that balance between the two?

CW: Generally not. I did get involved in various decisions in season one; the editor would come back [with a rough cut], but it was very secretive. [...] I would give notes to Lizzie about shots [where I felt something was missing], and she would go back to see if they belonged in. And then there's a reality, a truthfulness, [that plays a role]; I've seen some of the most beautiful shots go in the edit bin because they don't belong in there. You have to take that on the chin, that only the right shot needs to be in there. Especially with [showrunner] Bruce [Miller], we will do a lot of experimental stuff, and maybe only two shots out of ten will make it in. But if you stop doing that, then those two would never exist. So it's worth the eight going in the trash to get to those two in there. It makes the show very interesting to shoot. I directed one episode this year [S3E5, "Unknown Caller], and the edit process for that—I don't know if I would say I enjoyed it, because I would like to have had more time as a first-time director to really have just been able to take it in, to work out a couple of things myself as a first timer, but it's such an unbelievable pace. I think I had four days to edit [the episode]. Luckily, I went in there with [film editor] Chris [Donaldson]; I knew the editors at this point and we all had a great rapport. [...] So I went in there before I shot, laid out what I wanted it to be. I had an amazing script, and I think the editing will also bring their storytelling to it, which I really enjoyed. Some of the stuff I thought of, [Christopher Donaldson] could translate in his head. So [editing and directing offered] this whole new world, [...] and the process itself was really enjoyable. They want you to [contribute to the] edit, which I think is quite unique in television; the editors keep on top of each other, making sure that they maintain the show's aesthetic, and its storytelling sense, which is great. I love it.

SWL: Speaking of time constraints for editing, does the fact that this is streaming, and not network TV, does that impact the calendar you're given? Likewise, the fact that this was really their flagship series, could you speak to the relationship with Hulu?

CW: Hulu encourages creativity as much as possible and you always felt like Hulu had your back; they were encouraging and collaborative. […] Especially with little things, like when we went to shoot on this particular camera, Netflix wouldn't allow that camera, because it's not 4 K. And Hulu's question was: is it going to look great? Then yes, you should use what you want. That told me everything I needed to know about Hulu from the outset. But then you understand the machine: MGM with worldwide sales; Hulu; marketing to be bought or planned out; and then the post[-production] people. You're making ten hours of television, and you have to draw the line somewhere and make a plan. You only have so much money, and you have to work within [that framework] and be a part of it and not blow it all. It will bend, at times, when a script is not up to scratch, it will go back and then we'll push a week, or we'll do something else. The machine at MGM will bend when necessary, which is fantastic. But you have to work within the constraints.

And then you would just hire the right people, right? Hire people that are better than you at what they do, that's the key. Be impressed by them and get them to run [with their talent]. In fact, it's been an interesting show [given] how many people have raised their game with *The Handmaid's Tale*—people who should never have been there in the first place, including myself, you know.

SWL: That's very interesting. Why do you say that? Because to me, *The Fall* seems like it has a similar kind of inventivity, if not exactly the same aesthetic.

CW: In fact it was because of *The Fall* that Reed asked me to do it. She knows the director [Tarsem Singh], a great visualist. But there was talk of my work being too slick; they wanted a gritty sort of look. […] And then, you know, the gaffer—[film production in] Toronto is so busy, I couldn't hire the people that they first recommended, so we went with this guy that I really trust; he wanted to move into his style and he stepped up. All of the people involved stepped up. It was just fantastic to watch, even with Bruce Miller. I think they wanted a female showrunner to begin with. It was an Atwood show; it should be. But Bruce just kept going back, saying, "trust me, I know what this show is." And it was a huge decision to use Reed. And that was Warren Littlefield and [executives] from Hulu.

They stuck their neck out, going with a relatively new TV director. It was a huge gamble, and all these gambles paid off. I think it was very inspirational for the show, to start thinking about what you're making. I'll be very vocal about it: if it's shit, you need to say it's shit and make it better. Why is it not working? What bit is not working? You can't fix everything later.

SWL: So do you feel a responsibility to the show, or to the novel, or to the current political situation? We've all talked about how timely *The Handmaid's Tale* is.

CW: All of the above. The political situation was a byproduct that we didn't really see coming; I really wanted to see something made of that novel that suited it because it was such a seminal novel, it's so fantastic; and then all the people that were involved—I felt I needed to make sure that I maintained the show's high level. We're now working on season four, and Lizzie Moss is an amazing producer trying to maintain the show's integrity.

SWL: How did you treat the places that weren't described in Atwood's novels and try and make them coherent with the rest of the series?

CW: The colonies was a huge discussion, because they were never discussed exactly. What are the [Unwomen] doing? We had to try and create a whole backstory to explain what they were doing. And that was really tricky because it was never really discussed. So we looked at images from Fukushima; they would dig up the earth and make these big mounds of like radioactive earth and put them to one side. So that was the idea behind that. We had to try and create a fear factor, with the gas masks for the Aunts, creating this imagery to insist on the level of degradation that these women taken down to, and how little they thought of them. Little America, again, was influenced by current events. Refugees. What would a modern-day First World refugee look like? We just looked at things like clothing, food, all the basics that we all take for granted that are the first thing that goes out the window, and the chaos that creates. And Washington—at some point, Gilead had to expand, and I was happy they did it, made it scarier, giving an even more extreme version of religion. We've always thought that we should see the rest of Gilead. Margaret even drew up a map, of what she thought America might look like at these times, where there would still be areas that would be battlegrounds, fighting to secure areas and gray areas that didn't make it. It was an interesting map she made.

SWL: The fact that you're using real life examples from horrors of the past. I mean, that's very faithful to Atwood's process as well, isn't it?

CW: Everything that happened in the book happened some point in history. That was really Bruce's take, that everything that he wrote had actually happened at some point. He stayed truthful to that.

SWL: It's one of the reasons that it's so terrifying, that in the end, it is grounded in reality.

CW: Yes. The mass execution in the football stadium that was in season two. That was really scary. And it felt scary shooting it—that these things actually happen.

SWL: I was re-watching the first episode of each season, and S2E1 was still so moving, regardless of knowing what happened next. I was still tearing up; it was a terrifying moment.

CW: That's an example of what I mean about connectivity between people, on television. The best bits, the reason it makes you tear up, is when they look at each other.

SWL: Yes, one of the characters is trying to hold the hand of the person next to them, and that's what immediately brought tears to my eyes.

CW: Yes, it still does when I watch it. I remember shooting. That's what we had to have, and that's what makes people feel something. The editing was fantastic.

SWL: It was. But at the same time, it's very rare that we see characters actually looking at each other as they speak -.

CW: Yes.

SWL: So it's a fascinating balance that you're trying to find between people being unable to connect and at the same time trying nonetheless.

CW: Yes, it is an interesting factor. What we did was we didn't really want to do overs [over the shoulder shots]. Well, we do, though, as one directed point of view, it does happen. But it's not our default device for telling a story. I see why they're used: the camera's right here; the eyeline couldn't be closer. It works. But we didn't want to go down that road. Reed had just come from a show that used them all the time, and she wanted a change in this case. So where does the camera need to be? We started to learn that each degree a camera moves round, tells you a different story. Which opened up another whole can of worms for me, because sometimes you get it wrong. But then when you get right, and you literally have one character be full face, and the other side on, you can tell a completely different story than if you just do over the shoulder shots. So it became another fascinating tool born out of the desire not to do the usual TV, but instead to think about technique. In the early days, we thought about it so much, it hurt my head.

SWL: [Laughs] From a technical perspective, I can understand that that must be mind boggling. But as someone who's looking at the final product, it's really a fascinating idea that everybody is very isolated in their own head. I think it works really well with the story that you're trying to tell, a very effective technique.

CW: Yes, it's been an interesting journey in how to tell stories for sure.

"Adapting (to) Atwood"

Linda Hutcheon

As a reader both cursed and addicted to finding intertextual echoes in everything I read, I find Margaret Atwood, the wily, ironic, clever adapter, a total joy. Few writers allude, cite, and transform others' work with such brio; even fewer manage at once to respect and to contest both the priority and the authority of those earlier writers' works in the way that she does. Atwood provocatively challenges the hierarchical implications behind the idea of "fidelity" to a "source," because her adaptations may be second but they are never secondary. Others' works are indeed the specters that haunt her own writing, as Ruby Niemann here explores, but these are specters that both nourish and provoke in their haunting, as the chapters in this volume show so well.

Readers and reviewers have always noticed that Atwood "writes back" to the classics of Western literature, from Shakespeare to Milton, from the Bible to Susanna Moodie. She also, though, "writes alongside," if you like, other oppositional rewritings—using postcolonial, gendered, and class perspectives—from those of Aimé Césaire to prison plays. Like Pat Barker (*The Silence of the Girls*) and Madeline Miller (*Circe*), Atwood

---

L. Hutcheon (✉)
University of Toronto, Toronto, ON, Canada
e-mail: l.hutcheon@utoronto.ca

© The Author(s), under exclusive license to Springer Nature Switzerland AG 2021
S. Wells-Lassagne, F. McMahon (eds.), *Adapting Margaret Atwood*, Palgrave Studies in Adaptation and Visual Culture,
https://doi.org/10.1007/978-3-030-73686-6

often gives us women's versions of familiar stories. One might even say that she also "writes into (and out of)" or riffs on popular genres, from gothic romances to vampire tales, from the satyr plays of antiquity to current post-apocalyptic dystopias, from psychological thrillers to historical fiction, from dance films to fairy tales. Her adaptations and her parodies range in register and in tone from respectful to hilariously grotesque, but usually they wield the power of deeply critical satire.

Given the adaptational impulse and genius that Atwood so clearly demonstrates, it is either entirely appropriate or nicely ironic that her own works have been adapted so often. And, as David Roche shows in his article here, among the most discussed of the adaptations, the HULU television series is typical in that it too is in turn highly adaptive/intertextual in its directorial decisions and visual language. There seems to be something contagious about the Atwoodian urge to adapt. But it is also canny on her adapters' part. We know that classics of literature and opera were adaptation fodder for early cinema, used to legitimize a new art form and, en route, borrow their cultural capital. While Atwood is now a canonical writer, both in Canada and elsewhere, and is most certainly a celebrity, as Lorraine York has shown,[1] I suspect the motive for adapting her work may also have something to do with her uncanny ability to have her finger on the pulse of the *Zeitgeist*. It has to do, in a word, with relevance.

Atwood must have figured out well before writing the *MaddAddam* trilogy that nature adapts better than we do, but that we humans *do* adapt, mutate, transform. As a test case, I offer here my own experience of adapting to adaptations of Atwood's work, specifically of *The Handmaid's Tale*, a novel I've read multiple times. But each reading has been very different, in part because of the varied social, historical, political, and aesthetic contexts in which it occurred. As Heraclitus might have said, you can't read the same novel twice. But, more intriguingly for me, the different readings (and, frankly, experiences of reading) also came about because of various *adaptations* of the novel, specifically ones that moved from the novel's *telling* mode to a dramatized *showing* mode.

I first read the book when it first appeared. In 1985, Atwood was eager to tell her readers that there was nothing in this fictional story that had not already happened in our own world; there is a box of newspaper clippings in the Atwood holdings at the Fisher Rare Book Library at the University

---

[1] *Margaret Atwood and the Labour of Literary Celebrity* (Toronto: University of Toronto Press, 2013).

of Toronto to prove it. As she noted many years later, "The inclination toward tyranny—the wielding of absolute power by the few over the many—knows no ideological boundaries and is not confined to one time or space."[2] At the time, the premise of this dystopic work fed (and still does today) into our worst fears. An earthquake along the San Andreas fault causes a nuclear disaster; the resulting spread of toxic waste and dioxins brings on high levels of cancer and infertility; social and political instability follows. The US president and all members of congress are murdered; a fundamentalist Christian movement takes control, though the coup is blamed on "Islamic fanatics" at first. In the resulting mono-theocratic state, named (with biblical irony) Gilead, terror rules; dissidents are publicly executed; rights are curbed. As Atwood later put it, the novel's totalitarian dictatorship "emerged during a period of disruption: in such times, people are likely to trade in their rights in favour of militaristic governments that claim to be able to guarantee their safety."[3]

Like the real countries upon which Atwood says she modeled her Gilead in the 1980s—Iran and Afghanistan—her fictional Republic suppressed first the rights of women: women could not hold bank accounts; they were forbidden to read or write. As Atwood explained: "It is an axiom of most dictatorships that they control sexuality, both male and female, and that they suppress most men, but all women."[4] Those women in largely infertile Gilead who are still capable of conceiving children are indoctrinated at the "Red Centre" to become "handmaids" or what the narrator of the novel more cynically refers to as "two-legged wombs." They are sent out to live with childless couples of the ruling elite, and there they are made to undergo what is called the "Ceremony," a ritual copulation with the husband, in the wife's presence. Any child that results belongs to the couple only. The rationale in the mono-theocratic state is of course, biblical. In Genesis 30, Rachel says to Jacob: "Behold my handmaid, Bilhah. Go in unto her; and she shall bear upon my knees, that I may have children by her." Any handmaid who has failed to conceive after three postings is banished to what are called the Colonies to join the barren women in clearing toxic waste: a death sentence, in other words. Their only other choice is to

---

[2] Margaret Atwood, "For God and Gilead," *The Guardian*, 22 March 2003. https://www.theguardian.com/music/2003/mar/22/classicalmusicandopera.fiction
[3] Atwood, "For God and Gilead."
[4] Atwood, "For God and Gilead."

become a prostitute in the theoretically illegal (but actually very well frequented) brothels for the male elite of the regime.

In 1985, when I first read this novel, Atwood claims that the response to it varied from nation to nation: the response in the United Kingdom was "Jolly good yarn." In Canada, it was "Could this happen here?" In the United States, it was "How long have we got?"[5] Why? Because 1980s Reaganite America, with its Moral Majority, had historical roots in the nation's Puritan history and its Salem witch trials. It is no accident that Atwood set the novel in the historic heart of Puritan Massachusetts at Harvard University.

Before I read the novel the second time, I saw the 1990 film, directed by Volker Schlöndorff. Because he had already produced the astute film adaptation of Günther Grass's *The Tin Drum* in 1979, I was confident that with a script written by the Nobel Prize–winning playwright Harold Pinter, his film of *The Handmaid's Tale* would be impressive. Big-name stars of the day had been cast: Faye Dunaway, Robert Duvall, Natasha Richardson. Much to my surprise, before I saw the film, it was a popular and critical flop. Once I did see it, I understood why. For one thing, the film lost the rebellious, ironic, and emotionally gripping first-person voice of Offred, the handmaid of Fred. Losing the narrator's perspective and voice meant that the action played out as a frightening, but not very moving, dystopian vision. As the critic of *Rolling Stone Magazine* opined: "it's a piss-poor rehash of *The Stepford Wives* with delusions of grandeur."[6] While that is rather harsh, the cinematic story also had none of the open-endedness of the novel's first-person account. It ended not with the novel's academic conference in the future, speculating on the fate of the speaker of a series of tapes, whose transcription, we learn, we have been reading: that first-person voice was intended to be a real, recorded speaking voice. But the simple truth is that part of the problem with seeing the first (or any) adaptation of a novel you admire is that you realize that the director and the actors have interpreted almost everything in the world of that novel differently than you have: it simply doesn't look or sound the way you imagined it.

---

[5] Qtd. in Molly Young, "In the 2010s, *The Handmaid's Tale* Arrived: Margaret Atwood on Whether Anything Shocks Her Anymore," *Vulture*, 26 November 2019. https://www.vulture.com/2019/11/margaret-atwood-the-handmaids-tale.html

[6] Peter Travers, "*The Handmaid's Tale*," *Rolling Stone*, 9 March 1990. https://www.rollingstone.com/movies/movie-reviews/the-handmaids-tale-117518/

Of course, part of the difference between any novel and its film adaptation comes from the mode of engagement we have with each medium. When we read a novel, we perceive and then interpret black marks on white pages (or screens). We give the story life and form in our imaginations, which are simultaneously controlled by the selected, directing words on the page and yet also liberated, unconstrained by the limits of the visual or aural. We can stop reading at any moment; we can reread or skip ahead. But when we move from telling a story to showing it—in film or stage adaptations—we move from the world of the imagination to the direct perception of an aurally and visually realized world. In addition, we become caught up in an unrelenting, forward-driving story. Unlike in the novel, language is no longer the only means of expressing meaning or relating narrative. Visual and gestural representations are rich in complex associations; music offers aural "equivalents" for characters' emotions and, in turn, provokes emotional responses in the audience. Sound, in general, can enhance, reinforce, or even contradict visual and verbal aspects.

The major task of the film creators of *The Handmaid's Tale* was to dramatize the novel: description, narration, represented thoughts had to be transcoded into speech, action, sounds, and visual images. Conflicts and relationships between characters had to be made visible and audible. In the process, a certain amount of re-accentuation and re-focusing of themes, characters, and plots is inevitable. That the film lost more than it gained by this process was clear in the critical response—and my own, I admit.

Adapting a novel to an opera would likely be seen by most people as even more risky and difficult than moving to film. In 2000, however, composer Poul Ruders and librettist Paul Bentley tackled Atwood's novel. The challenge here was that, unlike film, opera is not a realistic art form, but rather one built on conventions and artifice. After all, everyone sings. In addition, unlike a film, which can be edited and shaped and has developed accepted techniques for showing different temporal dimensions—flashbacks, flashforwards—opera is a live staged art form that is resolutely experienced in the present tense.

When the Canadian Opera Company presented the opera in 2004, I read the novel for the second time. What fascinated me this time around was what happened when the entire story was set to music and then staged dramatically and forcefully by Phyllida Lloyd. To give only a brief example, in the handmaids' indoctrination scenes at the Red Centre, the young women are made to sing with a kind of inane and irritating simplicity in the key of C major. A version of what is sometimes called "holy minimalism," it is music that has been called "almost irritatingly tonal."[7] In powerful contrast, their indoctrinating teacher, the feared Aunt Lydia, sings in a kind of demented coloratura in the high upper ranges of her soprano voice, making her a fitting musical symbol of the fanaticism of the new regime. As Paul Bentley, the librettist wrote, "A searing top C on the word 'penetrated' was entirely proper for her."[8]

While clearly much is added through the music, in an operatic adaptation, much is lost as well. Because it takes so much longer to sing than to speak (or read) a line of text, libretti are, by definition, short. They lose words, characters, entire sub-plots. You might think they would lose the ability to present the interior psychological world of the characters. But, in fact, opera has a convention—the aria—that allows characters to stop the action and, as in Shakespearean soliloquy, reflect upon their situation and their emotional state. In this way, something of Offred's inner first-person voice is captured and is present in the operatic adaptation. The opera also tackles quite astutely the formal problem of adapting a novel written (or spoken) in the present tense, but consisting almost entirely of flashbacks. The novel moves backwards and forwards in time, but a staged opera has temporal limitations inherent in its "presentness" and in the forced linearity of its story presentation. As Helmut Reichenbächer studies in this volume in revealing detail, what the opera libretto does is to create two protagonists, both Offred, but one is in what is called the "Time Before" and another in the "Time Now." This allows the opera to juxtapose two political worlds as well as two psychic and emotional states.

What makes this work on stage is that the composer created two different musical worlds for the two times. The music of the Time Before is relatively conventional, melodic, soothing; that of Time Now, after the coup, is atonal, dissonant, and often terrifying—except when representing the sanctimonious piety of the regime through banal harmonic lines. The most pointed use of this difference, as Reichenbächer analyzes, is in the repetition of the familiar hymn, "Amazing Grace." As almost a leitmotif of the Time Before, it accompanies (ironically) love-making at its happiest: the protagonist and her lover (and the audience) hear it on the television in the background as they make love in the Time Before. When we hear it repeated during the ritualistic copulation of the Ceremony in the Time

---

[7] Paul Bentley, *A Handmaid's Diary* (Copenhagen: Edition Wilhelm Hansen, 2004), (140).
[8] *A Handmaid's Diary* (71).

Now, the hymn's now distorted form stands for love-making at its most perverted.

If operatic adaptations of the novel add music and dramatic action but subtract words and scenes, characters, and themes, a ballet version would obviously remove all words, and rely on the moving body and music to convey both narrative and emotion. This is what the Royal Winnipeg Ballet's adaptation succeeded in doing from all accounts, but since it was not part of my personal adapting experience of Atwood adaptations (though I wish it had been), I will move at once to the high-profile, critically acclaimed Hulu TV adaptation discussed so much and so well by others in this volume. But I want to use my personal experience and the impact of that particular adaptation upon my third reading of the novel as my focus here. The series began with a 10-hour retelling of the novel *and* the film, according to the writer, Bruce Miller. Why the (failed) film, as well? I would argue that, once a fictional world has been visualized and concretized, the creators' as well as the audience members' imaginations are effectively "colonized" by that first visualization.

That said, to be honest, the (not memorable) film did not have this effect on me. But, on the contrary, that first television series totally changed my experience of rereading *The Handmaid's Tale*; suddenly, I could not *not* see Elizabeth Moss as Offred. And, interestingly, this colonization continued into my reading of the sequel, *The Testaments*. My Aunt Lydia in both novels was now not the nasty "angular" woman, said to be "without flesh" in the novel, but was the fuller-faced and gradually more sympathetic Ann Dowd of the TV series. I will return to this experience later, but first I want to explore why the series succeeded as an adaptation (both in colonizing my imagination and in winning over the critics) where the film did not.

One of the reasons, and an important one, is that the series, unlike the film, kept Offred's first-person narration: using voice-over, she continues to *tell* us her version of the story, even as we watch the story's world being *shown*—that is, being created visually and aurally on the screen. We never lose that ironic, rebellious, often sassy voice of the novel; indeed, what is added in the screen adaptation's voice-over is the contrast between the conventionally Gileadean things Offred *says* and what she is *thinking* (which we also hear in the voice-over). The joke here is that all the major manuals on film adaptation, and most of the theorizing works on scriptwriting, scorn (or even ban) voice-over as disruptive and distracting, making audiences focus on words, not action. Voice-over is telling, not showing. But I would argue that it is precisely the mix of these two modes that makes the television series work and the film fail. And along with all the other arguments for the series' success offered in this collection, I would point to the same mixed technique for the success of Sarah Polley and Mary Harron's television adaptation of Atwood's *Alias Grace*.

There are other reasons for the power and success of *The Handmaid's Tale* TV series as adaptation, however. Its plot is much more linear than that of the novel, and its pace differs: after all, there are ten episodes to fill. It has been updated and modernized to seem like our current present, and Atwood herself was a consultant on these changes. But the alterations were not only to the visual world of Gilead. Instead of the Wife, Serena Joy, being presented as an Anita Bryant-like gospel singer and public spokeswoman for conservative family values, as in the novel, the series character is an active participant, with her husband, in the formation of Gilead's social forms and values—even if her sex then renders her their victim as well as their founder. Some of the characters have been made more glamorous for the TV screen: the Commander and his Wife are younger and more attractive than in the novel. Characters have been added and issues expanded (such as gay relationships, aka "gender treachery"); back stories have been provided to allow for future development in the subsequent series. Characters from the novel—like the protagonist's mother—do not appear in the first series, but do in later ones. Other characters, by implication white in the novel, are racially diversified. Offred's friend Moira, for one, is black; so too is the protagonist's partner Luke.

Inevitably, the television adaptation both gains and loses. Its Gilead gains a palpable reality so close to what we know today that it is deeply disturbing. Its oppressive surveillance culture is both audible and visible on screen. But it loses the other dimensions that the novel can provide through Offred's sensual descriptions of smelling the garden's flowers in the heat of summer, for instance. It also loses the poetic word play that extends from chapter to chapter in the novel. While the series is self-reflexive in its character's looks and addresses to the camera (as other TV series are as well, like *House of Cards*), there is less of a sense of the novel's narrator's need to tell her story to someone. As the novel's Offred says, "Because I am telling you this story, I will your existence. I tell, therefore you are."[9] Readers learn, in the epilogue, that the reason for this self-consciousness about narrating (and the need to do so) is that Offred has,

---

[9] *The Handmaid's Tale* (Toronto: McClelland & Stewart, 1985), e-book.

in fact, spoken her story into a tape recorder. The transcriptions of the 30 cassettes she used make up the text we learn we have just read.[10]

Readers find out about the tapes through the novel's framing device, an academic conference of the Gileadean Research Association in the year 2195. Clearly, therefore, the Republic of Gilead has fallen and is now an object of historical study. But the fate of the protagonist is not known: her own story in the novel (as in the first TV series) ends with her getting into a van, not sure if this is the end or a new beginning for her. The scholars at the conference can add little. She might have gone to the United Kingdom, via Canada; she might have been recaptured; she might have been killed by Nick. On the other hand, perhaps she was sent to the Colonies or to work at the nightclubs/brothels of the Commanders. It may be an apocryphal story, but it has been said that when Atwood was asked what happened at the end of her novel, she coyly stated that she too would like to know what happens next.

After 35 years, she gave us a sequel: *The Testaments*. Taking place 15 years after the first novel's time, it continues with first-person voices, but not of Offred (or June, as she was named in the television adaptation). There are three voices, all women's. Two are literal voices, in the sense that once again we read transcripts of oral witness testimonies by women whom we have to learn to know, for they are young and not, to our initial knowledge, part of the plot of the first book. But the third "voice" is a resolutely written one: that of the much-feared Aunt Lydia who has kept a secret autobiographical journal which she has hidden, most appropriately, in her library (for, unlike the handmaids, she is allowed to read and write) in a hollowed-out copy of Cardinal Newman's *Apologia pro vita sua*. As she notes, "I am well aware of how you must be judging me, my reader; if, that is, my reputation has preceded me and you have deciphered who I am, or was."[11]

Here, Atwood "corrects," if you like, the television version of this character, who is there said to be a religious elementary school teacher before Gilead. Atwood's Aunt Lydia, instead, was a family court judge who here, very self-consciously, records and judges both others in Gilead and herself. As Serena Joy did in the TV series, in the new novel Aunt Lydia helped

---

[10] All the tapes started with popular songs of the time (to throw off casual listeners/censors from their later spoken content), and this is a device that an audiobook adaptation of the novel has deployed to good effect.

[11] *The Testaments* (Toronto: McClelland & Stewart, 2019), e-book.

invent the "female sphere" of Gilead: its laws, slogans, hymns, uniforms, even its names—though she admits that all of this was a betrayal of everything she had been taught women could and should do in her earlier life.

We learn that Aunt Lydia's manuscript survived the fall of Gilead from yet another framing academic conference, a few years after the 2195 one in the first novel. Set in 2197, this one features the same scholar we met in *The Handmaid's Tale* who fills us in on the fall of the regime and the place of the two testimonies and the manuscript in that narrative. Indeed, he tells the participants (and us) that he and a colleague have prepared (for sale) a facsimile edition of the three documents, interweaved to make more sense—and, of course, that is precisely what we have been reading. Atwood's stress on the written nature of this text is, for me, a subtle reminder that this is *not* the television adaptation's version of the events after the end of Offred's story, but rather it is hers. I don't interpret this as an issue of her asserting intellectual or creative property rights, but rather of her reminding us *whose* imagination first created Gilead and its inhabitants, once again using only events that have precedents in our own human history.

I wish to return, however, to my personal experience of the television adaptation "colonizing" my imagination as I reread *The Handmaid's Tale* and read *The Testaments* for the first time. Offred will always be Elizabeth Moss for me now, and Aunt Lydia will always look and sound like Ann Dowd. I often wonder if Atwood had the same problem, when writing the sequel. But I think she has offered us a counter-colonizing move in a medium that both *shows* and *tells*: the graphic novel of *The Handmaid's Tale*. The words are all Atwood's; the images (the art and adaptation, that is) are those of Canadian artist Renée Nault. In this version, characters resemble Atwood's descriptions, not any of the mediated live incarnations. Serena Joy is not elegant and youngish; she is older, arthritic, with "knuckly" fingers, walking with a cane. Her husband, the Commander, is older and heavier-set than the television actor. The plot is not as linear as the film and TV versions, but rather follows that of the novel (though abridged). Reviewers have argued over whether the watercolors of the graphic novel adaptation are too beautiful to represent realistically the horrors of Gilead, but my own major interest is in this book as an attempt to recapture the imagination of the reader, to win it back from the potent visualization of the television version, to something closer to Atwood's version.

Some viewers of that series, of course, will not have read the novel beforehand. If they then do so, they likely won't be able ever to imagine Offred as looking and sounding like anyone but Elizabeth Moss. They will, in effect, be reading the novel as an adaptation of the TV series they first experienced: precedence implies source. That said, adaptations are often denigrated as secondary and derivative. As the articles in this volume show, they are actually imaginative reinterpretations and new creations in their own right. And it is Atwood herself who has taught us this by her contagious adapting example.

WORKS CITED

Atwood, Margaret. "For God and Gilead". *The Guardian*, 22 March 2003. https://www.theguardian.com/music/2003/mar/22/classicalmusicandopera.fiction.

———. *The Handmaid's Tale*. Toronto: McClelland & Stewart, 1985.

———. *The Testaments*. Toronto: McClelland & Stewart, 2019.

Bentley, Paul. *A Handmaid's Diary*. Copenhagen: Edition Wilhelm Hansen, 2004.

Travers, Peter. "*The Handmaid's Tale*", *Rolling Stone*, 9 March 1990. https://www.rollingstone.com/movies/movie-reviews/the-handmaids-tale-117518/

York, Lorraine. *Margaret Atwood and the Labour of Literary Celebrity*. Toronto: University of Toronto Press, 2013.

Young, Molly. "In the 2010s, *The Handmaid's Tale* Arrived: Margaret Atwood on Whether Anything Shocks Her Anymore," *Vulture*, 26 Nov. 2019. https://www.vulture.com/2019/11/margaret-atwood-the-handmaids-tale.html

Index[1]

A
Abbate, Carolyn, 199n25
Adams, Jeff, 173
Adaptation, 2–10, 35–47, 51, 56, 60, 63–89, 106, 143, 144, 148, 151, 153, 162, 166–169, 172, 173, 178–202, 213, 214, 218, 219, 221, 225, 230, 231, 233, 239, 251, 252, 254–261, 259n10
Adorno, Theodore W., 36
Agamben, Giorgio, 55
Ahmed, Sara, 37
Alias Grace (novel), 96, 97, 100, 105, 107, 108, 229, 231, 233, 235, 258
Alias Grace (series), 8, 10, 95–110, 229–230
Andersen, Hans C., 116, 117
Atwood, Margaret, 2–10, 5n10, 15–32, 17n5, 17n6, 17n7, 35–47, 49–60, 63–89, 96, 97, 100, 101, 103, 105, 107, 108, 110, 113–120, 124, 128n1, 128n2, 129, 129n3, 129n4, 138, 143–153, 159–162, 164–168, 170, 172–174, 178, 181, 182, 184, 188, 189, 197, 197n23, 200, 200n28, 213–215, 217–225, 227–231, 240, 242–244, 246–248, 251–261
Authorship, 2, 18, 30, 37, 182, 225

B
Bakhtin, Mikhail, 22
Balea, Ilie, 183
Balestrini, Nassim W., 188
Barthes, Roland, 37, 45, 162–164
Beckett, Samuel, 19, 19n10, 30n28
Bentley, Paul, 9, 178–202, 255, 256

[1] Note: Page numbers followed by 'n' refer to notes.

Beugnet, Martine, 129, 131, 132, 134, 136–138
Bible, 113, 114, 124, 132, 160, 226, 251
Bilous, Daniel, 25
Bordwell, David, 128
Bouson, J. Brooks, 74, 116
Boyd, Brian, 30n27
Boym, Svetlana, 41
Brook, Peter, 23
Butler, Judith, 139

C
Canadian history, 39
Césaire, Aimé, 16, 16n3, 16n4, 22, 251
Cinematography, 231, 239, 242
Clark, Caryl L., 181, 182
Colonial, 7, 36, 38, 39, 43, 46

D
Deleuze, Gilles, 138
Derrida, Jacques, 45, 46
Desblache, Lucile, 51, 51n3
Domville, Eric, 185n12, 198, 201
Donaldson, Laura, 43
Dystopia, 6, 18n9, 26–28, 57, 64, 69, 114, 115, 117, 119, 124, 143, 144, 252

E
Eagleton, Terry, 57
Ecology, 166
Emerson, Ralph Waldo, 6
Esquenazi, Jean-Pierre, 128

F
Fairy tale, 116, 117, 120
Feminism, 9, 79–89, 143–153, 160, 217, 218, 228

Fisher, Mark, 44
Forceville, Charles, 168, 168–169n10
Foucault, Michel, 37, 46
Frame, 3, 4, 10, 56, 70–73, 77, 99, 102, 103, 129, 136, 146, 165, 168–170, 188, 191–192, 240, 242–244
Frankenstein, Victor, 5, 52
Frost, Robert, 31
Frye, Northrop, 19, 63

G
Gender, 5, 9, 38, 43, 71, 81, 87, 88, 151, 194
Genette, Gérard, 16, 182n9
Goodman, Nelson, 183
Graphic novel, 8, 9, 157–174, 178, 260
Groensteen, Thierry, 169

H
Hag-Seed, 6, 7, 15–32
Handmaid's Tale, The (graphic novel)/ *Handmaid's Tale, The* (novel), 8–10, 18n8, 30, 80, 84, 85, 113, 116–118, 124, 143–153, 157–174, 178, 200, 252, 260
Handmaid's Tale, The (opera), 9, 85, 178–202
Handmaid's Tale, The (series), 5, 8–10, 15, 82–85, 87, 87n12, 88, 114, 119, 127–140, 143–153, 166–169, 219, 227, 239–249, 254, 255, 257, 258, 260
Harron, Mary, 8, 95–110, 258
Hartmann, Tina, 182, 184n11, 188n14
Heart Goes Last, The, 6, 15–32
Hendershot, Heather, 129
Horkheimer, Max, 36
Howells, Carol Ann, 4, 101, 103, 104

Hutcheon, Linda, 10, 25, 25n20, 39, 79, 80, 86, 87, 150, 172, 181, 182, 184, 189, 219
Hutcheon, Michael, 189
Huyssen, Andreas, 41

I
Irvine, Lorna, 4n8

J
Jadwin, Lisa, 159n2, 166
Jay, Martin, 132n6
Journals of Susanna Moodie, The, 35, 36, 39–41, 43, 45, 46

K
Klein, Naomi, 166
Kristeva, Julia, 6

L
Lapouge, Gilles, 20
Laycock, F.C., 179n4, 200n27
Lestel, Dominique, 50, 50n1, 51, 51n2, 51n3
Levinson, Jerrold, 20
Lighting, 18, 24, 86, 128, 129, 131, 136, 183, 190, 193, 222, 231–235, 242
Luther, Martin, 27

M
Maddaddam trilogy
  Maddaddam, 49, 59, 60, 64, 66, 73, 75, 77
  Oryx and Crake, 15, 49, 52, 64
  Year of the Flood, 49, 64, 66
Marks, Laura, 132, 132n7

Miller, Arthur, 16, 16n3, 16n4, 31
Miller, Bruce, 9, 83, 87, 87n11, 88, 115, 117, 119, 121, 143, 144, 146–150, 153, 245, 246, 257
Milton, John, 6, 16, 16n1, 17, 20, 26–29, 27n21, 251
Mittel, Jason, 128
Moodie, Susanna, 36, 38–41, 45, 46, 95, 101, 251
Moral Disorder, 25
Morano, Reed, 9, 130, 240
More, Thomas, 16n1, 17, 20, 21n11
Morra, Irene, 184

N
Nabokov, Vladimir, 30
Narrator, 6, 8, 10, 46, 52, 58, 60, 68, 70, 72, 96, 97, 107, 109, 114, 115, 119, 128, 136, 145, 165, 189, 233, 241, 253, 254, 258
Nature, 2, 3, 5–8, 15, 29, 35, 36, 39, 40, 42, 43, 50, 51, 58, 60, 63, 65, 66, 75n11, 79, 83, 99, 105, 106, 150, 151, 162, 165, 173, 180, 181, 218, 219, 227, 229, 238, 241, 252, 260
Nault, Renée, 9, 162, 166–169, 168n9, 171–173, 260
Nestruck, J. Kelly, 216n4
Northover, Alan, 70n7, 73–75, 74n10, 75n11

O
Odyssey, The, 36, 43, 44, 46, 80–82, 80n2, 217, 218, 223, 225, 226, 228
Opera, 5n10, 8, 9, 85, 166, 178–202, 179n4, 200n27, 252, 255, 256
Orwell, George, 17n7, 18, 20, 143, 144

P

Pacino, Al, 23
Palimpsest, 41
Paradise Lost, 6, 17, 20, 26, 27
Parody, 4, 25, 150–153, 199, 252
Peeren, Esther, 36, 38, 39, 45
Penelopiad, The (novella), 7, 8, 10, 16, 35, 36, 40, 43–47, 79–89, 213–228
Penelopiad, The (play), 80, 213
Polley, Sarah, 95–97, 100, 105, 229, 231, 234, 235, 238, 258
Pornography, 53, 145
Postcolonial, 7, 16, 37, 38, 251

R

Red Shoes, The, 9, 116, 117, 120
Rich, Adrienne, 8
Rigney, Barbara H., 116
Rozelle, Lee, 54, 56
Ruders, Poul, 9, 178–202, 255

S

Sanders, Julie, 80
Shakespeare, William, 2, 5, 6, 16, 16n3, 19, 20, 22–25, 23n14, 24n17, 25n19, 29, 30, 30n28, 36, 38, 39, 43, 251
Shallow focus, 9, 114, 234, 240
Shelley, Mary, 31, 52
Shelley, Percy Bysshe, 7, 16, 16n1, 30n26
Slattery, Mary F., 162–164
Spanjers, Rik, 167, 168
Spectral/spectrality, 2, 7, 35–47, 133
Speculative fiction, 7, 27, 64, 144–147, 153, 161, 161n3, 166, 172
Stam, Robert, 6
Stone Mattress, 18–20
Stoppard, Tom, 30, 30n28
Sullivan, Rosemary, 116
Survival (essay), 63

T

Television series, 8, 9, 82–85, 87–89, 88n13, 114, 115, 124, 146, 178, 219, 227, 252, 257, 258
Tempest, The, 6, 16n2, 20, 22, 23, 23n14, 29n25, 30, 36, 41–43, 46
Testaments, The, 10, 15, 18, 27, 30, 32, 87, 87n11, 88, 88n13, 119, 152, 153, 257, 259, 260
Theater, 5n10, 10, 19n10, 23, 23n14, 29n25, 85, 87, 168, 180, 185, 188, 189, 189n16, 192, 193, 202, 213, 215, 217n5, 218–222, 224, 226, 227
Thieme, John, 37–39
Traub, Courtney, 69
Turim, Maureen, 134n8

U

Ustopia, 64, 77
Utopia, 16n1, 17, 20, 127

W

Weiss, Allan, 197, 197n23
Wilderness, 46
Wilson, Emily, 44, 80n2, 116, 225
Wilson, Sharon R., 116, 119
Woodcock, George, 2
Woolf, Virginia, 57
Wunenburger, Jean-Jacques, 20

Y

York, Lorraine, 4n9, 252

Z

Zizek, Slavoj, 172, 173